Contents

Dedication

For Wolf and Beryl, travellers both.

Acknowledgements

Parts of this book had an earlier incarnation as a research thesis. This gives me an opportunity to thank my supervisor Barry Curtis for his help, enthusiasm and intellectual engagement with my Ph.D. I would also like to thank Artificial Eye and Parallax Pictures for generously donating, *gratis,* a still from *Land and Freedom.*

The Politics of Contemporary European Cinema

Histories, Borders, Diasporas

Mike Wayne

First Published in Great Britain in Paperback in 2002 by
Intellect Books, PO Box 862, Bristol BS99 1DE, UK

First Published in USA in 2002 by
Intellect Books, ISBS, 5824 N.E. Hassalo St, Portland, Oregon 97213-3644, USA

Consulting Editor: Robin Beecroft
Copy Editor: Holly Spradling
Typesetting: *Macstyle Ltd*, Scarborough, N. Yorkshire

Printed and bound by Antony Rowe Ltd, Eastbourne

A catalogue record for this book is available from the British Library
ISBN 1-84150-059-3 ✓

Preface

This book is about contemporary European cinema dated from around the mid-1980s onwards. It was during this period that large scale historical transformations were gathering pace within Europe. This decade saw the beginnings of the internal restructuring of national relations into a 'borderless' Europe that are still working themselves out today, with profound political, economic and cultural implications. Not the least of these will be the political and cultural relationship of Europe to the rest of the world and to America in particular. The year 1989 saw the fall of the Berlin Wall and in 1991 the subsequent collapse of the Soviet domination of Eastern Europe. All histories of film tacitly gesture towards some larger historical narrative. If some have read such momentous changes as the triumph of free market capitalism, this book will construct a rather different narrative. But this is the dramatic and traumatic macro-historical context within which we have to place contemporary European cinema.

Of course, this book is not remotely a definitive account of European cinema. Instead, filtered through a British perspective, it is organised around certain themes, events and theoretical debates. One theme is the importance of history, both as a latent force shaping events and as the *mise-en-scene* of many European films. If Europe has a shared history, it is one composed of numerous histories. While multiple, these histories often share a certain logic with each other, playing out similar tensions and triumphs (class conflict and industrialisation, for example), working in analogous ways (the importance of history in national identities) and impacting directly on one another (such as with wars and revolutions). If Europe exists as anything other than a vague ideal, it is presumably because its multiple histories have some relationship to a shared history. One reason, of course, that Europe and European cinema seems to be a category with little content, is because the *national* borders within Europe have historically been the prime mode in which social, economic, political and cultural life has been organised. Working from within such national parameters, thought, knowledge, culture, have often struggled to transcend them. Just as European cinema has been primarily understood in terms of national cinemas, so the multiple histories of Europe are usually understood as national histories. Yet at the same time, the moves towards political and economic integration, a dynamic driven by corporate capitalism's need to access ever larger markets with fewer legal discrepancies between them, forces us to think of the relations between these national histories and the increasingly porous borders which 'contain' them. This book has been organised to weave such links and comparisons, often reading films for what they can tell us about such cross-border similarities and differences.

This book is not just concerned with the politics of contemporary European cinema, but also with the politics of contemporary cultural theory that has influenced critical writing of the cinema and, in some instances such as Black and Asian British cinema, European films themselves. The great theme or motif which runs through so much contemporary cultural theory is precisely the idea that borders, whether cultural, social, national or pan-national, are becoming increasingly porous. Because the formation of so many borders and divisions has historically been the product of dominant institutions and official politics, the concept of porosity and the notion of border-crossings, has acquired a certain radical cache.

Against the fixity and rigidity of many conceptions of identity (just think of the fixed and exclusive identity implicit in the telling of many national histories) contemporary cultural theory emphasises the transitional, improvisational and shifting nature of identity, national or otherwise. This is the obverse side of the homogenising effects of the transnational culture industries. The movement of people and cultures – particularly as the latter are made through small producers – provides some significant counter to the corporate centres of cultural control on the one hand and the cultural insularity of nation-states on the other. On the latter, Paul Gilroy questions whether 'cultures always flow into patterns congruent with the borders of essentially homogenous nation states.'[1] Gilroy wants to develop a 'transnational and intercultural perspective'[2] on Black culture and politics and quadrangulates Black identity between America, Britain, the Caribbean and Africa (the four points of the slave trade).

This book shares this interest in thinking about transnational histories and cultures and the changes and shifts they undergo. But too often such considerations of culture have become uncoupled from material life, the real divisions and conflicts, the real pressures and constraints, the real forces and counter forces that shape all culture, but particularly an industrial and co-operative one such as cinema. This is why the first chapter will begin by exploring the economic and institutional determinants at work on European cinema. One of the key debates turns on whether there should be state intervention and regulation of the market and, if so, what its objectives should be. For some, European cinema is in a parlous condition because it is overly protected from the rigours of the market. For others, it is precisely the industry's exposure to current market conditions and organisation that is responsible for the industry's fragility. This chapter explores Eurimages, Europe's largest public subsidy for production funds that has invested in a number of high profile European co-productions since its inception. How far has Eurimages encouraged the production of films, which address aspects of European culture, history and identity? What kind of cultural identity should European films articulate and how might these be affected by the industrial strategies pursued?

Chapter two develops a model for thinking about how (British) national cinema operates within an international market for images of, in this case, Britishness, and how this interlocks with a dominant/official internal history which narrows the range of representations of the past circulating within and about Britain. This contrasts with a case study of recent French national cinema, which seeks out the *unofficial* histories of the nation, producing in effect what I call an anti-national, national cinema. Chapter three explores the emerging sense of Europe as a shared context and determining presence within a number of European films and again returns to the question of the politics of identity, culture and society which these film work over. Chapter four continues the pan-European theme exploring cinematic representations of Central and

Eastern Europe after the fall of the Berlin Wall and the Soviet Empire, as well as the implosion of Yugoslavia and the subsequent wars in the Balkans. Since the rise of virulent nationalism in the former Yugoslavia constitutes the nightmare antithesis of the liberal multiculturalism which underpins much cultural theory today, the Balkans functions as something of a test case for the politics and adequacy of such theory as well as examining the cinematic representations of these events. The final chapter returns to the question of British national identity and culture as it has been reconfigured by the cross-border flows of people and culture evidenced in Black British, but particularly British Asian, films. Again the debate will be structured around the tensions between culture as transient and perpetually mutable and the obdurate material determinants on life which it is necessary to recognise in order to formulate a politics dedicated to substantive change.

References

1   P. Gilroy, *The Black Atlantic, Modernity and Double Consciousness*, Verso, London, 1993, p. 5.
2   P. Gilroy, *The Black Atlantic*, p. 15.

1 European Cinema: In The Shadow of Hollywood

This chapter begins by mapping out the economic reasons for Hollywood's global domination and explores the UK film industry's subordinate position within that hegemony. I will situate the European film industry and film policy within the contemporary and contradictory drive towards economic and political union. The European Community has implemented a number of strategies designed to help sustain the European film industry in its unequal struggle with Hollywood. I will focus on a case study of one film, *The Disappearance of Finbar* (Sue Clayton, 1996), to show in detail, how the Eurimages scheme works to encourage European co-productions and what its limitations might be. This chapter focuses on questions of industry, its structures and strategies, for the simple reason that conditions of production, distribution and exhibition help shape the kinds of films which get made. But we must also engage with the cultural debates circulating around European cinema, since these also shape the kinds of films which get made, not least by shaping the industrial arrangements which make film production and consumption possible in the first place. On the one hand we must call into question the arrogance, the complacency, the assumptions and self-delusions involved in an uncritical celebration of Europe as the source and guarantor of Enlightenment ideals. On the other hand (and much less fashionably) we must call into question the mirror image of this position which is common amongst the western intelligentsia. This postmodern position can best be described as post-Enlightenment liberalism, in which cultural difference becomes the Holy Grail, the only debate in town worth having. It is an important theme throughout this book that questions of cultural diversity, while quite proper and important, must not be formulated in such a way that notions such as social progress, justice, and questions around social solidarity, become marginalised. Within this broader cultural debate, I will plot some of the cultural positions implied by various strategies for European cinema. We shall find a number of tensions particularly around 'big' filmmaking vs. 'small' filmmaking; tensions between commercial and cultural ambitions; between popular and high culture, and between Europe's differentiation from or influence by Hollywood.

Globalisation and National Culture

Before plunging into the details of European cinema and its economic and cultural relations with Hollywood, it would be useful to situate the debate within the wider context of debates around globalisation and national culture. For Hollywood is of course a major globaliser of symbolic material. In order to provide some focus to a large subject, I want to concentrate on an essay by the American Marxist critic Fredric Jameson. This essay, 'Globalization as a Philosophical Issue',[1] is a typically Jamesonian mix of eloquently crafted insights and curious blind spots. This combination will help identify some of the problems and issues surrounding current thinking on global, national and pan-national cultures.

Jameson's central concern in this essay is to try and formulate why globalisation appears to be simultaneously about two contradictory dynamics. This, as Arjun Appadurai has noted, 'is the tension between cultural homogenization and cultural heterogenization.'[2] Jameson defines globalisation as centrally about the export and import of culture.[3] At one level, globalisation appears to be the process whereby all the world's cultures are being drawn together in new creative combinations. Here globalisation links to a postmodern celebration of heterogeneity, with cultural differences jostling in 'tolerant contact with each other'.[4] Linked to this expanded and extended communication network is the emergence 'into the speech of the public sphere' of a whole range of formerly marginalised groups and cultures.

However, the duality of the concept of globalisation means that the term also has a dark side insofar as it is associated with the coercive integration of national economies, markets and cultures into a homogenous, essentially American dominated culture. Here we are reminded that the import and export of culture does not take place on a level playing field. While Hollywood captures at least 70% of the British film market, the British film industry captures only 1% of the American film market.[5]

Jameson suggests that the homogenisation/heterogenisation couplet is applied across the global/national culture couplet depending on where 'a malign and standardizing identity is discerned.'[6] If it is perceived to be the state (or the culture industries) using the nation as its sphere of legitimacy, to be an agent of uniformity in which difference is marginalised or concealed, in which the hierarchies of power which structure the nation are masked, and where the interests of political and economic elites are projected as general interests when in fact they are not, then it is at the level of the nation where a despotic homogenisation may be said to accrue. Here then the market, with its cosmopolitanism and its transnationalism, can be mobilised as a site of resistance and difference to a national culture which is in fact the class, gender and ethnic encoded culture of a national dominant. And this is of course precisely the way in which Hollywood has functioned for the working classes of Britain[7] and Europe,[8] for many decades. However, Jameson suggests that when we move 'to a higher level globally, then everything changes: at this upper range, it is not national state power that is the enemy of difference, but rather the transnational system itself.'[9] Here then, nation-states are called on to protect the difference of national cultures and to affirm their particularity in the face of global homogenisation.

I think this is a very useful way of formulating the problem and plotting the different responses of commentators to the global vs national culture tension. However, we need to explore the implications of the relations between the global and the national in a bit more detail. Jameson's own position within this formulation is problematic because, as his language about moving to 'a higher level' suggests, the main threat to cultural diversity comes, for him, from the corporate interests which dominate the transnational markets. While I would not disagree with this diagnosis, within Jameson's essay, it is a diagnosis premised on a rather uncritical support for the nation-state. It is also premised on some problematic assumptions concerning American cultural domination.

The latter is worth exploring not least because Jameson takes as his example, the case of Hollywood. Jameson falls into the problematic assertion that the consumption of Hollywood films breaks up the 'seamless web of habits and habitual practices' of a national culture. Here, Jameson presents Hollywood film, particularly in the context of the Third World, as 'the apprenticeship to a specific culture', a kind of Trojan horse that lays the ground in converting unique national cultures into an American global cultural hegemony.[10] Here Jameson seems quite unaware of the critiques of this kind of simplistic notion of cultural imperialism.

One scrupulously detailed critique of this argument has been made by John Tomlinson. He notes that discussions of cultural domination often locate the media as central to cultural imperialism.[11] However, we cannot conflate media products with culture per se. The former may enter as 'foreign' bodies into another cultural matrix, but be 'indigenised', which is to say, read not in accordance with the American cultural framework from which they have originated and now exited, but read in relation to the cultural framework they subsequently enter. As Tomlinson notes:

> media texts of Western origin are massively present in other cultures. But the key question is, does this presence represent cultural imperialism? Clearly the sheer presence *alone* does not. A text does not become culturally significant until it is read.[12]

This argument is equally applicable to Hollywood films playing in European cinemas or on European television. This distinction between media products (films, television programmes, books, etc) and culture (which draws on a broader repertoire of meaning making resources and interpretive codes) opens up the space for the audience to become active rather than merely passive consumers of culture.This has been a familiar theme in the populist turn in much contemporary cultural theory.[13]

Yet while this position rightly deals a blow to any simplistic cultural imperialism model, what it often fails to address is whether it would be desirable to have media forms which *are* rooted in and sensitive to more local, national or regional (in a pan-national sense) realities and cultures. This is not to deny that there may be 'universalist' or at least transnational themes and concerns in global cultural products such as provided by Hollywood, or that Hollywood films may well be inflected differently according to the cultural frameworks into which they enter; yet neither of these possibilities are a substitute for cultural plurality to be rooted in thriving production units outside Hollywood/America. Without access to indigenous production, cultural consumption is always having to work with symbolic material fashioned elsewhere under material and cultural determinants that may be quite different and remote from the place(s) of reception.

As Hollywood's global hegemony expands, the resulting homogenisation of world film culture is complexly coupled with Hollywood's own differentiation as it incorporates stylistic elements and the creative personnel it sucks up from the film cultures it gradually displaces or marginalises. But this internal differentiation is not, I would argue, an adequate compensation for the diminishing scope which other film cultures have to develop in. Even under conditions of economic inequality between film industries (to be explored below) cultural exchange has its benefits, but it is a skewed and one-sided process, with Hollywood conceding rather less culturally, than its competitors, and with losses that are entirely avoidable if we were operating outside the economic metabolism of capital.

There are two arguments running along here which it is worth drawing out more explicitly. In part, my argument is a geo-cultural one, that it is desirable for there to be film production that displays a familiarity with local, national or pan-national realities and cultures. However, 'local' production (at whatever geographical scale) is not necessarily desirable in and of itself. Ideally, local film production should adopt a critical and questioning perspective on the material and cultural realities it is in proximate contact with.

It is precisely this critical stance that does not come through strongly enough in Jameson's valorisation of the nation. The nation-state of course has often provided the legal power, the financial resources and the institutional apparatuses to foster and sustain indigenous cultural production. Yet as I have already indicated, Jameson's text acknowledges that the national sphere may well be the site of a 'despotic' domination by elites. Yet this is interestingly displaced in Jameson's essay onto a critique of the pan-national ambitions of the European Community.

> I happen to find the effort, stimulated by the EEC, to conjure up a new European cultural synthesis, with Milan Kundera substituting for T. S. Eliot, an [...] ominous [...] pathetic symptom.'[14]

Now one can certainly be critical of the bureaucratic, top-down attempts to create a 'Euro-culture', and many critiques of the new Europe rightly point to its 'democratic deficit', which is to say the lack of popular involvement and legitimacy in the actions and policies of its institutions. Yet this seems to ignore the extent to which the nation-state has accommodated a great variety of political forces and movements, some of which have been progressive and increased popular participation in decision making and cultural life, and some of which have been reactionary, conservative and elitist, closing down popular involvement in political and cultural life. Similarly, in principle, the supranational European polity could be coupled with different political and cultural projects. The French sociologist Pierre Bourdieu sees a European wide body able to defend the social (and for our purposes, the cultural) dimension once won at the level of individual nation-states, as the logical strategy for the working class, since this is the international level at which the forces they are fighting are operating.[15] But, if it is the case that European institutions cannot be bent in a more democratic direction, then still less can the nation-state, penetrated as they both are by an increasingly rampant capitalism.

We have seen then that any evaluation of globalisation, the nation and a prospective supranational European polity, is very complex. Globalisation is both at once a phenomenon which involves homogenisation and differentiation. It indicates a vast arena of creative cultural exchanges which have often undermined cultural inequalities within nation-states, providing the culturally disenfranchised, resources with which to contest their domination. This is a theme in films such as *Young Soul Rebels* (Isaac Julien, 1991) and *Wild West* (David Attwood, 1992), where Black and Asian youths respectively, draw on American music to contest their subordination within a racially structured Britain. But the nation state is also ambiguous, providing the legitimacy and material resources for the indigenous production which is threatened by the globalisation unrolling from Los Angeles. *Young Soul Rebels* was funded by the British Film Institute and Channel Four invested in *Wild West*. Both organisations have state sanctioned obligations to address aspects of life within the nation which have not been adequately serviced by the dominant media. Just as the nation-state is an ambiguous entity, a site of struggle, so too is the proto-European polity presently under construction.

I do however have to enter a caveat about the terms which have dominated the discussion thus far. The *cultural* issue of homogeneity vs heterogeneity appears to be the absolute horizon within which to discuss culture, with the latter category (heterogeneity) being understandably preferred as a promotor of liberalism and pluralism. The problem with this is that the dominance of the question of cultural diversity tends to make awareness of the context in which culture operates, sporadic at best. I do not think that we can understand the politics of European film culture by confining ourselves to a discussion of cultural politics. Culture has to be situated in a broader political and material struggle. It has to be contextualised in the struggle for material resources (of cultural production as much as employment, consumer goods, welfare systems, etc) made scarce by the social relations of capitalism. It is this context, rather than the promotion of difference in and of itself, which provides the material conditions in which a productive engagement with cultural difference will be sustained or harmed. It is indeed extraordinary that a social and economic system which *levels* civilisation down rather than up, as global capital chases wider profit margins, can still retain, in the ranks of the intelligentsia and the wider population, any credibility. And yet it does. This suggests that we must couple the debate about standardisation *vs* heterogeneity with a less fashionable but still pertinent cultural question: what contribution does film make to the *legitimation* or otherwise of this social and economic (dis)order.

Hollywood: the economics of domination

It is important to stress that my analysis of Hollywood's domination is focused on the structural, enduring features of the film industry. The empirical figures, the changing policy initiatives, the up and downs of the industry, the mergers, the new technologies, all testify to a constantly protean environment. I am not concerned to give a detailed chronological survey of that environment. Rather I want to illuminate the persistent, obdurate, structural characteristics of the system. This is important because the economics of domination is political but it is precisely the politics of writing about this domination which has been deeply bourgeois. Angus Finney's investigation of the film industry for example tends to treat companies like bourgeois individuals, as if they were free-standing agents determining their lives in isolation from the social and economic relations around them. Hence this comment:

> Traditionally, smaller European companies have not enjoyed a promising track record when trying to run ambitious production, international sales and distribution outfits.[16]

In order to understand why the odds are weighed against European film companies enjoying large-scale success, we need to map out the institutional – these are in fact *social* – and economic relations of European cinema and how it operates within the shadow of Hollywood:

a) *Hollywood is a powerfully capitalised industry.* The size of the American home market and the fact that it is dominated by a small cartel of large corporations provides the launchpad for global domination with expensive products which can be sold cheaply abroad, undercutting competitors. Thus the US film industry accounts for 74% of worldwide film production investment.[17] The shift of American capital into the culture industries is exemplified in the course charted by Gulf and Western. This conglomerate which had interests in sugar, zinc, fertiliser, real estate, etc, acquired Paramount in 1966. By the 1980s it was shedding its interests in manufacturing, property and agriculture to concentrate on becoming a major player in the culture industries: in effect, Paramount, once just a small corner of a multinational, had absorbed Gulf and Western.[18]

Hollywood majors are vertically integrated and horizontally integrated: they have interests in property, theme parks, television, video, satellite, retail outlets, music, book publishing, etc. This allows economies of scale, cross subsidy, spreading of risk, cross promotion of products, and substantially raises the barriers of entry into the market. As Garnham notes, 'it is now necessary to be large enough to have a significant stake across a whole range of leisure markets.'[19] For example, marketing spin-offs for *Batman* (Tim Burton,1989) made an estimated $1 billion from merchandising, four times box-office takings, while *Malcolm X* (Spike Lee, 1992) took $100 million in *X* products in the U.S. alone.[20]

b) *Rising production costs.* This is a deliberate and long-term strategy within the industry to squeeze out competitors. Escalating production costs are another way of raising barriers to successful entry into the market. Average production costs for Hollywood films rose from $9 million in 1980 to $24 million in 1989.[21]
c) *Soft Loans.* Hollywood's strength in the marketplace means that they get bank loans at very favourable rates of interest, as low as 2.75%. British companies by contrast, operating in a much more risky environment, pay between 8-9% a year.[22]
d) *Marketing.* Huge promotion and advertising campaigns running into many millions of dollars help to make smaller competitors virtually invisible to consumers. The average promotional budget for a British film is currently around £250,000-300,000.[23]
e) *Volume.* Many Hollywood films do not break even but the few successes (re)cover the costs of the rest.
f) *Poaching.* The size of the industry and the opportunities it offers for regular and well renumerated work means that Hollywood sucks up talent from around the world.[24]
g) *Distribution.* A worldwide distribution system is, as Garnham notes, the key to Hollywood's long-term success. For it is distribution which links production to

exhibition. Since the highest investment in the making of the film commodity goes into the original negative, multiple prints are marginal extra costs rewarded many times over by massively increasing the exchange value of the commodity through wide exposure to as many people as possible.[25] Maintaining a worldwide distribution network is hugely expensive however. In chapter two I will discuss how the European company, PolyGram films, tried to penetrate the US market. During the 1990s they spent the best part of a staggering $1 billion trying to set up a profitable US distribution arm.

h) *The Superpower State.* Hollywood has the enthusiastic backing of the American state, which as a superpower has enormous economic leverage (in terms of trade and loans) over other countries. After the Second World War, Hollywood's Motion Picture Export Agency referred to itself as the 'little State Department' so intertwined was it with US foreign policy and ideology.[26] The world film industry generates revenues of about £30 billion,[27] so the stakes are reasonably high. France expelled two CIA agents when they were found trying to gather information on the strength of the French bargaining position at the General Agreement on Tariffs and Trade (GATT) talks. Given that the unequal trade flows are self evident, systemic and long term, we cannot underestimate the role of *realpolitik* in the quietest acceptance by governments around the world to this domination.

i) *Ancillary Markets.* The growth of the video market has produced a dramatic new revenue stream but has been dominated by Hollywood. Only 4.6% of video rentals in 1991 were UK releases.[28] In 1983, revenues from video for the major Hollywood corporations on both their domestic and foreign markets were worth only $750 million. By 1988, they were worth $3,725 million. Worldwide sales to foreign television had also increased in value from $125 million to $550 million over the same period, indicating increased penetration of foreign television markets.[29] While revenues from cinema are more or less static, Hollywood will fight to retain its domination over the cinema exhibition circuits because only cinema generates the high profile marketing and publicity of a film which means that when it is sold into other markets (video, television) its high market profile increases its exchange value. This forging of what John Ellis calls the 'narrative image' of a film, its cluster of expectations and enigmas, means that in the future, cinema could 'be preserved as a loss-making arena for promotion of individual films which will make their real profits in other arenas.'[30]

The UK

The domination of the British market by Hollywood has been exacerbated by the fact that Britain is underscreened. France, for example, has twice as many screens. A multiplex building programme worth £560 million built up the number of screens in the late 1980s from a low base. However, this investment was mostly American. As one commentator noted, '[t]he promise of wider choices, regularly made by the multiplex owners before they were built, has not been kept.'[31] The multiplexes increased the number of people watching films in cinemas from a low point of 55 million in1984 to123 million in 1996.[32] Unsurprisingly though, audiences are seeing more American films.

Increased direct investment and ownership in the exhibition sector is reinforced by Hollywood's domination of distribution. The US majors, UIP, Buena Vista (Disney), Columbia Tri Star, Warner and 20th Century Fox took just under 80% of the UK box office takings in 2000, totaling around £456 million with 143 films.[33] The two 'independent' distributors, Pathé and Entertainment, made most of their money distributing American funded films such as *Chicken Run*, *Final Destination* and *Sleepy Hollow*.[34] The rest of the independent sector, made up of around two dozen companies distributing one or two films a year took around £45 million or 9% of the box office (this is actually a good year for the independents). Average takings for the independent sector is around £29,000 as against a £3.1 million average for the Hollywood majors.'

Is this domination due to the fact that the British cannot make popular films? *The Full Monty* is an instructive example. It made £26.8 million in 8 weeks. Culturally it is clearly a British film. In terms of storyline, style and acting it is in the tradition of British *television* drama,[35] which informs (detrimentally some would argue)[36] so much British cinema. It was a success though because it was distributed by Murdoch's 20th Century Fox and given a 300 print distribution in the UK.[37] By contrast *The Disappearance of Finbar* had six prints in circulation for its independent distribution.[38] *Brassed Off* (Mark Herman,1996) similar in theme to *The Full Monty* but a much more complex film in terms of how it asks the audience to respond and a much more politically angry film, had a minimal US distribution. Meanwhile the success of Damien O' Donnell's *East Is East* with a budget of £3 million was no accident. Film Four Distribution marketed the film very heavily in the cinemas, with a large poster campaign and on the television. The marketing budget was very high by British standards at over £1 million.[39] The thrust of the advertising strongly stressed the film's comedic qualities using the dalmation which is in fact rather marginal in the film. The problem with this is that it tends to reinforce a certain narrowing in the range of representation, so that minority cultures tend to get pidgeon-holed in the 'it's those crazy ethnic types' category. And while the film does have a comedic strand running through it, there was something of a discrepancy between the marketing campaign and the actual film which is rather darker in tone and more serious than suggested by the advertising.

While controlling the means of distribution and exhibition cannot guarantee success, without a profile in the marketplace and without access to audiences, one can guarantee that even the possibility of success is out of the question. Thus the percentage of British films unreleased a year after production has been rising since the mid-1980s, peaking at 50% in1993, while the number of British films which achieve a wide release has fallen over the same period to as little as 20% in1995.[40] The structural weakness of the British film industry means that companies are posed with an insoluble dilemma. They can choose to stay small and creatively ambitious and resist the lure of economic expansion: but in that case, small, far from being beautiful, is weak, vulnerable and insecure. Alternatively, they can try and expand economically, and thereby expand their leverage in the marketplace. But here too there are dangers. The structural weaknesses of the British film industry means that expanding production makes the producers exceptionally prone to the classic cyclical patterns of capitalist industry: boom turns to bust. Expansion of output in turn requires increased borrowing from the banks. However, producers can quickly overstretch themselves. One or two difficulties can have a knock-on cumulative effect. The levers to rescue the company with a product successful at the box office (control of distribution) are not in their control. From there the company experiences a 'credit crunch'; the banks pull out and the receivers are called in. This was the story of Korda in the 1930s and it was also the story of Palace Pictures in the early 1990s.[41]

Contrary to popular opinion, ploughing money into the production side of British cinema is not and never has been the main problem. Certainly City investors have been fickle in their relations with the industry (although arguably no more short termist than British capitalism is generally) but the real problem, and indeed the real source of City nervousness, is in distribution and exhibition – which is dominated now, as it was in the late 1920s and 30s, by the Hollywood majors. The recent channelling of money from the National Lottery shows that it is relatively straight forward to devise a system that pours money into production (although exactly who gets the money is always open to controversy).[42] But unless the unequal power and control in distribution and therefore unequal access to exhibition is addressed, British cinema will be perennially characterised by short-lived success and painful contractions.

The domination of the British film industry at the point of distribution and exhibition is a typical feature of 'mature' capitalism where free market competition between numerous small units of capital is gradually replaced by monopoly domination. United International Pictures (UIP) for example was set up in 1981 by Paramount, Universal and MGM to pool their power in the marketplace. Such explicit co-operation between three giants might have been expected to face scrutiny at both the level of the European Commission and national watchdogs. However the EC gave UIP an exemption to operate which it regularly renews, while the UK Monopolies and Mergers Commission, which seems to understand its remit as one of encouraging rather than investigating monopolies and mergers, also waved the UIP venture through.[43] This institutional failure to tackle American domination of distribution and exhibition is matched at a critical level by a continual downplaying of this domination and a sliding towards production as the key problem.

Although Stuart Jeffries noted of French protectionist measures that trying to halt the 'Godzilla-isation of French cinemagoing' was like trying to catch water, his own figures show that France is far less dominated by Hollywood than Britain. In 1997, 53.8% of films shown were American, 34.5% French and 11.7% other.[44] By contrast, the Conservatives were intent on abandoning the film industry to the tender mercies of the very unfree market. Quotas requiring distributors and exhibitors to handle a proportion of British films, dating back to the 1927 Cinematograph Act, were axed in 1983. The Conservative budget of 1985 withdrew tax incentives, terminated the Eady Levy, shut down the National Film Finance Corporation (NFFC), and replaced it with British Screen, which despite some notable successes, is funded by private capital and so has proved sensitive to economic downturns. None of the existing arrangements were working particularly well in part because they had been set up many decades previously. However, instead of devising new mechanisms appropriate to present circumstances, the Conservatives simply abolished state support.[45]

European Cinema: the political context

The drive towards political and economic union has its modern roots in the post-war Treaty Of Rome (1957). The goal of convergence in terms of laws, politics and economics and the removal of internal barriers to the free flow of goods, services and capital within Europe accelerated decisively in the 1980s. This had a triple aim: to compete globally with those outside Europe; to pool sovereignty as nation-states sought to empower themselves in the face of transnational corporations and global financial markets; and to bind Europe internally after centuries of war and conflict. It is crucial to understand the political dynamics at work within the European Union since these *set the parameters for cultural policy*.

Politically, the integrationist agenda within the EU is deeply contradictory. Two conflicting philosophies can be identified within the elites driving the process. On the one hand the goal of European integration appears to be an attempt to sustain, albeit in a modified and scaled down form, the traditions of social democracy, the ideals of a compact between capital and labour and some regulatory role for the state. This political tradition knows that there will have to be concessions to capital on social spending and labour 'flexibility', but it hopes to retain some legitimacy for social democratic class compromise within the ruling political and economic elites. This is evident in the will to intervene in current market outcomes to help the European film industry, as well as in broader policy areas such as enviromental and employment law.

The second political tradition, which is almost certainly the dominant one, is the neo-liberal doctrine. This is 'liberal' not in a social sense, but an economic one, since it seeks to liberate capital from as many commitments and obligations to social values as possible. Business sees such social values as parental leave and maternity rights as government interference in their operations which pander to sectional interests (like the majority) whereas capital, which lavishly rewards a minority, apparently represents, in the topsy-turvey world view of industrialists, the general interest.[46] This political philosophy is evident in mainland Europe but is best exemplified by the Anglo-American model. Alan Greenspan, the US federal reserve chairman has openly called for the power of European unions to be broken in order to shore up investor confidence in the Euro currency. The neo-liberal utopia, Pierre Bourdieu notes, includes individualising the wage relation (performance related pay), reducing labour costs ('red tape'), cuts in public spending, 'flexible' labour markets (night work, weekend work, short-term contracts,), in short *'a programme of methodical destruction of collectives'*.[47] Bourdieu identifies the social forces pushing for the neo-liberal agenda as shareholders, financial operators, industrialists, much of the political class and senior officials within the various financial ministries and national banks.[48]

The stronger the social democratic tradition, the more space there is likely to be for a progressive agenda for the cultural industries. The stronger the free-marketeers' agenda, the more likely purely commercial values and objectives will dominate. One theme in Bourdieu's intervention is precisely how the generalisation of market principles is undermining whatever autonomy from unregulated commercial diktat had been won for cultural and knowledge production.[49]

The resistance from below to either a scaled down social democracy or its effective dismantling, is also crucial. The level of protest sets the ground tone in which cultural work is undertaken and some cultural workers at least will attune their creative practices to the political struggle for the good life. The 1987 Single European Act ushered in the ambition towards a Single European Market by 1992. This timetable proved far too ambitious, not least because of the reuniting of Germany after the fall of the Berlin Wall (1989). The 1990s has seen the goal of political and economic union oscillate violently between being an apparent inevitability, to it almost collapsing as resistance was mounted to it, at least on the terms of its initial formulation which was, essentially, a bankers' Europe. In referendums, demonstrations, and strikes–the epicentre of which has been, characteristically, France, people challenged the neo-liberal agenda. Now, political and economic integration once more appears to be on track, but the terms of integration have shifted a little or at least been opened up as a site of struggle between conflicting social forces. These wider questions concerning what kind of Europe the Europe of the future is to be, the tensions between economic and social (or cultural) agendas have been and will be crucial for the shape of European cinema.

European Cinema: an economic challenge to Hollywood?

The goal of creating 'a unified economic territory undivided by either customs or trade barriers'[50] holds out the prospect of creating a larger market for films than the one which has sustained Hollywood's global domination. On the other hand, since the Treaty Of Rome enshrines, as Buscombe notes, 'a commitment to the doctrines of the free market'[51] integration may just as easily facilitate Hollywood's complete domination of European cinema. It all depends on whether one believes that the free market is always free so long as state interference is kept to a minimum or whether one believes that the market itself, with its monopolistic tendencies, may produce a market that is substantially unfree.

These debates are reproduced within the political and policy-making elites themselves. For example, the document on European broadcasting, *Television Without Frontiers* (1984), argued for some level of protection against US domination. But four years later, another EU document, *The audio-visual media in the Single European Market* (1988) in turn criticised the import quotas advocated by *Television Without Frontiers.*

> Quotas are definitely not an adequate method for the support of an industry. When adopted, they are evidence of an extreme weakness in the sector involved. As a remedy they are, in fact extreme.[52]

This document, which is extraordinarily coy about American domination does in fact let slip from whose perspective such measures would be 'extreme'. 'The USA put impressive pressure on Community institutions and on Member State authorities on this issue.'[53]. These differences within Europe and between America and Europe came to a head towards the end of 1993 around the GATT talks. Here, those arguing for some form of protection for a production base within Europe and for cinema and other media being regarded as a cultural good, rallied. (The question of what arguments can and should be made concerning the 'cultural' dimension of film is something we will come to later).

GATT Crisis

Hollywood's success requires domination of foreign markets to the detriment of local producers.[54] As Tunstall and Palmer note, 'in the 1980s Hollywood finally eliminated all other national film industries as serious competitors.'[55] The 1960s and 1970s saw brief film renaissances from Italy, France, West Germany and the UK. In 1967, 220 films from these four countries entered the US. In 1987, the same 4 countries could only get 83 films into the US market.[56] Today, while Hollywood operates globally, 80% of films produced in Europe do not leave their country of origin.[57] In 1990, US exports to the EC were worth $3.75 billion while EC exports to the US were worth $250 million. Such unequal trade flows have a long history. In 1913, *before* Hollywood's global hegemony had been built, 32 million feet of film was exported *from* America. The figure had increased exponentially to 235 million feet by 1925. Conversely, the US *imported* 16 million feet in 1913 but a mere 7 million by 1925.[58]

With the fall of the Berlin Wall, the countries of the former Eastern bloc are now also opened up for Hollywood penetration. While investment in Russia has been slow because of its political and economic instability, Poland, Hungary, Czechoslovakia and the Baltics have all seen Hollywood investment in movie theatres and a retail infrastructure. Eastern Europe has, like India, signed up to the copyright convention which means that they will crack down on the software piracy that might dent Hollywood's profit margins. With revenue growth fairly static in the US and western Europe, Eastern Europe opens up new lucrative markets for Hollywood.[59]

Although Hollywood penetrates other markets with ease, as Toby Miller notes: 'Washington/Hollywood/New York preside over the most closed television and cinema space in world history.'[60] Despite this, Hollywood, backed by the American state, were adamant that the cultural industries should be included within the terms of trade set out in the General Agreement on Tariffs and Trade talks. Essentially, GATT represents the institutional face of the expansion of the principles of neo-liberalism into every corner of social, cultural and economic life. If film were to be included in the GATT's terms of trade, then that would outlaw any protectionist measures which countries might adopt towards their own threatened film industries. The battles around this issue came to a climax towards the end of 1993. What is extraordinary is that it was a cultural question which almost brought a gargantuan economic treaty, with little interest in the pressing issues of social justice and environmental protection, to its knees.[61] The importance of culture at GATT reflects in part the shift in America from export of goods to 'exporters of textuality'.[62] By contrast, the stubbornness of French politicians in risking the wrath of the American state by defending what is for them an economically small industry, derives from a long history of state protection for cinema as a cultural good, and a recent vigorous (although not entirely successful) campaign by Jack Lang, Minister of Culture, to promote indigenous cultural production.[63]

Although the fight against GATT was presented by some as French chauvinism, it was widely supported across Europe's 12 member states by a petition of over 4000 artists, directors and producers.[64] The outcome of GATT was that culture industries were excluded from the free trade obligations of the treaty. That does not in itself guarantee that European film at national and supranational levels will achieve sufficient protection – only that it would not be illegal under the terms of international trading law, if they were to achieve such protection. Both sides agreed to disagree, both sides will regroup and engage again. It was a victory for neither side – more of a draw.

MEDIA/Eurimages

Two programmes that might have been threatened by GATT are the MEDIA programme and Eurimages. The MEDIA programme is a raft of initiatives which aim to stimulate the European audio-visual sector, especially, cross-border projects. Between 1991 and 1995 it had a 200 million ECU budget to provide seeding capital across three areas: the economic and commercial training of producers and script development (the latter is routinely identified as a weakness in European films); distribution, via the European Film Distribution Office which also helps with the promotion and marketing of European films; and exhibition.[65]

However, it is Eurimages which is my main concern since it is a pan-European fund for direct investment in European multilateral co-productions. Established in 1988 within the Council of Europe in Strasbourg it is, in fact, Europe's largest public-sector film financier. The fund comes from the subscription which member countries pay to join. The subscription is calculated on a scale according to GDP (it cost the UK around £2 million a year). Members include countries both inside the European Union but also outside, such as Turkey, Poland, Bulgaria, the Czech Republic and Hungary. The fund has been involved in a number of major European films, many of which will be discussed in this book. These include Kieslowski's *Three Colours* trilogy, *La Reine Margot* (Patrice Chereau, 1994*), Land and Freedom* (Ken Loach, 1995), and *Ulysses' Gaze* (1995)*.

Eurimages has a cultural remit, seeking festival awards, critical praise and perceived contributions to cultural life from the films it funds. In particular Eurimages exists to facilitate new co-production networks, aiming in particular to bring companies from smaller film producing countries into contact with larger producer countries in order to foster audio-visual production in small markets. This ambition in turn depends on encouraging tri-lateral production between two big producers and a third producer from a smaller country. Persistent pressure for a shift towards more manageable bi-lateral co-productions secured a change to Eurimages rules at the end of 1997. A bi-lateral co-production is defined as having one partner investing no more than 80% into the film and another partner investing no less than 20%. In order to encourage European wide circulation, the producers must show one or more presale contract to a reputable distributor in at least one European country *outside* the co-producers' countries. While the tri-lateral scheme continues, the adoption of the bi-lateral scheme is likely to be more attractive to the bigger producers who have in the past struggled to find a third partner who could make a meaningful material contribution to the film. This in turn is likely to have a negative impact on smaller countries, particularly the Balkan countries.[66] However, as we shall see, there are real logistical difficulties with multiple-partnered co-productions, and the cultural ambitions of smaller producers are not necessarily protected by the larger players.

It is important to note that although Eurimages offers a public subsidy to European films, on average it only constitutes around 10% of the investment in any one film. Contrary to the popular myth that European cinema survives by shunning private capital and existing on 'soft subsidy money' (as Angus Finney would have it)[67], around 50% of the investment into Eurimages films comes from the private sector. The percentage contribution of public television into Eurimages films has declined in the 1990s while capital from commercial television has increased and outstripped public sector television involvement.[68] The cultural implications of the limited financial contribution which Eurimages makes, means that it cannot draw films into the kind of progressive cultural brief which was once associated with, for example, Channel Four.

The UK joined Eurimages in 1993. UK participation in co-productions increased from 8 in 1990 to 32 in 1994,[69] a rise from just under 4% of total production in 1990 to just under 50% in 1994. In 1995, 34% of all UK films had Eurimage money. Another percentage of co-productions on top of that were made simply because Eurimages was there and provides a fall back position if money elsewhere drys up.[70] However, after a 3% cut in the Department of National Heritage's Budget,[71] the Conservative government minister, Virginia Bottomly, pulled out of Eurimages in November 1995. In just under three years it had paid £5.5 million to Eurimages, which had in turn invested £12.5 million in UK co-productions, helping to generate, according to one estimate, £40 million worth of filmmaking activity.[72]

Valuable as the MEDIA programme and Eurimages are, they are attempting to stimulate European filmmaking in a wider policy vacuum which has failed to address the structural inequalities and vested interests that have squeezed European cinema to the very margins of cultural life in Europe. Garnham quotes an industry analyst from the 1930s who argued that it was, 'folly to believe that, no matter what developments take place in the industry, the American producers and distributors will be able to maintain as a mere matter of course, the commanding position which they at present possess.'[73] It was believed that European-wide production and distribution cartels, backed by European states, would use US access to European markets as a bargaining position to create more favourable terms of access to the US market.[74] We are still waiting.

The Disappearance Of Finbar: case study of a co-production

A case study helps us to explore one of the major conundrums of the study of the medium: how determinants at the point of production shape the types of films that are available.[75] As a production paradigm, co-productions can be distinguished from co-financing deals. The former involves a genuine input – although not necessarily equal in volume and weight – into the key factors which shape the film from pre-production to post-production. Co-financing involves financial contributions from more than one source, but beyond agreed contractual commitments, only one partner has a creative input across the production process.[76]

Co-productions between unequally sized markets raise questions of power and the extent to which such co-productions involve the overwhelming domination of one or two partners over a third.[77] Co-productions are culturally contentious as well as logistically difficult. Everett writes of 'the inevitable watering down of differences and resulting blandness of these films.'[78] Although my case study is of a film which tells half its story in Lapland and Stockholm, it does not, as we shall see, contribute to Nordic aspirations to avoid an English language takeover.[79]

The film that I want to concentrate on is called *The Disappearance of Finbar.* This was one of the last British films to benefit from Eurimages funding before the British exit in 1995. Yet the *The Disappearance Of Finbar* is perhaps a British film in a financial and production sense only. The film's major investor was Channel Four, the main production company was British and the director, Sue Clayton, is also British. The story however begins in Ireland and concerns itself with the disappearance of Finbar from a housing estate and the effect this has on the community. Finbar cannot be forgotten about even though he himself has apparently forgotten about them. Three years later, a pop video is made about Finbar's disappearance and it is this example of travelling culture which motivates Finbar to phone his friend Danny and tell him that the video was rubbish and that they should all just try and forget about him. But contacting Danny produces the opposite effect and Danny leaves for Sweden in search of Finbar. Arriving in Stockholm, he finds that Finbar has already left and so he heads north, tracking him eventually to Lapland. In many ways *The Disappearance of Finbar* is a textbook example of a co-production and one which makes use of the then newly installed mechanisms to facilitate European co-operation.

A case study of the production process raises the complex issue of authorship which remains a persistent and privileged term in European cinema.[80] Thus Channel Four told Sue Clayton to make a 'personal film' – and saw the project throughout as an art film. Whatever the limitations of auteur theory as it was developed in the 1960s and however incomplete even a modified and reworked approach to the question of directorial agency would be *on its own*, authorship is clearly important in European cinema and has, as Elsaesser notes in relation to German art cinema,[81] institutional, material infrastructures to ensure that directors produce work that can be seen to bear the mark of some sort of authorial signature.

The question of authorship also raises some questions about my own methodological procedure. In order to construct this case study, I interviewed both the film's British producer (Martin Bruce-Clayton) and its director (Sue Clayton, no relation) in order to piece together the production process in some detail. This raises questions of authorship, motivations and agency and the status we give to the self-reflections of those involved in the very processes which we seek to understand.

Clearly there is a danger here of reducing meanings and motivations to individual perspectives and biographies which simply reproduces the worst aspects of auteurism. On the other hand, the empirical data generated by interviews with key participants in the production process, provides the researcher with a wealth of information and potentially real insights into a process academics are often rather ignorant of. The way to handle such empirical data it seems to me is to try and integrate motivations, agency, and individual perspectives into the wider institutional structures and cultural dynamics in operation, using these objective phenomena (i.e. existing independent of our will) as a way of assessing the weight, merit and contradictions of the empirical evidence gathered by interview. As John Tulloch notes, cultural producers, like all human subjects, must be accredited with some sense of agency. They do not simply, unconsciously conform to their given structures and uncritically reproduce their cultures. To varying degrees, 'authors' (producers and directors, just like academics) can 'reflexively monitor their conduct, and are *partially aware* of the conditions of their behaviour.'[82]

So, to the case study proper. *The Disappearance of Finbar* derives from a script of a book by an Irish writer, Carl Lombard, called *The Disappearance of Rory Brophy*.[83] The director Sue Clayton has a preference for working from novels but avoids English literary fiction which she feels is both dominated by middle-class values and is too domestic in its orientation to translate into visually exciting cinema.[84] The producers, a British company called First City, submitted Clayton's treatment of the story to the MEDIA programme's European Script Development Fund and the Irish Film Board. Both these organisations stumped up script development money which in turn augmented Channel Four's interest in the proposal. The film was to be shot both in Ireland and somewhere in Scandinavia. The Irish location was Tallaght. On the edge of Dublin it is one of the biggest housing estates in Europe. Sue Clayton:

> I was looking for a 'anywhere' in Europe location. There was this idea that Europe was on the way to becoming lots of housing estates [...] places that aren't quite cities and aren't quite countryside. People's sense of identity in these places is ambiguous. They retain some of the old sense of community, but also they are losing it.[85]

An Irish company called Samson Films was brought on board which was crucial for accessing Ireland's Section 35 funding, i.e. the tax break, worth £160,000 to this film's overall budget. The Irish Film Board came up with £240,000 and £25,000 came from RTE as their license fee.

First City then set about finding a Scandinavian partner. In doing this they had to weigh up logistical and financial factors. In financial terms, the Scandinavian countries do not have film industries of a comparable size to the UK's. During this period, the UK had 13.7% share of all films produced in Europe; Denmark had 2.7%, Finland and Norway 2.5%.[86] After initial enquiries, neither Norwegian or Finnish companies could provide the required capital. Nordisk, a Danish company was prepared to invest in the film and offer good facilities but it was felt that Copenhagen looked too much like a Northern European city rather than a Northern Scandinavian city which the director wanted. There was also the additional logistical factor that the location provide plenty of snow, which Denmark could not. For Sue Clayton, the location of Lapland that was eventually used was especially symbolic, since Lapland, like a United States of Europe, is an imaginary country that has no formal existence. Instead, like the imagined Europe of the future it is a place where the borders of different countries intersect.[87]

A deal was finally made with Victoria Films in Sweden who started the ball rolling with Swedish television and other Scandinavian funds. For example, £120,000 came from the Swedish Film Institute and a further contribution from TV2, the main Danish broadcaster. There was also funding in kind from Lapland through the Midnight Sun Film Investors, who offered the use of facilities. In the end there were approximately 10 sources of cash. This included £300,000 from Eurimages, providing just under 10% of the film's overall budget, which is the average proportion of budget supplied by Eurimages. In fact, because it costs money to communicate with overseas producers, involving as it does transport costs and translation fees, co-productions actually add about 10% to a film's budget. Therefore, Martin Bruce-Clayton argues, the money from Eurimages is not really a net gain, but a vital compensation for engaging in co-productions in the first place. The film's total budget was £3.3 million.

One of the problems of having so many partners involved in such a project is that the film may be pulled in quite different directions according to the different backers' perceived audiences. For the director, Sue Clayton, this meant trying to reconcile several conflicting interests.

> We would have meetings where the different backers would say, make it faster, slower, shorter, longer, funnier, more serious, more elliptical, more straight forward, more linear, more Postmodern, and we'll be back next Friday to see the next cut – and they'd all get back on their planes and I would just sit there and scream.[88]

The Swedish Film Institute, for example, invested on the understanding that at least parts of the film would be in the Swedish language. Channel Four however subsequently refused to have any subtitles in the film – so the Swedish and Finnish language could only be used where it was obvious to English language speakers what the meaning of the dialogue was, or alternatively, where humour is generated by the English language spectator sharing the Irish character's bewilderment and confusion. Pandora, a French sales company that had invested £575,000 for European and Japanese distribution rights, were convinced that the film was a teen-movie and were concerned that First City do all they could to help market the film to adolescent girls. Channel Four however insisted that it was an adult art movie. Thus the film was originally scripted with the intention of starting in Sweden and having flashbacks to Ireland, but Pandora felt that this complex structure would be unintelligible to their idea of who the core audience was. 'You could say' suggests Sue Clayton, 'that the film was scripted for Channel Four and edited for Pandora.'

Such multiple voices, interests and pressures can make for a confused end product and the classic 'Euro-pudding'. The critical reception in some quarters to *The Disappearance Of Finbar* implied precisely this.[89] As I have noted, European producers successfully lobbied Eurimages to revise its guidelines and make bilateral co-productions eligible for funding. One difficulty with the trilateral rules is that the third partner is often very small and is unable to supply adequate finance, forcing the co-production to broaden still further the number of investors. All of which can make for a culturally and economically unwieldy operation. However, while a revision of the rules makes economic sense, it would cut against the cultural remit of Eurimages, which has the *ambition* (it may not be entirely successful) of safeguarding indigenous audio-visual production in countries and regions (such as Scandinavia) with very small industries and markets.

Funding, whether multiple or single in source, whether private or public, whether high budget or low budget, always brings with it investor pressure and influence. Take Sue Clayton's experience whereby investor pressure led to the dropping of a key scene that would have helped make the link between Finbar's disappearance and the film's allegory of political and economic exile which is part of the hidden story of migration into Europe.[90] From Finbar's phone call, Danny learns that he is in Stockholm. The scene that proved contentious for the investors is as follows: Danny, looking for Finbar, finds out where the migrants' quarter is. Now, in Stockholm, the migrants' quarter is in a district on the edge of the city called Rinkeby. Here the displaced are ghettoised on mega-estates, where dozens of nationalities have come together and have formed informal structures like their own football teams. Danny goes to the fictional equivalent, telling anyone who will listen that his friend is 'missing'. A Moroccan asks him whether he's got a campaign and a poster, because 'all the missing are here.' Meanwhile, a white racist is shouting in the market square at the immigrants telling them they are not really Swedish. The Moroccan meanwhile informs Danny that the Swedish authorities have made him watch all of Ingmar Bergman's films. This neatly juxtaposes two common and contradictory European attitudes towards the outsider. On the one hand there is the attempt to absorb the outsider into what is thought to be a 'superior' western culture (Ingmar Bergman films in this case) and on the other, there is the declaration (via the market square racist) that they can never really be 'one of us'.

The investors however found this scene too blunt, detracting from the 'magical realist' qualities of the film. Here the 'fantasy' components of the film (the quest, the idiosyncratic characters) are used by the investors to displace the critique of European racism that the film's 'realist' project was trying to depict. This is a clear case of investor bullying. It raises very acutely the question of whether film is to be no more than a mode of regional boosterism or whether it can adopt a more critical interrogation of society . Given that it is precisely the migrants' story that is often cut out of the media, the pressure exerted on Clayton to leave this scene on the cutting room floor, has clear political ramifications. What this episode also tells us is that the average 10% contribution to film production, which Eurimages offers, is not enough to formulate and enforce a progressive cultural agenda against the pressures of commercialism, cultural tourism and sensitivities concerning national images.

Having negotiated a fraught production process, the low-budget European co-production then has to fight to get decent distribution. This is made all the harder if the film does not have – as is likely in a low-budget film – a star around which to hang the marketing of the film. However, *The Disappearance Of Finbar* was fortunate enough to have cast Jonathan Rhys Myers in the role of Finbar. Back in 1995–96 when the film was shot, Rhys Myers was an unknown actor, but subsequently starred in *Velvet Goldmine* (Todd Haynes, 1998) and *The Governess* (Sandra Goldbacher, 1997). *The Disappearance Of Finbar* was deliberately held over in the UK and released at the same time as these two films in an attempt to cash in on the publicity being generated around Rhys Myers as a rising star. Yet Channel Four had by that time decided not to distribute the film, a reflection less on *The Disappearance Of Finbar* than on a market in which it is desperately difficult to give a quirky, non-generic film much of a chance. However, Channel Four did contribute money to its independent distribution by Robins Cinemas, a tiny company which owns the Prince Charles cinema in Leicester Square, the film's main venue in London.[91]

European Cinema: a cultural challenge to Hollywood?

Thus far I have been discussing the industrial and institutional context in which European films operate. But we now need to turn to the cultural context and the debates there which also help shape the kinds of films which get made. When it comes to British government film policy across the decades, the implicit, largely unstated and unexamined cultural implications inscribed into the policies, tend to be a confused mix of crude nationalism and unfeasible commercial ambitions. The same has been true of much of the debate concerning a European film industry and culture. The kind of explicit debate about the cultural values, meanings and identities (the kind, for example, that took place before–and informed the setting up of–Channel Four), in short, what and who a British or European cinema would be for and what it would do, has been noticeable by its absence.

A document such as *A fresh boost for culture in the European Community* [92] is similarly characterised by this confusion of conservative pan-Europeanism and commercial banality. The former simply sees culture as a form of regional boosterism, propagandising on behalf of and trying to secure the popular support necessary for the 'considerable changes […] in living conditions' which integration will bring.[93] The document waxes lyrical about European culture ('a shared pluralistic humanism based on democracy, justice and freedom')[94] and seems ripe for Walter Benjamin's riposte that '[t]here is no document of civilisation which is not at the same time a document of barbarism.'[95] At the national level, some of the best European cinema has been attacked by those who thought that film should 'promote' the image(s) of the nation rather than document the barbarism, say, of poverty and unemployment. Thus Italian Neo-Realism met with the hostility of powerful political and Church elites and in 1949 a law was passed preventing the export of films which showed a 'negative' picture of Italy.[96] Decades later, Norman Stone, the Thatcherite historian, launched an attack on such 'worthless and insulting' films as *Sammy and Rosie Get Laid* (Stephen Frears,1987) and *The Last Of England* (Derek Jarman, 1987)[97] because they were angry testaments to the social barbarism of Britain under Thatcherism. In one version of the future Europe circulating among policy makers, the ambition appears to be no more than the conservative national model of identity and politics scaled up to a supranational level. As Morley and Robins note:

> The language of official Euro-culture is significant: it is the language of cohesions, commu-
> nity, unity, integration, security. What is invoked, though never avowed, is the possibility
> of a new European order defined by a clear sense of its own coherence, and integrity.[98]

An emphasis on unity, integration and cohesion is likely to produce at the level of European film culture, a somewhat affirmative, consensual, and uncritical cinema. Alternatively, film could engage in the complexity of life as lived, teasing out, acknowledging and debating the tensions and contradictions within Europe.

Within European film, the commercial and cultural emphases have helped shape two somewhat polarising attitudes or strategies: the cultural emphasis differentiates itself from Hollywood cinema, defining itself to some extent by what Hollywood is not. Everett lists self-consciousness, irony, slower tempo, reflective tone, challenging editing and open-endedness, as some of the qualities of the European film.[99] This sounds like the European art film. But is this a useful model for the new European context? John Hill has suggested that the European art film is defined largely by its formal features rather than exhibiting any engagement with a shared Europeaness.[100] However while this is historically true, this could, and possibly is altering given changing funding arrangements and wider political and economic integration. *The Disappearance of Finbar* may be taken as one example of this. Chapter three is devoted to exploring an emerging sense of Europeanness in both popular and art cinema.

The commercial strategy seeks to compete with Hollywood on its own terms: push up budgets, build and utilise stars and emulate the narrative structure of Hollywood films. Yet advocates of this strategy need to address the economic and cultural problems which that involves. At the economic level, the British film industry has suffered too many implosions because of big budget films failing in the American market for this strategy to be uncritically adopted. Even if the structural problems which inhibit commercial success were addressed, (and that is a very big 'if') there are still enormous cultural problems with an uncritical pursuit of a commercial and 'popular' cinema. The problem with the word 'popular' and its association with 'the people' is that we forget to ask, 'which people' are being represented here at the core of this or that project, political or cultural? This is particularly relevant to British cinema, which finds it difficult to mobilise the popular without situating at the heart of its vision of the people, the white, male, middle class and/or the attitudes associated with them. Thus 'the people' turn out to have a very particular class, gender and ethnic identity. Even Hollywood cinema, often praised for its multicultural awareness, ranks ethnic identities hierarchically, with the whites at the top.

A similar problem for the 'blockbuster' argument is posed elsewhere in Europe. Hungarian Cinema has been recently and rapidly penetrated by Hollywood. Small independent cinemas which once housed indigenous Hungarian films have been marginalised by the American multiplexes which mushroomed all over the country in the late 1990s.[101] In response, Hungarian films have attempted to simulate the Hollywood formula with such films as *Europa Expressz* (Csaba Horvath, 1998) and *Kalozok* (Tamas Sas, 1997) despite the fact that Hungarian cinema neither has the financial infrastructure to make blockbusters or the cultural traditions of the American cinematic idiom. Falling between two stools, such films, Andrew Horton has argued, are neither American enough to make it in the American market or European enough to attract attention in Europe.[102]

On the other hand, making arguments for a more culturally and politically ambitious cinema always risks making an alliance with elitism, although, as I have indicated, beneath the escapist, 'merely' entertainment-led model of popular cinema, there often lurks a class, gender and ethnic politics that is hardly very inclusive. Asian and Black British cinema, while not unproblematic, offers much from which the mainstream and independent wings of the film industry could learn in the way it combines a popular cinematic idiom with an address to the culture and lives of 'minorities'.

Nevertheless, there are cultural and institutional problems within the 'independent' sector, particularly around audiences and cultural capital, which introduce questions of class and tend to stigmatise reaching wider audiences. As an example of the cultural capital at work in the independent art house sector, take this editorial from the film magazine *enthusiasm*, published by the independent film and video distributor, Artificial Eye:

> There is a debate going on about the future of cinema in Britain. Again. And again it seems to come down to the simple blunt confrontation of cinema versus the movies i.e. art versus commerce. We, who insist that alternatives to pap, dished out unremittingly by the dominant sector, must be kept alive, have to make ourselves heard […] The most pressing problem to be addressed is exhibition outside London. Without a properly funded network of independently programmed cinemas, choice will be further reduced and mass culture will prevail – very likely for a very long time. And that would be bad. Worse, it would be a mistake.'[103]

While the emphasis on exhibition is welcome, the fear of popular culture is palpable, the exclusivity of the 'we' who speaks, very clear. It is this kind of elitism which makes some commentators impatient with the thought of any public subsidy being used to further middle-class film consumption.[104]

Such attitudes as exhibited by the editors of *enthusiasm* and Artificial Eye are deeply rooted in material structures of class difference and industry specific divisions of production and consumption. And such attitudes have real material effects which perpetuate class divisions. That Artificial Eye who were distributing *Land And Freedom* (Ken Loach,1995) refused to allow the film to move into the multiplexes even though they had (for once) asked for the film, is hardly surprising. Thus the film had only a 15 print UK release but 85 in France.[105] This suggests that the distributors had a vested interest in preventing the film from making an art house/multiplex crossover. They wanted, one suspects, to keep their product clearly differentiated in order to retain their exclusive middle-class market for both *Land And Freedom* and future art house products. A film then may have intrinsic properties that excludes wider audiences; that is to say, it may be heavily coded for middle-class consumption only. Alternatively, a film like *Land and Freedom*, which is not exclusively coded for niche audience consumption, may become an art house product for extrinsic reasons to do with its conditions of distribution and exhibition.

In contrast to the big budget 'blockbuster' paradigm, the low-budget film has the advantage of spreading economic risk across numerous films and opening up the possibility of taking more cultural risks. Yet there is often a sense in which telling 'smaller stories' gets conflated with telling rather inconsequential stories and losing sight of what Jonathan Freedland calls 'big picture' filmmaking; that is, weaving into stories the grand themes of modernism. As he puts it:

> The likes of *Lock, Stock and Two Smoking Barrels* or *Divorcing Jack* may be skillfully-made, but their focus is narrow. They are attempting only to tell small stories well. Much of our contemporary fiction is in the same vein, zeroing in on the miniature, the detail of human relationships, while shying away from the big picture.[106]

He contrasts this with recent Hollywood films like *Pleasantville* (Gary Ross, 1998*), The Truman Show* (Peter Weir, 1998), and *Antz* (Eric Darnell, 1998). This celebration of 'big themes', of freedom, progress, struggle and change, is similar to Alan O' Shea's celebration of Hollywood films for their attunement to some of the progressive currents within modernism.[107] O'Shea does not uncritically valorise Hollywood's modernist utopianism, entwined as it is with nationalism, racism, individualism and masculinism,[108] but he notes how contemporary Hollywood films place a liberating emphasis on human agency, the capacity to transform self and environment, progress and emancipation. These big modernist themes, which the editors of *enthusiasm* appear to be completely blind to, can all too easily get lost in small picture filmmaking.

There is also the danger that the small story, while it has the chance to focus in on what Hill describes as the specificities of culture,[109] must also guard against a tendency, slightly evident in *Bhaji On The Beach, Wild West* and *The Disappearance Of Finbar* (Irish cowboys, dancing the tango in Lapland, etc) to emphasise cultural eccentricity which risks becoming, in a globalised variation of Ealing cinema at its least interesting, a kind of cosmopolitan whimsy.

The Antinomies of Cultural Theory

The difficulty in reconciling these polarities is evident not only in industrial strategies and cinematic texts but a postmodernised cultural theory as well. Ien Ang, for example, argues that Europe's 'grand narratives' are over – collapsing the Enlightenment, May 68, Empire, Thatcherism and the Third Reich together as a symptom of a single will to power.[110] This is a characteristic feature of postmodern thinking. On the one hand it celebrates difference and heterogeneity, abhoring big social projects and ambitions; on the other, it is prone to lumping very different phenomena (May 68 and the Third Reich?) together with breathtaking homogeneity. Ang calls for 'the abandonment of the search for the universalising 'big story' which should open up the space for the telling of smaller, more particular stories.'[111] For Ang, the 'big story' is associated intrinsically with reconfirming already dominant identities and histories.

I suggested earlier in my discussion of globalisation, that on its own, the question of cultural difference or particularity, tends to be rather blind to the material conditions of life. This is true of Ang's advocacy of smaller, more particular stories. For the problem remains how this rejection of more 'general' themes allows one to address or even in fact to acknowledge that the world today is, as Ang herself notes, 'a thoroughly interdependent but unequal world system.'[112] This statement –if it is to mean anything - presupposes some sense of 'universal' or standard against which inequality is measured. For differentials in income, life chances, infant mortality rates, nutritional diets, etc, to be seen as *unequal*, the comparison between X and Y must assume some historically determined standard that would be more acceptable, and presumably some 'big story' that would move in the direction of correcting such inequalities. Otherwise, differentials cannot be interpreted as 'inequalities', they simply become examples of the rich field of particularities which the advocates of difference celebrate. It is not grand narratives and big stories per se that need to be rejected, but particular types of big stories which need to be interrogated.

One term that has been useful in trying to overcome this antinomy is 'critical regionalism'. Martin McLoone deploys it in order to argue that 'the particular problems in Ireland are regional and national *inflections* of problems that exist elsewhere.'[113] A *critical* regionalism would then be one which investigated these problems as ones which were inflections of more general conditions. But contrast this definition with Morley and Robins who define critical regionalism as a 'local regional culture that sees itself not introspectively but as an inflexion of global culture […] that favours diversity, plurality, discontinuity.'[114] Here the relationship between the local and the global is a largely cultural one with heterogeneity as the defining feature of a *critical* regionalism. Yet if critical regionalism is only or primarily about 'diversity, plurality, discontuinuity' then it cannot be an inflexion of problems or cultures that exist elsewhere. To be able to measure that 'elsewhere' requires some sense of continuity, some sense of connection between different points in space. The multiple stories and histories of Europe and indeed the world, must have some connection with a 'universal' or shared story and history. The exclusive emphasis on 'difference', which it is much easier to achieve with an emphasis on the cultural, provides no basis on which to make comparisons, make links, forge solidarities.

Why does cultural theory find it so difficult to reconcile cultural specificity to grand narratives, the particular to the general, the local to the global, diversity with unity? There are theoretical and political roots to this problem. The theoretical roots of the contemporary fetishisation of 'difference' derive from post-structuralist readings of Saussurean linguistics. It is based on a formalistic binary opposition between identities that parade themselves as unified and which are on that basis considered fictions or myths, and identities based on difference which are considered more real and/or more desirable. This discourse has a very pervasive influence. Andrew Higson, who writes on British Cinema from a left perspective, critiques national identity in these terms:

> The process of identification is thus invariably a hegemonising, mythologising process, involving both the production and assignation of a particular set of meanings, and the attempt to contain, or prevent the potential proliferation of other meanings.[115]

The problem with this is that all cats turn black in the postmodern night (another example of postmodernism's homogenising effects). Certainly it makes sense to argue that *dominant* versions of national identity usually (although surely to varying degrees) have strong mythological elements to them. They are prone to being ahistorical, affirmative rather than critical, concealing tensions and contradictions within the nation because these discourses have a *structural, systemic vested material interest* in misrecognising the governing social relations. But are all attempts to pin down meaning, make identifications, construct certain solidarities or collectivities equally mythological? Here the fixing of meaning is assigned the status of a 'mythologising process' while the proliferation of meanings is implicitly loaded as the real state of things (non-mythological) and therefore 'better'. While the concept of 'difference' has some value in countering the consensual, centripetal tendencies of national identity, this is too abstract and formalistic a model to help us make *political* choices and decisions. The model suggests that the potential proliferation of meanings equals 'good' because that is the reality of cultural identity, and any attempt at unity/unifying around a set of commonalities, equals 'bad' because it disavows the 'reality' of perpetual difference.

What particularly concerns me is not the impossibility of cultural commonalities within this paradigm, but the impossibility of social commonalities or a commonality of material interests. Within this model, one has to ask why, for example, gender, ethnic and class differences are more 'real' than the 'fictions' of national identity? For while these categories fissure national identity, do they not seek to establish some *internal* unity required to define for example, a class identity and gender identity; do they not in other words impose a certain homogeneity on the seething heterogeneity that is life?

Such a model of identity, so cut off from questions of material interests and social being, cannot sustain any substantive form of solidarity, collectivity and bonding. Politically it is very suited to a new souped up liberalism. An older liberalism preached tolerance of cultural difference but saw these cultures as existing peacefully but discretely with one another. Today's postmodern liberalism has a much more dynamic conception of cultural interaction and transformation. Morley and Robins commit themselves to this model of identity arguing for the importance of living with difference (this was the old liberal message) *and* letting difference live within the self (the new postmodern liberalism, premised on a new theory of the decentred subject). Now, plurality and commitment to diversity is not to be snorted at and indeed it is one of my arguments that if we are committed to diversity, then capitalism constitutes a problem. But a liberalism based on the cultural politics of difference makes solidarity recede to vague notions of sympathy, empathy and agonised calls to recognise the suffering of our fellow human beings.[116] In other words an uncritical commitment to particularity or difference flips over into an uncritical universalism ('uncritical' because the appeal to our humanity disguises how some human beings systematically exploit other human beings). What is needed is an approach to identity which is grounded materially and historically.

Making The Case For Protection of Indigenous Culture

There has been a concerted attempt by ideologues of the free market to undermine the case for cultural protection. Finney, for example, argues that economic risk is good for cultural creativity. This free market dogma has a terrible time trying to make the fantasy economics of the free market fit the realities of oligopolistic capitalism where risk is bad for profits and so is minimised. Having just made an argument for risk being good for creativity, Finney then flatly contradicts himself and admits that capital is cautious about investing in European cinema precisely because of 'the inherent risks of production.'[117] Well, not quite. The risks are there not because they are 'inherent' but largely because Hollywood has minimised its own risks and therefore displaced them elsewhere: onto the rest of the world.

Richard Collins meanwhile has argued that the attempt to make European culture 'fit' with political and economic realities, simply seeks to take the nationalist model (which assumes that polity and culture must be congruent) and scale it up to a Europe-wide level.[118] This imagines culture as being a) hermetically sealed off from influence and comparability with others, and b) as unified and formerly 'national' in its culture as the political and legal structures. Collins yokes the postmodern arguments concerning the hybridity of culture and the transnational exchanges associated with globalisation, to champion the 'free' market as the best guarantor of an international cosmopolitanism. Thus anything which interferes in the market is taken as a sign of *nationalism.*

> Europe's proactive production and quota initiatives exemplify the nationalist aspiration to make culture and polity congruent within a Greater Europe.[119]

The term 'congruent' suggests that rather consensual, seamless fit between culture and pan-national institutions which represents the *dominant* (but not uncontested) cultural politics within European elites. Collins' description of a 'Greater Europe' has deliberately imperial echoes which aid to further discredit attempts to protect the European audio-visual culture industries.

A similar defense of the market is espoused in the mainstream press by Stuart Jeffries in his attack on French protectionism:

> isn't a culture without frontiers based on transnational capitalism, better than lots of nations fighting for their misplaced cultural virility?[120]

Yet why should some protection for European cultural production be cast in terms of national 'virility'. It is clear that any attempt to do so can be immediately denounced as insular chauvinism by the free marketeers. What neither Collins or Jeffries see or admit to is that there are other cultural politics to be defended other than those based on cultural superiority and virility, at either a national or pan-national level. There is a grain of truth to the argument that capitalism and cosmopolitanism go hand in hand. The market is certainly no respecter of the parochial insularity which certain versions of national belonging display. However, it takes a rather large step to move from this observation to then valorise the market as the guarantor of diversity. As I suggested earlier, Hollywood produces a homogenisation *across* nations every bit as insular and parochial as the 'vertical' homogenisation which nationalism produces *within* nations. But in truth the problem is not Hollywood but the market system in which it operates and which allows and encourages Hollywood to *dominate* cultural production and consumption so one-sidedly. This could only be seen as unproblematic if you believe in the capitalist myth of consumer power or sovereignty. Of course consumers make decisions within the marketplace, but they do so within a field which has already been powerfully pre-structured, as my economic analysis has shown, by corporate interests.

It is clear that without cultural policies diversity is threatened. But in broad terms, what should the aims of such a cultural policy be? My argument suggests that they must avoid the antinomies of blockbuster vs small-scale filmmaking. The blockbuster strategy is economically risky and culturally problematic insofar as a) it does not seek to offer an alternative to Hollywood and b) in its representations, it betrays that it is not quite the cinema for all people that it claims to be. While low or modest budget filmmaking makes better economic sense in many ways, it often equates budgetary restrictions with small-scale ambitions and a lack of engagement with the kind of big themes which can strike a chord with broad based audiences. Closely linked with this antinomy is the one between high culture and mass culture. The way out of this antinomy is not to opt for a middlebrow culture, a 'quality' but rather conservative cinema. A progressive cultural policy would seek to engage with those aspects of mass culture which do give some expression to the lives and interests and styles of (what shall we call them?) 'the masses' or 'ordinary people'. But this vernacular needs to be yoked to a project of greater political and cultural ambition than can often be accommodated within mass culture. Such a cultural policy would have to be particularly alive to the dangers of formulating an exclusive film culture coded for the middle class.

At a national level, the argument for policy to develop structures which would foster such films should not be conflated with nationalism. John Hill has made this point very effectively:

> [...] it is quite possible to conceive of a national cinema which is *nationally specific* without being either nationalist or attached to homogenising myths of national identity.[121]

Higson has argued that advocates of a progressive national cinema, such as Hill, are really in effect talking about a 'critical (and implicitly left-wing) cinema, a radical cinema'.[122] I think Higson is right. Such a cinema is essentially an *anti-national* cinema insofar as it would challenge the myths of national belonging and unity. Yet it is still *national* in a pragmatic sense of being attuned to the specific social, political and cultural dynamics within the territory of the nation. I will explore this kind of cinema, what I call an *anti-national, national cinema*, in the next chapter.

The same argument concerning a diverse, critical and questioning film culture also applies at a pan-national, European level. The arguments for a critical and diverse national and pan-national film culture are in fact linked, rather than separate or opposed. Higson severs the link for example when he argues that cultural diversity 'may just as easily be achieved through encouraging a range of imports as by ensuring that home-grown films are produced.'[123] Yet the range of imports into national cinemas is precisely restricted by the same force (Hollywood) which makes 'homegrown' film production precarious.

We need to turn again to this question of 'critical'. The notion of critical regionalism is useful in capturing a spirit of 'indigenous' cultural production (whether indigenous refers to a sensitivity to local, national or pan-national) cultural resources and expressions. However, we do need to be clear what is meant by 'critical'. It cannot, I think, be simply about cultural plurality and 'difference', important as they are. I do not think we can make what are primarily cultural categories the absolute horizon for cultural analysis. 'Critical' needs to be defined in more substantive terms which means paying attention to the *material social* structures which determine life so unevenly and unequally.

Hill argues that what European cinemas share is a set of common problems and needs rather than a common culture.[124] The language is significant: *problems* and *needs* immediately starts to orientate us in a more materialist direction. These problems and needs we could say are both specific to the institutions of cinema but also more general social problems and needs. This lays the basis for constituting audiences 'horizontally' across national boundaries, 'binding them into cultural unities that are transnational' as Collins puts it, and not simply or exclusively national or 'vertical'.[125] For Collins this, of course, is an argument for Hollywood's relevance to audiences around the world. But why should Hollywood have *sole* rights to constitute audiences 'horizontally'?

If European policy developed so as to guarantee more equitable access to audiences, cultural producers could work towards developing not a common (homogenous) European culture, but 'horizontal' correspondences between different points within

"Europe's working class estates constellated using stills from *La Haine* which features the Chanteloup estate and the Scottish film *Small Faces* which is set on Glasgow's Easterhouse estate. © *The Guardian*, E. Clouston and P. Webster

27

Europe. Such *constellations* in social space would be both rooted in the specifics of a particular time and place, but (and here we return to a version of telling 'big stories') would have correspondences in other places within Europe and, in all likelihood, beyond.

Take for example *La Haine* with its tale of conflict, solidarity and deprivation in a French housing estate. Is this only a peculiarly French story? Recalling Sue Clayton's aim for an 'anywhere in Europe' feel to the Dublin housing estate in *The Disappearance of Finbar*, evidently not. Confirmation of this comes from a *Guardian* report on French President Jacque Chirac's 1996 visit to Glasgow's Easterhouse estate which was montaged on the same page with images from *La Haine* and a report on the Parisian estate La Noe, which was the central location in the film. Culturally, La Noe and Easterhouse are as far apart as one is likely to get within western Europe.[126] Yet the paper itself has made the link between two deprived *conditions of life* and used the film to imaginatively cement the constellation. The report notes that a year after the film, there has been little change on the French estate. This is only a surprise to those who think that film has a direct cause and effect impact on the world. Does this lack of change in La Noe mean that the film has in some way 'failed'? Surely not. It is not possible generally to measure the impact of film in such a crude way. Rather it can produce the ideas and images and values which help percolate through into a wider collective consciousness and provide at some point in the future, fuel for utopian desire, without which (and this much is certain) there will be no progressive change.

This chapter began by discussing how the question of homogenisation and heterogenisation plays out across national and global cultural markets. A progressive cultural politics takes up an ambivalent position on the national question. On the one hand the national is still the practically indispensable (although by no means only) site where material support structures can be developed to resist the cultural homogenisation unrolling from Los Angeles. It has to be stressed that it is not the culture of Hollywood itself that is the main problem, but rather the free market system in which and through which it dominates and marginalises all other film cultures. Of course the global market system does impact and standardise Hollywood film culture to a significant degree, but even then one cannot read off the value of Hollywood from its enabling economic structures. Making the distinction between Hollywood culture and economics does help move the analysis from middle-class snobbery to political and economic critique proper. For whatever the value of Hollywood films, its economic domination of the global film market and the consequences that has for cultural plurality can be measured fairly exactly. I explored the material infrastructure which ensures that Hollywood enjoys an overwhelming economic advantage in a very unfree free market. On the other hand, the national cultural space has equally been critiqued as prone to a homogenisation dynamic, the monopoly of dominant elites. We have seen that cultural unity and cultural diversity have become the key antinomy around which cultural theory has fashioned itself. Underpinned by a liberal politics, it unsurprisingly advocates the latter. We shall see in chapter three that there are theorists prepared to explicitly argue for a measure of cultural uniformity rooted at the level of the nation-state, against the advocates of cultural pluralism. But neither position will quite do, although cultural pluralism is preferable to cultural homogeneity. We have already seen that the advocates of cultural difference do not, and cannot within the terms of their conceptual underpinnings, address questions around social solidarity and shared material interests, which cut across cultural differences. This will be a reoccurring theme in the chapters that follow.

Between the national and the global there is the emerging economic, political and cultural space of Europe. The same debates get played out at this level too. There is the same argument to be had over whether Europe will be conceived in culturally exclusive ways or culturally diverse ways. I have argued though that culture cannot be the ultimate horizon within which to discuss the issue of homogeneity vs heterogeneity. Trapped within a culturally hermetic discourse, the heterogeneity that the advocates of cultural plurality advocate, will reach no further than the middle class for whom the material conditions for the good life are already to some extent in place. Travel further down the social ladder and it is clear that a discourse about cultural heterogeneity must be articulated with a critique of the material conditions in which people live and culture is produced. Thus the infrastructural mechanism of Eurimages which has sought to protect and promote European cinema, while welcome, lacks a certain economic muscle and cultural political agenda. The most important disappearance in *The Disappearance of Finbar*, that of the migrants in Stockholm, testifies to the pressures and limits which capital and national cultural pride put on exploring difference at the bottom of the class structure. It is this interlocking between multinational capital and national culture which will be explored in the next chapter.

References

1   F. Jameson, 'Globalization as a Philosophical Issue',*The Cultures of Globalization* (eds) F. Jameson and M. Miyoshi, Duke University Press, 1998.

2   A. Appadurai, 'Disjuncture and Difference in the Global Cultural Economy', *Global Culture, Nationalism, Globalization and Modernity* (ed.) M. Featherstone, Sage, London, 1995, p. 295.

3   F. Jameson, 'Globalization as a Philosophical Issue', *Cultures of Globalization*, p. 58.

4   F. Jameson, 'Globalization as a Philosophical Issue', *Cultures of Globalization*, p. 57.

5   L. Elliott, *The Guardian*, August 7, 2000, p. 21.

6   F. Jameson, 'Globalization as a Philosophical Issue', *Cultures of Globalization*, p. 74.

7   P. Swann, *The Hollywood Feature Film in Postwar Britain* St. Martin's Press, New York, 1987.

8   S. Schou, 'Postwar Americanisation and the revitalisation of European culture', *Media Cultures: Reappraising Transnational Media* (eds) M. Skovmand, K. Schroder, Routledge, London, 1992.

9   F. Jameson, 'Globalization as a Philosophical Issue', *Cultures of Globalization*, p. 74.

10 F. Jameson, 'Globalization as a Philosophical Issue', *Cultures of Globalization*, p. 63.

11 J. Tomlinson,*Cultural Imperialism*, Pinter Publishers, London, 1991, p. 22.

12 J. Tomlinson,*Cultural Imperialism*, p. 42.

13 N. Garnham, 'Political Economy and the Practice of Cultural Studies', *Cultural Studies In Question*, (eds) M.Ferguson, P. Golding, Sage, London, 1997, pp. 67–8.

14 F. Jameson, 'Globalization as a Philosophical Issue', *Cultures of Globalization*, p. 67.

15 P. Bourdieu, *Acts of Resistance, Against The Myths of Our Time*, Polity Press, Cambridge, 1998, p. 41.

16 A. Finney, *The State of European Cinema: A New Dose of Reality*, Cassell, London, 1996, p. 77.

17 *Screen Digest*, June 1995, p. 131.

18 T. Balio, 'Adjusting To The New Global Economy: Hollywood in the 1990s', *Film Policy, International, National and Regional Perspectives* (ed.) A. Moran, Routledge, London, 1996, p. 29.

19 N. Garnham, 'The Economics of the US Motion Picture Industry', *Capitalism and Communication: Global Culture and the Economics of Information* Sage, London,1990, p. 202.

20 *The Observer,* June 20, 1993, p. 53.

21 T. Balio, 'Adjusting To The New Global Economy', *Film Policy,* p. 24.

22 A. Finney, *The State of European Cinema,* p. 70.

23 A. Pulver, *The Guardian 2,* July 24, 1998, p. 5.

24 L. Friedman, (ed.) *British Cinema and Thatcherism,* University College London Press, London, 1993, p. 2 for a list of British talent that has sought regular employment in Hollywood.

25 N. Garnham, 'The Economics of the US Motion Picture Industry', *Capitalism and Communication,* p. 183.

26 T. Miller, 'The Crime Of Monsieur Lang, GATT, the screen and the new international division of cultural labour' *Film Policy,* p. 76.

27 L. Buckingham, *The Guardian,* October 19, 1996, p. 26.

28 J. Hill, 'British Film Policy' *Film Policy,* p. 107.

29 N. Garnham, 'The Economics of the US Motion Picture Industry', *Capitalism and Communication:* p. 205.

30 J. Ellis, *Visible Fictions, Cinema, Television, Video* Routledge, London, 1992, p. 35.

31 D. Malcolm, *The Guardian 2,* August 5, 1993, p. 5.

32 D. Putnam, *The Guardian 2,* July 5 1997, p. 5.

33 E. Dyja *BFI Film and Television Handbook 2002,* BFI 2001, p. 47.

34 E. Dyja *BFI Film and Television Handbook 2002,* BFI 2001, p. 39.

35 E. Forrest, *The Guardian 2,* October 27, 1997, p. 5.

36 A. Parker, *The Guardian 2,* October 27, 1997, pp.8–9.

37 D. Glaister, *The Guardian,* p. 15.

38 M. Bruce-Clayton, interviewed by the author on November 5th, 1998.

39 D. Leigh, *The Guardian 2,* December 10, 1999, p. 19.

40 A. Pulver, *The Guardian 2,* July 24, 1998, p. 5.

41 S.Woolley, *Time Out,* November 4–11, 1992, pp. 20–2.

42 A. Pulver, *The Guardian 2,* July 24, 1998, pp. 4–7.

43 D. Glaister, *The Guardian,* February 10th, 1998, p. 15.

44 S. Jeffries, the *Guardian,* July 24th, 1998, p. 15.

45 J. Hill, 'British Film Policy', *Film Policy,* pp. 101–13.

46 L. Elliott,*The Guardian,* September 5, 2000, p. 23.

47 P. Bourdieu, *Acts of Resistance,* pp. 95-96.

48 P. Bourdieu, *Acts of Resistance,* p. 96.

49 P. Bourdieu, *Acts of Resistance,* p. 37.

50 K. D. Borchardt, *European Integration: The origins and growth of the European Union* Luxembourg, 1995, p. 34.

51 E. Buscombe, 'Coca-Cola Satellites? Hollywood and the Deregulation of European Television', *Hollywood In The Age Of Television* (ed.) T. Balio, Unwin Hyman, Boston, 1990, p. 400.

52 European Commission, *The audio-visual media in the Single European Market* Luxembourg, 4/1988, p. 38.

53 European Commission, *The audio-visual media in the Single European Market,* p. 38.

54 T. Balio, 'Adjusting To The New Global Economy', *Film Policy,* p. 23.

55 J. Tunstall and M. Palmer, *Media Moguls,* Routledge, London, p. 25.

56 J. Tunstall and M. Palmer, *Media Moguls,* p. 25.

57 European Commission, *The audio-visual media in the Single European Market*, p. 26.

58 T. H. Guback, 'Hollywood's International Market', *The American Film Industry* (ed.) T. Balio, University of Wisconsin Press, Wisconsin,1985, pp. 465–9.

59 J. Coles, *The Guardian* May 11, 1992, p. 35.

60 T. Miller, 'The Crime Of Monsieur Lang, GATT, the screen and the new international division of cultural labour', *Film Policy*, p. 76.

61 P. Lennon, *the Guardian*, November 12, 1993, p. 30.

62 T. Miller, 'The Crime Of Monsieur Lang', *Film Policy*, p. 74.

63 S. Hayward, 'State, culture and the cinema: Jack Lang's strategies for the French film industry', *Screen*, 34 (4) 1993.

64 J. Carvel, *The Guardian*, September 29, 1993, p. 8.

65 European Commission, *Media Programme*, 5th edition, October, 1994.

66 M.Blaney, *Screen International*, May 1997, p. 8.

67 A. Finney, *The State of European Cinema*, p. 84.

68 *Screen Digest*, June 1995, p. 136.

69 *Screen Digest*, June, 1995, p. 130.

70 M. Most, *Eyepiece*, vol. 17, no. 1, Feb/Mar 1996, p. 21.

71 M. Most, *Eyepiece*, p. 20.

72 *Sight and Sound*, v.6, no. 2, February 1996, p. 5.

73 N. Garnham, 'The Economics of the US Motion Picture Industry', *Capitalism and Communication*, p. 188.

74 See also, A. Higson, 'A Film League Of Nations': Gainsborough, Gaumont-British and 'Film Europe', *Gainsborough Pictures* (ed.) P. Cook, Cassell, London, 1997.

75 V. Porter, 'European Co-production – Aesthetic and Cultural Implications', *European Cinema Conference* (ed.) S. Hayward, AMLC/Aston University, 1985, p. 1.

76 V. Porter, 'European Co-production', *European Cinema Conference*, p. 2.

77 J. Tunstall and M.Palmer, *Media Moguls*, pp. 27–30.

78 W. Everett, 'Framing the fingerprints: a brief survey of European film', *European Identity In Cinema* (ed.) W. Everett, Intellect Books, Exeter, 1996, p. 15.

79 W. Everett, 'Framing the fingerprints', *European Identity In Cinema*, p. 23.

80 W. Everett, 'European film and the quest for identity',*European Identity In Cinema*, pp. 9–10.

81 T. Elsaesser, *New German Cinema, A History*, BFI/Macmillan, London, 1989.

82 J. Tulloch, *Television Drama, Agency, Audience and Myth*, Routledge, London, 1990, p. 11.

83 The following information concerning the production process derives from an interview with Martin Bruce-Clayton on January 24th, 1997, unless otherwise stated.

84 Sue Clayton, interviewed by the author on February 6th, 1997.

85 Sue Clayton, interviewed February 6th, 1997.

86 *Screen Digest*, June 1995, p. 129.

87 Sue Clayton, 6th February, 1997.

88 Sue Clayton, 6th February, 1997.

89 R. White, *Sight and Sound*, November 1998, p. 46.

90 Sue Clayton, interviewed on November 10th, 1998.

91 M. Bruce-Clayton, interviewed by the author on November 5th, 1998.

92 European Commission, *A fresh boost for culture in the European Community*, EC supplement, 4/87, 1988, Luxembourg.

93 *A fresh boost for culture in the European Community*, pp. 5–6.

94 *A fresh boost for culture in the European Community*, p. 5.

95 W. Benjamin, 'Theses On The Philosophy Of History', *Illuminations* Pimlico Press, 1999, p. 248.

96 M. Liehm, *Italian Film In The Light Of Neo Realism*, Princeton University Press, Princeton, New Jersey, 1986, p. 27.

97 N. Stone, 'Through A Lens Darkly', *Black Film, British Cinema* (ed.) K. Mercer, ICA, 7, 1988, pp. 22–4.

98 D. Morley and K. Robins, *Spaces of Identity*, p. 23.

99 W. Everett, 'Framing the fingerprints', *European Identity in Cinema*, p. 14.

100 J. Hill, 'The Future Of European Cinema: The economics and culture of pan-European strategies', *Border Crossing* (eds) J. Hill, M.Mcloone, M. Hainsworth, p. 55.

101 A. J.Horton, 'Csardas and cash: Why money alone won't help Hungarian cinema', *Central European Review* 1 march, 1999, online at www.ce-review.org/kinoeye/npkinoeye4old.html.102. A.J. Horton, 'Crushing Defeats (Part II): Hungary vs Hollywood',*Central European Review* 16 March, 1999, online at: www.ce-review.org/kinoeye/kinoeye25old2.html.

103 *enthusiasm*, no. 2, summer 2000, p. 1.

104 L. Elliott,*The Guardian* August 7, 2000, p. 21.

105 P. Keighron, *The Pact Magazine*, no. 50, March 1996, pp. 11–12.

106 J. Freedland, *The Guardian*, November 18th, 1998, p. 22.

107 A. O' Shea, 'What A Day For A Daydream, Modernity, cinema and the popular imagination in the late twentieth century', *Modern Times, Reflections On A Century Of English Modernity* (eds) M. Nava and A. O'Shea, Routledge, London, 1996.

108 A. O' Shea, 'What A Day For A Daydream', *Modern Times*, p. 244.

109 J. Hill, 'Introduction' *Border Crossing*, p. 4.

110 I. Ang, 'Hegemony-In-Trouble, Nostalgia and the Ideology of the Impossible in European Cinema', *Screening Europe, Image and Identity in Contemporary European Cinema*, (ed.) D. Petrie, BFI, London, 1992, p. 27.

111 I. Ang, 'Hegemony-In-Trouble', *Screening Europe*, p. 28.

112 I. Ang, 'Hegemony-In-Trouble', *Screening Europe*, p. 22.

113 M. McLoone, 'National Cinema And Cultural Identity: Ireland And Europe', *Border Crossing*, p. 170.

114 D. Morley and K. Robins, *Spaces Of Identity*, p. 2.

115 A. Higson, 'The Concept Of National Cinema', *Screen*, vol. 30, no. 4, 1989, p. 37.

116 D. Morley and K. Robins, *Spaces of Identity*, pp. 39-40.

117 A. Finney, *The State of European Cinema: A New Dose of Reality*, Cassell, 1996, p. 71.

118 R. Collins, 'National Culture: A Contradiction In Terms?' *Television: Policy and Culture*, Unwin Hyman, London, 1990, pp. 206–7.

119 R. Collins, 'National Culture', *Television*, p. 208.

120. S. Jeffries, *The Guardian*, July 24, 1998, p. 15.

121. J. Hill, 'The Issue Of National Cinema and British Film Production', *New Questions of British Cinema*, (ed.) D. Petrie, BFI, 1992, p. 16.

122. A. Higson, 'The Limiting Imagination of National Cinema', *Cinema and Nation*, (eds) M. Hjort & S. Mackenzie, Routledge, 2000, p. 71.

123. A. Higson, 'The Limiting Imagination of National Cinema', *Cinema and Nation*, p. 71.

124. J. Hill, 'The Future of European Cinema: The economic and culture of pan-European strategies', *Border Crossing*, p. 67.

125 R. Collins, 'National Culture', *Television*, p. 214.

126 P. Webster, *The Guardian*, May 13th, 1996, p. 3.

2   National Cinema/International Markets

This chapter will explore how British national cinema has been operating in the context of international image markets in the 1990s. This will require adopting a critical stance towards both the idea of the nation, national culture and (some versions of) national cinema, as well as the international market and the way in which it diminishes cultural plurality and marginalises certain critical voices. I am going to explore how the dominant market and cultural relations structure the production and profile of representations of Britishness. I will not be focusing on the detailed institutional arrangements of British cinema in this chapter, but the discussion of production, distribution and exhibition in chapter one should be borne in mind. Instead I am going to be operating at a fairly macro economic and cultural level in order to explore how perceptions of Britishness held by *others* (Americans specifically) are a key determinant in the kind of imaginings produced by UK filmmakers. These imaginings, I will suggest, are dominated by a certain nostalgic and archaic quality. However, there is a 1990s twist to this familiar story. We can trace a debate and shift within business and political circles which has sought to *modernise* an archaic image of Britishness. I will argue that the cultural and economic strategies of one key multinational player in the British film industry during the 1990s, PolyGram Films, can be understood within this wider context of Britishness as an international commodity-image. In particular, PolyGram Films sought to *modernise* a traditional image of Britishness for international/American consumption. I will question how far such modernisation really challenged social myths (it is, in other words, a pseudo-modernisation), while also suggesting that there are, on the margins of British cinema, films which do question both the past and modernity. However, in order to really appreciate the limits within which British cinema currently operates, I will offer a comparative assessment of French cinema from the mid-1990s. Again, the argument is of a more cultural and historical kind than a detailed assessment of institutional arrangements. What I want to demonstrate is the greater space that has opened up since the mid-1990s, for a French cinema which is sensitive to and interrogative of the social, political and cultural dynamics going on within France. However, we also need to situate this internal dynamic in the context of France as the epi-centre of contemporary struggles against a neo-liberal Europe.

National Identity

A defining component of modernity is the formation and conceptualisation of the nation-state, where a centralised political authority claims sovereignty over a clearly defined territory and where the formation of a national culture becomes a crucial underpinning to the national polity. So crucial is the cultural dimension, in fact, that Benedict Anderson famously defined national identity as an imagined community. This has been an influential and in many ways fruitful formulation, because it orientates analysis to the cultural making of national identity. It has also been criticised by Schlesinger as a formulation which shares nationalism's own 'internalist' assumptions. This is the idea that the key processes responsible for the construction of national identity happens within its own borders and beyond the reach of 'external' influences.[1] Schlesinger argues that similar assumptions have dogged the study of national cinemas. My account of British cinema in this chapter will therefore try and explore the internal and external dynamics involved in its production.

Let us start with Anderson. He argues that the nation is an imagined community in several senses. It is an imagined community because the nation is too extensive for its members to 'know most of their fellow-members, meet them, or even hear of them'. Thus national identity requires *cultural* resources by which to construct representations, and to imagine from those representations, the nature of their community and connectedness.[2] Anderson suggests that in the crucial period of national formation in 18th- and 19th-century western Europe, the emerging print media of the novel and the newspaper played the central role of imagining the national community.[3] Today, of course, the cultural resources for imagining the national community are more extensive and include radio, film, television, music, the heritage industry and so on. Despite this, imagining the nation has become a good deal more complex, and indeed contradictory, than ever before.

Anderson notes that all nations are imagined as 'limited', which is to say that nations have 'finite, if elastic, boundaries, beyond which lie other nations.'[4] This is problematised, however, when the nation is increasingly pulled into larger geopolitical spheres of influence, as is happening with the construction of economic and (very likely) political convergence within Europe. It is also problematised when those boundaries become increasingly porous. For as Ernest Gellner has argued, nationalism 'is the political principle which maintains that similarity of culture is the basic social bond'[5] and that 'the boundaries of social units and of cultures [...] converge.'[6] But what if the imaginings by which the community comes to understand itself are no longer primarily self-generated? In a situation where transnational corporations and international communications networks are responsible for a global flow of images and ideas, then clearly cultures no longer neatly fit social or political units. Even when signifying practices, such as films and television programmes, are indigenously made, they are often locked into a relationship whereby perceptions of the nation that are held by *others*, are a key determinant in the kind of imaginings produced. (We shall explore this dynamic further later on). As communication networks expand, so too does the potential for migration, another key force penetrating national 'limits', often despite severe barriers and obstacles placed before the migrants by national politicians. Here again this complicates the nationalist ideal that social or political units converge with cultural ones.

Linked to the crisis over the limits and effective boundaries of the nation is the crisis of sovereignty. Ideally the national state is understood as the guarantor of a chosen mode of life and the representative of the people, even where electoral representation has been severely or totally curtailed. Yet clearly the sovereignty or autonomy of the nation is in crisis, drawn as it is into the sphere of influence of such powerful forces as the United States, the sole remaining superpower after the collapse of the Soviet Union; multinational corporations whose investment decisions affect large swathes of national populations quite outside the power and control of national governments; the financial markets, whose global and unregulated activities (the buying and selling of currencies, speculation on prices and so on) and periodic crises once more call the ideal of the sovereign nation acting alone and through its own internally generated processes, very much into question; financial organisations, like the World Bank, the International Monetary Fund (IMF), the European Central Bank and so forth, again operate outside the control of, but have a significant impact on national governments. Just as the bourgeois ideal of the individual subject operating according to their own autonomous laws has been called into question (in different ways) by Marxism, psychoanalysis and post-structuralism, so the nationalist ideal of the sovereign autonomous nation, is increasingly being called into question by real world developments within global capitalism.

Anderson notes that the nation is imagined as a *community* 'because, regardless of the actual inequality and exploitation that may prevail […] the nation is always conceived as a deep, horizontal comradeship.'[7] This is a crucial point. While liberal commentators on nationalism such as Gellner and Zygmunt Bauman restrict their critiques of the nation to its intolerance of cultural diversity, they tend to play down this contradiction between the comradeship with which the nation is imagined and the inequality and exploitation which actually fractures this community. Gellner for example has virtually nothing to say about how the political elites which dominate the state apparatus are functionally linked into national and transnational capital. Within film theory, the nation has been increasingly critiqued for its smoothing over of internal differences within the community. Yet the way in which such 'differences' are conceptualised is politically crucial and there are some important choices which need to be made. One could characterise the internal differences of the national community in the way Higson does:

> those communities consist of highly fragmented and widely dispersed groups of people with as many differences as similarities and with little […] real physical contact with each other.[8]

What gets evacuated from such a conception of the nation's differences (which here derive from geography and individuality) is any sense of the systemic, structured and structuring unequal power relations which constitute the nation. For me, cultural difference and specificity become interesting (and explicable) when they are articulated with the social power struggles which fracture the nation. The contradiction between the national ideal that all members share the same or similar *material* interests (backed up by cultural uniformity) and the actual division of interests within the nation, is central to my definition (and advocacy) of what I call anti-national national films.

At a political level, the nation constitutes a shared frame of reference within which struggles over the nature of the state and national society are conducted. This has implications for thinking about national culture and identity. So, too, does the fact that many practices take place within the nation-state but are hardly 'national' in the sense of being widely shared across various groups. Thus there are cultural practices which take place within the national territory but are particular to certain groups, whether defined by class, region, gender, ethnicity and so on. In this sense, the 'national' is a somewhat empty category. Such cultural practices obviously might spread more widely and so at one level they may be legitimately described as 'national', for instance, the way curry has become the British national dish. But many other Indian cultural practices remain particular to British-Asians and so one has to ask, in what sense such practices are really 'national'? Other cultural practices (such as cinema going, football) though are more widely 'shared' across numerous groups and so at one level could be described as 'national'. However, we need to use this term in a neutral descriptive sense and should on no account assume that a shared cultural reference is the same as shared cultural meanings. Although various groups may converge in watching films or around the various practices and discourses of football, because they are different groups, they may well participate in, experience and consume these cultural practices in different ways. The task of cultural analysis is to identify the continuities and differences in the actual uses and meanings which different groups make of shared and particular cultural resources and, crucially, how those cultural resources and meanings are articulated with unequal relations of power. The term 'national' often short-circuits that kind of precise investigation by assuming too much, while the notion of difference, on its own, equally has a truncated explanatory power.

The final characteristic of national identity that is important to understand is the dynamic between tradition and modernity. Anderson notes the historical fact that nations (insofar as they have been defined above) are comparatively recent phenomenon, around three hundred odd years old and often involving, in the course of their histories, fundamental geographical, political and cultural re-alignments. Just sketching the case of Britain gives some sense of how national identity has been transformed and adapted over time. The 1707 Act of Union incorporated Scotland for the first time in an English dominated British nation, which included an already subordinated Wales. The 1800 Act of Union brought Ireland under direct rule. In 1922 Northern Ireland was established after the rest of Ireland achieved independence from Britain. In 1931, the Statute of Westminster began to shift Britain's Empire towards the status of a self-governing Commonwealth. In 1935 the Government of India Act granted a limited self-government to India (the jewel in the colonial crown) in response to Indian nationalism. The 1939–45 war and the post-war Labour government were defining moments in the formation of a post-war national identity built around the welfare state. The post-war period of decolonisation, the end of Empire and the rise of a multicultural Britain through immigration from the former colonies, brought further transformations. The 1980s saw the rise of the neo-liberal economics which has privatised most areas of public service and seen the emergence of a market dominated society of the type characterised by America.

Thus national identity is marked by discontinuities, transformations, accretions and the contradictory jostling between various components which have accumulated in the course of history. Yet despite this, national identity is almost always seen as having roots deep into antiquity and, as a result, there is a strong tendency to dehistoricise national identity, downplaying the changes and transformations that national identity has undergone or only acknowledging and incorporating those changes when they can be slotted into a mythical timelessness.

The emphasis on tradition provides a crucial resource of legitimation when the imagined community is buffeted by crises and riven by internal fissures. Tradition stresses continuity, and, if there is to be any change at all, gradualism. In *The Invention of Tradition,* a collection of authors identify the increasing tendency towards the invention of rituals, practices and symbols in Imperial Britain, particularly around the monarchy and in colonial India and Africa, towards the end of the 19th century. This *modern* investment in invented traditions attempts to link relatively *novel* forms of power relations and exploitation, with continuity, with the past, with what has been, as a form of legitimation for what is, in a world premised on transience and change.[9] Here modernity uses tradition to legitimise social relations, but conversely, as we shall see, tradition can adopt a veneer of innovation and modernisation; the social motive behind this *reinvention* of tradition is, however, exactly the same.

According to Stuart Hall, the Englishness which was forged in the period of the Empire was a classic binary one, a 'highly exclusive and exclusivist form of cultural identity' in which essentialising characteristics (mostly positive) were ascribed to the English and essentialising characteristics (mostly inferior) were ascribed to the other. The English were white, the other was not, the English were masculine, the other was feminine, the English were disciplined and rational, the other was emotional or spiritual, the English were administrators, the other was administrated, the English were bourgeois, the other was not.[10] Best of all, the English were modern *and* traditional, while the other (if American) was either *too* modern or, if the colonised, *too* traditional and backward. One of the defining characteristics of all national identities within capitalism is this struggle to negotiate the tensions between tradition and modernity. It is this tension which has dominated political and business derived discourses in the 1990s.

National Identities and International Markets

We live in a world dominated by images. The perceptions they construct and the values and meanings which they assign to products, companies, even nations are absolutely central to the workings of modern capitalism. This is not a new phenomenon. The early domination of world film markets by Hollywood was widely recognised as a means by which to sell all kinds of American products and ideals.[11] More recent phenomena, such as the rise of the branded product, extend this logic further. Naomi Klein has shown how the process of branding invests material products (Nike Shoes, Starbucks coffee, Disney, GAP, Body Shop, etc) with culture: that is with a particular set of meanings and values which sell much more than the product, but rather signify a way of life. Multinational corporations are spending an increasing amount of their investment in the expensive business of this *cultural* production. In fact branding is even more of a priority than manufacturing and so multinationals have been downsizing their own industrial base and subcontracting production out, often overseas to the Third World where labour costs are low. This means that products can be made cheaply which leaves plenty of surplus capital around to build brands.[12]

Yet while multinational capital operates globally, the image bank which they draw on to brand their goods, taps much of their meaning and resonance from the master-images which constitute the *national* image. The 1990s have seen a debate within British capitalism as to whether the national brand is good for business or bad for it. The Walpole Committee, for example, was set up in the early 1990s to promote a traditional Britishness. The committee's members are primarily luxury goods and service companies like Savoy, the perfumer Penhaligon, Mulberry (bags and belts) and Asprey (jewellery). Many are foreign owned, others are part of huge international conglomerates, but they all see an old style Britishness as a valuable commodity in the international image markets. For companies like the National Trust, Beefeater Gin and Walkers Shortbread, this means exploiting heritage, pageantry and the stately home imagery associated with Britishness.[13] However, others think this image is a liability. British Airways spent £60 million in ditching its Union Jack tail fins and designing 50 'global images' to replace them. Famously, they were admonished by Margaret Thatcher for doing so. Yet this switch to a 'modern' cosmopolitan identity did not not help shore up British Airways in a competitive market and they subsequently brought the Union Jack tailfins back.

The problem is that while a traditional branding of Britishness can signify quality, luxury and craftsmanship, research has shown that it can equally signify a backward looking, amateur cottage industry, unable to provide the reliable quality which modern professional businesses need. Shortly after New Labour's 1997 election victory, Tony Blair, who had made 'modernisation' a keyword in the party's vocabulary, attempted to rebrand Britain around 'modern' industries such as design, architecture, fashion, film, television and music. Blair argued that the image which British people had of themselves and others had of them, was that of being 'stuck in the past', wonderful at pageantry, 'less good at new technology'.[14] However, Blair did not declare an all-out war on tradition. He was careful to call for a delicate blend of the two.

> When I talk about Britain as a "Young Country", I mean an attitude of mind as much as anything. I mean we should think of ourselves as a country that cherishes its past, its traditions, and its unique cultural inheritance, but does not live in the past. A country that is not resting on past glories, but hungry for future success.[15]

Here is an example of that continual and delicate negotiation between tradition and modernity, that I discussed earlier. Blair does not want to reject tradition but instead he wants to give an expanded role for the modern within conceptions of British national identity. As we shall see later, this reworking of the traditional and the modern can be detected in British cinema during the 1990s.

One of the reports, which was influencing opinion on the possible negative equity of the traditional British brand, was drawn up by an advertising agency, BMP DDB NeedHam. (Significantly, the agency was PolyGram's marketing advisor in the early 1990s). The report explored perceptions of Britishness held by people outside Britain.

Its sample was, of course, professional business people, so it hardly counts as a representative sociological survey, yet it makes for interesting reading and has important implications for thinking about British cinema.

The report found that Western Europe had the strongest sense of Britain as a country 'with many differentiated characteristics'.[16] While the traditional images of Britain had a strong profile, it was their paradoxical combination with various signifiers of modernity, such as a multi ethnic population, which fashioned a picture of 'contrasts and contradictions'. While perceptions of Britishness varied around the world, the most 'limited views of Britishness came from the US, they lacked depth and were single dimensional.'[17] For America, the typical associations of Britishness were: croquet, teatime, Robin Hood, tweed, castles, Henry VIII, Charles Dickens' London, aristocracy, Shakespeare, Eton, etc. The report notes that often fact and fiction, reality and myth were blurred.[18] The report identifies the centrality of film and television images in shaping the perceptions of Americans. 'Britain is admired for its history, its culture, its traditions and its great literature and the visualisation of this in BBC drama has a big and appreciative market abroad.'[19] Americans value the green landscape ('a manageable outdoors rather than the mythical outdoors of the US'), the history and the culture; but these positive associations also shade into negatives, even for the Americans.

There is a lack of vitality, excitement and aspiration associated with the British whose reserve and formality indicate a certain lack of warmth and intimacy. Note the importance of the audio-visual industries in constructing this image and conversely, how this image in the international markets must also set the parameters for what is produced by the audio-visual industries. Now, if we add that the American market is the most important for British film and that it is in this market that Britishness is seen in its most one dimensional, stereotypical version, then we can see that there are powerful commercial pressures determining what images of Britain get produced. This situation also implies that a more diverse space for the production of images set in Britain might be created if the main market was western Europe. Yet that, of course, as we saw in the previous chapter, would require a greater space within the European market for European films, currently dominated by Hollywood.

The report notes that the traditional version of Britishness 'has achieved a near mythical status abroad and has pervaded all perceptions of Britain'.[20] This image has been 'sold hard' and while it benefits certain companies and products, it also narrows the British brand. 'By only projecting a sense of tradition and letting nothing else through, Britain is failing to associate itself with progress'.[21] This failure to modernise means Britishness is increasingly linked with the negative associations of conservatism: decline, elitism, hierarchy, male dominated, white and class ridden. The report calls for restoring the balance between tradition and modernity and concludes that:

> British media output is like a national advertising campaign. If the parent brand is to be kept strong, healthy and relevant so that it can provide unique umbrella support to a broader range of brands and product categories, it is critical that Britain plays to new-found strengths which are rooted in the reality of the country today.[22]

As the report goes on and it explores the various characteristics of Britishness, it reads more and more like an analysis of British cinema. The report notes that the British are uncomfortable with the unknown, the unfamiliar and the foreign (see *Another Time, Another Place, Letter To Brezhnev*); they insulate themselves from other social classes (certainly one of the characteristics of British cinema is the lack of mobility and communication between classes). This insularity manifests itself in British humour which 'is essentially insular – it is self-lampooning, ironic, dry and lateral and many jokes are 'in-jokes'. John Cleese and Monty Python are its main exponent and export.'[23] While enjoying a good joke, the British 'are not seen as being good at enjoying the sensuous pleasures of life, food, wine, good company, intimacy'.[24]

Curiously, there is a perception abroad that the British display a certain individualism and idiosyncratic quality. This is curious because it seems to be paradoxically combined with the reserve, inhibition and tradition-bound aspects of Britishness. Yet this paradox, this combination of individualism vs social convention, is the dramatic structure for many British films, particularly the heritage genre. In *A Room With A View* (James Ivory, 1985) the narrative trajectory of the heroine, Lucy Honeychurch, is one which moves from the restricted social order of late Victorian Britain, with its firmly delineated class distinctions and expectations for women, to a more 'modern' class and gendered order where the individual subject's authentic desires (Lucy's cross-class romance with George Emerson) are not snuffed out by social convention. This movement forward is achieved however via a movement 'backwards' in time. Via the source novel by E. M. Forster (written in the first decade of the 20th century), *A Room With A View* taps into the late-19th-century bourgeois vogue of romantic primitivism,[25] by beginning in underdeveloped Florence, Italy. The ideological project of the film – encapsulated in the title– is to achieve a reconciliation between the motif of the room, that interior space symbolising all the refinement, culture, and civilisation of bourgeois society, but also its repressions, with the motif of 'the view', the exterior space of nature where desire can be expressed unembarrassed by social conventions. Exactly then the sort of narrative that could travel well in the American market.

(Inter) National Cinema

I want to now map out a model of the kinds of films which get made by a national cinema operating in an international environment. The model (see Fig. 2.1) turns on four categories: embedded films; disembedded films; cross-border films; and anti-national, national films. They are not mutually exclusive categories; films can occupy more than one category, but the arrows radiating out do give some sense of the different directions which national film production can take in terms of what it produces and for which audiences. The model is built largely around the UK, but with modifications, it could apply equally to the output of other European national cinemas. The criteria for including films in the embedded, disembedded and cross-border categories, are a mixture of economic and cultural factors which determine what markets they are primarily pitched at. The fourth category, however, is defined primarily by the political combativity of the films; their critique that is of the nation as a site of shared interests and values. I am not implying that political combativity is impossible in films belonging largely to the other categories. Here, however, my key concern is with positioning films in relation to national identity.

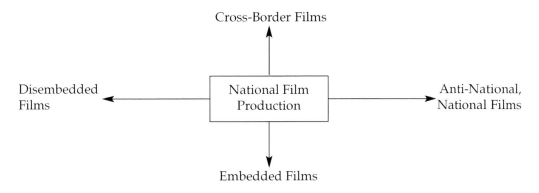

Figure 2.1 National Cinema/International Market

1) Embedded films. These are films which are pitched primarily (although not exclusively) for the national market, either because the budgets (including the marketing budgets) for the films are not sufficiently high for there to be a reasonable expectation that it will gain a profile abroad, and/or because the cultural material which the film is dealing with has not had sufficiently successful prior circulation in the international market. Anne Jackel gives a fascinating account of the French comedy, *Les Visiteurs* (Jean-Marie Poire, 1993) for example, which was a box office success at home but in general, struggled to find audiences outside Francophone areas on the international market.[26] Comedy films within Europe are often strongly anchored in their national cultural contexts and while they enjoy success there, they often fail to cross borders. British films about football such as *When Saturday Comes* (Maria Giese, 1995), *Fever Pitch* (David Evans, 1996), and *The Match* (Mick Davis, 1999), also tend to suffer from a certain inexportability. The British gangster movie however has been, as we shall see, increasingly successful in the international market place, but again, if the budgets for the film are low, this international potential is unlikely to be fulfilled (*You're Dead* (Andy Hurst, 1999), for example). The financial backing for these kinds of films comes largely from national sources, often television as in the examples of *Twenty Four Seven* (Shane Meadows, 1997), and *A Room For Romeo Brass* (Shane Meadows, 1999), both BBC funded. National subsidies are another source for these low budget films. Indeed a number of films funded by the National Lottery appear to be the 'quota-quickies'[27] of their day and have attracted much criticism for being made with little care or expectation that they will find even a national audience.[28] Elsewhere though the National Lottery has had more success with *Beautiful People* (Jasmin Disdar, 1999) and *Ratcatcher* (Lynne Ramsay, 1999).

However, international capital does plug into this low-profile cultural production. Global companies must retain some sensitivity to cultural trends happening locally. In this way, international film companies may be able to tap into unexpected hits or at least keep in touch with current trends that could be exploited (i.e. disembedded) within international markets. Thus the Belfast-based romantic comedy *With Or Without You* (Michael Winterbottom, 2000) (a film which, like *Divorcing Jack*, is a product of the Northern Ireland peace process) was funded by Film Four and Miramax, the Walt Disney subsidiary. Unfortunately for Miramax, despite poaching senior executives from Channel Four and giving them a £30 million production fund,[29] *With Or Without You* was six re-writes short of having a good script. It signally failed to explore the French, British/Protestant and Catholic/Irish culture clash which the story and setting suggested and which Channel Four Films have done so successfully in the past.

2) Disembedded films. These are those films which have the budgets and the cultural potential to succeed in the American market. Generally, only the UK and France have the economic and cultural resources to gain access to America's huge audience. The cultural material which they exploit in doing this are, as we have seen, the repertoire of national imagery that has already achieved or may achieve wide circulation in the international market. It is in this sense that the films are disembedded from the national context. We have seen that in the case of the UK, the narrowness of the imagery, which conventionally represents Britishness, has been the subject of much debate, within political and economic institutions. The advertising report by BMP DDB NeedHam called for images more rooted in the reality of contemporary Britain, but there is a real sense in which images designed for international consumption find it difficult to be attuned to the social specificities and diversities of national life. Two questions arise therefore: to what extent has the somewhat archaic branding of Britishness in the international market been corrected by more modern images? And how far has this 'modernisation' of Britishness (if it has occurred) challenged the strong commercial compulsion which disembedded images have of mythicising national identity?

During the 1990s, the Dutch-owned PolyGram Films were particularly active in attempting to plug into joint ventures with British national based talent to lift embedded cultural material into the international market, or give cultural material already well established at international level, a kind of modernising make-over. PolyGram hoped to exploit the global domination of the English language and Anglo-American cultural links to access Hollywood's domestic market. PolyGram Films is another example of a great hope for European cinema to compete with Hollywood. But in 1998 it was sold to the Canadian company Seagram who own Universal. PolyGram's parent company, Philips, the electronics giant, had decided that it needed to streamline its operations and increase shareholder returns.

Thus the profit motive claimed another interesting, if not unproblematic, cultural experiment. PolyGram had made a disastrous foray into Hollywood in the late 1970s, but their 1990s film strategy sensibly did not involve pouring money into pockets of Hollywood moguls. Instead PolyGram films adopted the model of the PolyGram music division which was to work through production subsidiaries or 'labels'.[30] PolyGram purchased Working Title for their UK production base in 1991. Philips, which owned 75% of PolyGram, invested over $1 billion in film production over the decade, much of which included setting up a US distribution arm (Gramercy). Thus it was PolyGram's ambition to become the first European investor to succeed over the long term in Hollywood. Although PolyGram had distribution arms in the UK, France, Germany, Spain, the Netherlands and Australia, the colossal investment in US distribution meant two things: firstly, they needed to make around 15 films a year to supply the distribution arm, up to four of which would be 'wide releases' on more than 2000 screens;[31] secondly, the films had to be geared towards success in the American market as an absolute prerequisite for financial viability.

PolyGram invested in the football film mentioned above, *The Match*, which was clearly intended to have some Atlantic cross-over appeal (it starred the American actor Tom Sizemore), but they were more successful in bankrolling and disembedding *Bean: The Ultimate Disaster Movie* (Mel Smith, 1997). At $15 million, *Bean* was clearly intended to do well in the international market. This meant translating Rowan Atkinson's television character into cultural material with blockbuster appeal. In part the film could use the international disembedded profile which the *television* series had achieved in some territories (Australia, for example, but not America) as a profitable launching pad (the film was first released in Australia where it took $5 million in its first week).[32] *Bean* eventually grossed $235 million worldwide.[33] PolyGram's most successful film of the 1990s was a kind of heritage movie in contemporary guise. *Four Weddings and a Funeral* (Mike Newell, 1993), starring the American actress Andie Macdowell alongside a then fairly unknown Hugh Grant, took more than $250 million worldwide. PolyGram's *Plunkett & Macleane* (Jake Scott,1999) tried to hybridise the heritage film, fusing it with the crime caper movie and slotting in the Hollywood actress Liv Tyler as a co-star for the American market. *Trainspotting* (Danny Boyle, 1995) is a more complex case of disembedding. It was funded by Channel Four but marketed and distributed by PolyGram to the tune of £850,000. As with *East is East*, this was a large marketing budget, almost half as much again as the film's production budget.[34] Drawing on PolyGram's connections and experience with the music business, the film was marketed through 'outlets and sites connected with the pop and rock music culture.'[35] The film went on to take $75 million worldwide.[36] Murray Smith has explored the way *Trainspotting* draws its cultural reference points from every geographical scale, from the very local, to the regional, up through the national and then onto the global. In terms of my production model, the film has elements of all four categories. It can be seen as an example of an anti-national, national film (Renton's famous 'It's shite being Scottish' speech); embedded film (it has strong local, regional and national cultural references and inflections that have not had huge prior international circulation, e.g. the working class Scottish accents are fairly strong); disembedded culture (the film draws on international American and British popular music culture as well as displaying British and Scottish national heritage culture); and cross-border films. Murray describes the film's aesthetic as 'Black magic realism'. Certainly the film's aesthetic code depends on juxtaposing two traditions, the realistic (images and stories of social deprivation) and the surreal (for example the toilet bowl sequence) which European audiences have been receptive to in the past.

PolyGram's cultural strategy bears a remarkable resemblance to the debates that I discussed earlier, where a one-sided over reliance on traditional images of Britishness was beginning to be seen as a potential liability, but where a simple assertion of the modern and the cosmopolitan was also, as British Airways found out, problematic. The solution for British capital (and by extension, transnational capital using/selling images of Britishness) was to try and negotiate some blending or reconciliation between the traditional and the modern. The advantage for PolyGram of this strategy is that it would diversify the brand they were using to try and crack the American market while also hopefully proving popular in European and other world markets, which, as the BMP DDB Needham report found, had already a more diverse sense of Britishness in circulation.

While historically, high profile representations of Britishness have been dominated by the heritage genre, drawing on literary sources, iconic imagery and historical narratives, recent developments have seen the repertoire of imagery pitched at the international market place, diversify slightly. However, this slight advance on standardised images is still largely in thrall to mythicisation. Both *The Full Monty* (Peter Cattaneo, 1997) and *Billy Elliot* (Stephen Daldry, 2000) deal with cultural material that might once have been an example of an embedded film or an example of anti-national, national cinema. But both add to working class life the all important ingredients of aspiration, individual ingenuity and transcendence of class boundaries (just like *Room With A View*), which help these films travel into the American market. The British gangster genre or crime film – which has long had thematic and stylistic links with its American cousin – has also been revived as an international commodity via *Lock Stock and Two Smoking Barrels* (Guy Ritchie,1998) while Mike Hodges *Croupier* (1998) succeeded in America after the film's British backers (Film Four) refused to help its British distribution.

An interesting example of the figure of the British gangster circulating in the American market can be found in *The Limey* (Steven Soderbergh, 1999). The use of British stars in American films are examples of fragments of British culture crossing the Atlantic as star *images*. Even when they are not playing British protagonists, their Britishness still functions as a signifier of some alien or foreign sensibility– Alan Rickman playing a German in *Die Hard* (John McTiernan, 1988) or Anthony Hopkins, playing a psychotic American in *The Silence of the Lambs* (Johnathan Demme,1990). In *The Limey*, Terence Stamp arrives in LA to the sound of a Who song ('The Seeker', appropriately enough). The film very self-consciously takes an element of 1960s British culture – the hard Cockney gangster – and translates it into a modern American setting. This makes Stamp's character doubly incongruous, both temporally (he has been in prison for three decades) and culturally. Stamp's presence in the film, directed by Steven Soderbergh, seems to license *The Limey*'s Boormanesque/*Point Blank* (1967)/European New Wave aesthetic (flash forwards, flash backs, a-synchronic sound and so on). But perhaps most audaciously, and most knowingly, the film's conceit is that Stamp/Wilson, is a continuation of the protagonist from Ken Loach's realist classic, *Poor Cow* (also 1967). *The Limey* includes several sequences of borrowed material from *Poor Cow* including the younger Stamp and Carol White, the mother of the daughter whose death in America, Stamp/Wilson has come to investigate in *The Limey*. The latter film even splices into the footage from *Poor Cow* shots of the daughter as a young girl that are not from the original film (there was a son, but no daughter).

Stamp's double incongruity in 1990s Los Angeles is the occasion for a number of jokes concerning cultural misunderstandings and sheer incomprehension on the part of the Americans. In one scene at a party, Stamp/Wilson informs his American friend that he's going to take a 'butchers' around the house, to which his friend inquires: 'Who you goin' to butcher?' In *The Limey* we have an example of both cultural exchanges and border crossings in the international image markets (the mythic construction and relocation of a certain very hard British masculinity which the American villains are constantly underestimating) and, in an intertextual nod/homage to *Poor Cow*, a very different mode of film practice, that of a British anti-national, national cinema that is rarely to be found circulating with any profile in the United States.

3) Cross-Border films. These are those films which travel in the international market outside America, particularly, although not exclusively, the European market. This category may include national art films, but increasingly, in the context of the European market, it includes films which inscribe travel and a certain porosity of national identities within their narratives as a precondition of the co-productions which funded them and the broader European identities which they are exploring. Such a category would include the films which I will discuss in the next chapter: *The Disappearance of Finbar* (Sue Clayton, 1996), *Land and Freedom* (Ken Loach, 1995) and *The Name of The Rose* (Jean-Jacques Annaud, 1986). Interestingly, the latter film, a West German, Italian and French co-production, was made with the kind of budget, $30 million, which indicates that the producers and financial backers were expecting the film to score well in the American market (and, indeed, the presence of Christian Slater in the cast was aimed as facilitating this, although he was not a major star at the time). Thus Twentieth Century Fox bought the film's theatrical and television distribution rights for North America and worldwide video rights. However, the film did poorly at the US box office but was financially very successful with European audiences. It took $45 million in Germany alone and was equally successful in France and Italy.[37]

Anti-National National films. The films in this category are defined by their critique of the myth of *community* which underpins national identity; the myth that is of that deep horizontal comradeship which overlays the actual relations of a divided and fractured society. The myth of unity and shared interests is a powerful means for legitimising the social order. These films are national insofar as they display an acute attunement to the specific social, political and cultural dynamics within the territory of the nation, but they are anti-national insofar as that territory is seen as a conflicted zone of unequal relations of power. The scandalously under-appreciated work (within the UK) of Ken Loach with such films as *Riff Raff* (1991), *Raining Stones* (1993), *Ladybird Ladybird* (1994), would be examples, as would *Brassed Off* (Mark Herman, 1996), *Face* (Antonio Bird, 1997) *Century* (Steven Poliakoff, 1993) and *Mansfield Park* (1999). The latter film radically updates Jane Austen's source novel by, among other things, imaginatively filling in the silences within Austen's text concerning the source of Sir Thomas' wealth (the slave plantation in Antigua). One could make a case for *Trainspotting* as an anti-national national film while the British Asian films discussed in the final chapter also fit into this category insofar as the nation-state has imagined itself as being underpinned by a homogeneous culture. Insofar as the films situate themselves within an international geo-cultural space (British *and Asian*, British Cinema *and* Bollywood) these films also belong in the category of cross-border films.

The Politics of the Historical Drama

Representations of British history have been dominated by what came to be known in the 1980s as the heritage film. While these films may not represent the majority of the type of British films that are made, they do, as we have seen, have a disproportionate impact on perceptions of Britishness. The heritage film has attracted plenty of critical attention. Tana Wollen provided an early analysis of the genre (and it can fairly be labelled a genre, with its consistent iconography, cluster of themes, and even a familiar repertoire of British actors and actresses). Wollen criticises the taken-for-granted wealth which is on display in the films[38] and the exclusive and hierarchical society which they tacitly uphold.[39] Wollen notes that there are 'hints of something rotten' in the nostalgic representations of the past, but generally she calls for 'old ghosts' to be left behind and for contemporary stories to be told. Yet while contemporary stories are important, the past, tradition, should not be left to the political right to define. There are stories and perspectives buried in the past which have to be redeemed by the present just as urgently as articulating marginalised voices in the present. Indeed the two are intimately linked.

Andrew Higson has argued that there is a tension within the heritage genre between a nostalgic image constructed at the level of *mise-en-scene*, with its 'reassurance of apparent continuity with the past', and narratives which suggest this past is already in decline.[40] However, Higson has argued that in general, 'the satire or ironic social critique' evident in the source novels of these films, such as Forster's, are blunted by the 'pictorial qualities' of a lovingly recreated *mise-en-scene* of the past.[41] Sarah Street by contrast argues that the social critique does sometimes come through from the source novels. In *Howard's End* (James Ivory, 1991), for example, adapted from Forster's novel, Leonard Bast's fate 'highlights the hypocritical norms of the upper-middle class'.[42] We could put this a little more strongly, I think. What comes into view in *Howard's End* is the capricious nature of the capitalist economy, with Bast losing his income after he swaps banking jobs on the advice of the upper- middle-class characters he has befriended. In another analysis of the genre, Claire Monk's empirical study of audiences has called into question the assumption that heritage films are peculiarly or exclusively films watched by the middle classes.[43]

Nevertheless, while we can find tensions and contradictions within these films and even moments of disgust, as Street notes, at the class nature of British society, critics should not let the dominance of these films inhibit us from imagining and indeed pointing to alternative modes of representing history (and here the composition of the audience for these films is secondary to a broader political point). A comparative analysis is therefore useful in alerting us to the *limits* within which the heritage film operates. I will suggest in the next section, that contemporary French cinema produces representations of the historical past that are radical in a way that the dominant

British culture finds difficult to support and foster. The domination of the aristocracy and the landed bourgeoisie in these films, the at best muted criticism of these social stratas, the virtual exclusion of the labouring classes whose exploitation the wealthy depend on, and the resistance to acknowledging the forces of change and modernity that exist within the past, are all characteristic of the British heritage film. Where the British film, *The Madness of King George* (Nicholas Hytner, 1994) focuses sympathetically on the ailing monarch, the French film, *Ridicule* (Patrice Leconte, 1996), also set in the 1780s, indicts the irrational madness of the entire French aristocratic and feudal class.

The juxtaposition of these two films suggests that it is not only the contemporary international market which shapes the narrow range of Britishness for export, but the *internal* dynamics of the nation: in this case the very different legacies of the English and French Revolutions. It is indeed extraordinary how the events of the past persist in having profound effects in the present. The English revolution of 1648–9 generated an intense debate as to the nature and scope of the envisaged transformations of the social order. Groups like the Diggers, the 'Ranters', elements within the Levellers, Fifth Monarchists and Quakers sought to extend the political revolution, which had seen the abolition of the monarchy and the House of Lords into a more thorough-going social revolution that would benefit the plebeian masses and not just the embryonic middle classes. As Brian Manning notes, such radical political traditions were:

> [...] characterised by class feeling, dreams of equality, schemes for the decentralisation of power, 'practical christianity', and hopes for the redistribution of wealth. It foreshadows socialism.[44]

However, such radical arguments had little effective social base. The industrial working class was still nearly two hundred years away. Cromwell effectively marginalised and oppressed these more radical elements *within* the revolution, while the restoration of the monarchy in 1660 set the seal on the re-establishment of a conservative *official* national identity. The radical arguments of the left of course re-emerged in the wake of the French revolution, amongst the artisans of the 1790s, the immediate forerunners of the industrial working class.[45] But the gestation and evolution of capitalism in England had been developed over two centuries before the industrial working class emerged. Thus the bourgeoisie consolidated its relationship with the aristocracy, while the English working class – the first proletariat, 'coincided with the minimum availability of socialism as a structured ideology'.[46] The persistence of history is such that the after-images of this course of events is still very much part of the cultural fabric of Britain's national identity.

By contrast, the French revolution was more successful in incorporating 'equality, fraternity, and liberty' as part of the *official* identity of revolutionary France. In addition, such radical traditions could be coupled, within two generations, to an emerging social base, wage labour, that could at last have the leverage which could turn what had once been utopian ideals into a practical force. Of course, the ideals of the French revolution could be and were reconciled to the dominant interests that

47

drove the revolution, the property-owning middle classes. But the official French political culture has always been a great deal more ambiguous and open to more radical inflection than the British one, which so successfully built itself around hierarchy, privilege and deference. It is important to stress the distinction between official representations of national identity and the actual realities of life that make up the nation but which do not get readily acknowledged. I would not, for example, want to set up an equally mythic opposition between the radical, revolting French and the passive, acquiescent (or depending on the point of view, law-abiding), British. It was after all, striking British miners that lost Edward Heath the 1974 election, while de Gaulle survived the French revolts of 1968. And it was the British who sank Margaret Thatcher without an election when they rebelled against her flagship policy, the Poll Tax.[47] But clearly *these* aspects of life in Britain are regarded as somehow 'un-British', while in France such acts are regarded, even by a sometimes resigned media and political class, as distinctly French.

Radical representations of history depend in part then on the political nature of the cultural resources and identities which history bequeaths the present. Yet while the present is influenced by the past, it is not in absolute thrall to it. The political context of the present is always to some degree, an opening, a space where contending social forces actively struggle to *make* history. As we shall see in the next section, the French political context of mid-1990s onwards, is crucial in understanding the more radical representations of history and of contemporary society which have emerged and which have consigned, for the time being, a conservative period of French cinema, to the dustbin of history.

However, in this section, the cinematic comparison that I want to explore takes its evidence from within British cinema and from within the period drama. *Century* (Stephen Poliakoff, 1993) is set at the dawn of the twentieth century, but although it occupies familiar heritage territory (the Victorian and Edwardian period), it is I will argue, a very different kind of film and, for that reason, achieved a negligible distribution and cultural profile. *Elizabeth* (Shekhar Kapur, 1998) was funded jointly by Film Four and PolyGram and had a budget of over £9 million. Film Four of course operates within Channel Four's government-enforced public broadcaster remit and thus has a long tradition of funding low-budget, radical, alternative or just plain quirky filmmaking. PolyGram, as we have seen, developed a cultural strategy for tapping into marginal aspects of Britishness (*Trainspotting*) for the international market, or giving already established traditional cultural material a new 'modernising' twist. With such backing it is hardly surprising that *Elizabeth* was considered to be a little 'different' from the standard heritage fare. *Time Out* declared that the 'costume drama escapes its mothballs in this labyrinthine conspiracy movie'.[48] The film's prowling camerawork, rapid cutting and disorientating camera angles (particularly the overhead shot) certainly graft a very modern sensibility of intrigue and politicking onto its historical content. My argument is that while the film is certainly different, both stylistically and thematically from other heritage films, it is still operating well within the national myth of monarchy generally and Elizabeth specifically.

Elizabeth

In *Mythologies,* Roland Barthes defines myth as the process whereby signs are lifted out of a complex of social and historical determinants. Decontextualisation and dehistoricisation and therefore naturalisation, are the typical features of the disembedded film, at least in relation to national specificity. For Barthes, myth is a form of 'language-robbery'[49] in that it operates by turning a sign (say a rural landscape) into the signifier of another set of signifieds. This new sign is filled with the connotations of bourgeois ideology. In the case of the rural landscape, myth turns it into a terrain outside history, production, industry, conflict and populates it with a certain class and ethnic exclusivity.

There are three interwoven mythical strands in *Elizabeth*. Firstly the film purports to be the 'backstory' to the mythical figure we have of Elizabeth; that is, the film is about the process by which the young Queen is transformed into the mythic Virgin Queen. The terms of this process, however, are highly mythical. Secondly, the film represents Catholicism as foreign and alien to the country and Elizabeth's ascension to the throne as a deliverance from dark times. Thirdly, the film completely excludes the common people from the frame, a move which is typical of British cinema and which facilitates the disavowal of class conflict between the Tudor regime and the peasant masses.

The religious conflict at the centre of the film is certainly unusual, not only for the heritage film but for British cinema generally. The 16th-century break with the Catholic Church and the Pope and the establishment of the Church of England and Protestantism as the state-sanctioned religion has been little dwelt upon in British cinema, not least, one suspects because of the conflict within Northern Ireland. At one level, *Elizabeth* is a film that comes out of the context of the peace process in Northern Ireland. For perhaps only now is it possible to explore the historical roots of British Protestantism.

However, the strategies which the film deploys to tell its story fully dehistoricises those roots and so pulls the film towards myth. The myths surrounding Elizabeth were often constructed contemporaneously to her reign. She ascended the throne in 1558 and in 1563 John Foxe's *Actes and Monuments* was published. According to Roy Strong this book was familiar to every Englishman for three centuries. Copies were placed in every Parish church. The book:

> not only narrated the sufferings of Protestants under Mary but went on to cast England and the English into an heroic role, that of the chosen nation of God [...] English history was cast into a dramatic story in which light overcame darkness, Protestantism Catholicism, and the valiant kings of England the wicked popes of Rome.[50]

This is a fair description of the film's representation of Mary's rule and Elizabeth's ascension to the throne. Queen Mary's chamber is a noirish cavern, dark with shards of light coming through the windows. She herself is dressed in black and cared for by a dwarf. The film opens with an overhead shot of the persecution and burning of three Protestants. The martyrs call upon the common people to throw more wood on the fire for the flames are not sufficiently fierce to ensure a relatively quick death. The crowd respond, braving the soldiers. This is the only time that we see the common people and it serves to establish the cruelty of Mary's reign and the resistance of the people to her.

When Mary dies of a tumour, the Royal ring is passed onto her. Elizabeth receives the ring, the symbol of the transfer of power, in an exterior scene resonating English iconography and contrasting starkly with Mary's dark interior scenes. A large oak tree dominates the left side of the frame. Elizabeth, right, stands atop a hill overlooking the trees and countryside below. The tree confers to Elizabeth, at this key moment of her ascension, all the qualities associated with the oak: strength, endurance, nature, rootedness, Englishness. Yet the film itself has told us using titles at the beginning that England is divided between Protestantism and Catholicism. At the same time, Elizabeth's pragmatic Protestantism is represented as embodying Englishness. Since the narration never descends amongst the common people, the divisions appear to be between Elizabeth who embodies Englishness and a minority of Catholic nobles around her court, allied with foreign powers (France, Spain and the Pope). There is little sense of residual or strong support for Catholicism amongst the broader population, even though, upon Mary's ascension in 1553, 'images of the Virgin and saints had immediately reappeared to be displayed in people's windows, having presumably been hoarded in cellars and attics.'[51] I am not arguing that the film must be judged against a strict catalogue of facts. Nor that one cannot make the judgement that Elizabeth's reign laid the foundations for a more moderate role of religion in daily life than a reactionary Catholicism linked to Rome. Yet what we have here is a good example of how myth works. Elizabeth is *naturalised* as the embodiment of Englishness, the complexities of history evaporates and in its place we have a binary opposition:

> Elizabeth=good=Protestant=light=England.
> Mary=bad=Catholicism=dark=foreignness

It is not as if I am imposing historical evidence on the film which it itself does not recognise. It does recognise (using titles) that England was divided, but its *cinematic* language is in contradiction with this recognition of historical reality.

Elizabeth's transformation into the Virgin Queen turns on familiar heritage territory, indeed it is a classic motif of British cinema: the individual sacrificing their desires for social duty, obligation and responsibility. Elizabeth is separated from her one true love by the pressures of state diplomacy and the various factions around her which try to marry her off to either French or Spanish royalty to shore up England's fragile position. Lord Dudley's access to Elizabeth is increasingly difficult once she becomes Queen. After an assassination attempt on her, for example, Dudley is refused entry to her chamber. This separation from Elizabeth makes him vulnerable to being drawn into the intrigues being spun by the Duke of Norfolk and the Spanish ambassador.

The denouement of the film is strikingly 'modern' in conception and has strong intertextual links to the *Godfather* films. In both, the climax of the struggle between contending forces is presented by cross-cutting between the central protagonist (Michael Corleone in the *Godfather* series and Elizabeth) and their enemies being assassinated by their agents (Walsingham, in *Elizabeth*), or in *Elizabeth* being arrested before they are officially executed. As in *Godfather I* (Francis Ford Coppola, 1971) the soundtrack to the murders is choral. In Coppola's film, there is an ironic juxtaposition between the religious sanctity of Michael Corleone's marriage ceremony, but in *Elizabeth*, the choral music is aligned with Elizabeth because we see her ferverently praying. Interestingly, she is now in the same dark chamber as Mary was earlier, except now the meaning of the mise-en-scene is very different. This is Elizabeth's moment of greatest danger, when she will succeed or fail against the conspirators. Apart from the ever loyal Walsingham, she is all alone, except for her faith.

The only figure to escape the meticulous attentions of Walsingham is Lord Dudley. Elizabeth keeps him alive and free, despite his involvement with the conspirators, as a constant memory of how close love brought her to danger. Her repudiation of sexual intimacy as compromising her independence and power, her repression of feeling and desire, lays the basis for her visual transformation into the mythic figure of the Virgin Queen. In a key exchange between Elizabeth and Walsingham under a statue of the Virgin Mary, Walsingham advises her that in effect she too must be made of stone in order to reign supreme. Elizabeth notes that the Madonna had such power to move men's hearts. Walsingham suggests that men must be able to 'touch the divine here on Earth' and that Elizabeth must replace in men's hearts, the Catholic worship of idols with the profane worship of rulers. In the next scene we see the process by which Elizabeth is transformed into the myth of the Virgin Queen. The long flowing hair of her youth is cut off by her tearful lady-in-waiting. This emotion already contrasts with Elizabeth's stony facial expression. The displacement of emotion to the lady-in-waiting marks the passage Elizabeth is already making from desire to duty, from self to social obligation. This is the archetypal self-legitimising myth of Britain's social elites. We see the preparation of the distinctive white face paint that will turn pink flesh into a cold white pallor. 'I have become a Virgin' Elizabeth intones. When she enters the court her figure is strongly backlit with a blinding white light signifying her transformation and transcendence beyond mere men. 'Observe', she instructs one of her trusted advisors, Lord Burleigh, 'I am married to England.' Now, for the first time we see the iconic representation of Elizabeth that has been handed down in numerous portraits: her hair is now fanned distinctively over the top of her head, decorated with crowns and jewels, her face has been caked in white make-up and she wears a vast ruff. Elizabeth the young woman has become Elizabeth the myth.

Interestingly, the conversation between Walsingham and Elizabeth draws on a view widely held by historians, that representations of Elizabeth attempted to construct her as a Protestant substitute for the Virgin Mary, filling, as Helen Hackett notes, 'a post-Reformation gap in the psyche of the masses.'[52] This of course is Walsingham's interpretation and there is nothing in the film to contradict him because the masses have been effectively screened out. The problem with this historiographic analysis, as Hackett observes, is precisely that it constructs that horizontal comradeship which Anderson noted conceals the vertical power relations between rulers and ruled within the nation. Panegyrical paintings, poetry and songs were the propaganda product of the Court aimed at securing Elizabeth's rule at particular moments of weakness or vulnerability.[53] Thus here we are, at the start of the twenty-first century, with the means of advanced mass technological representation at our disposal, recycling myths some four hundred and fifty years old. If the aura of an institution like the monarchy has at times been undermined by exposure to the mass media, *Elizabeth* revives the aura (with its attendant myths of national unity between the ruling and subaltern classes and the ruling elite's favourite myth that their privileged position is channelled into duty and self-sacrificial social obligation) with a vengeance.[54]

Century

Stephen Poliakoff's film deploys a number of strategies by which to de-mythicise British Cinema's conventional treatment of late Victorian Britain. Made in the early 1990s and set at the turn of the twentieth century, the film constellates the *fin de siecle* with our own millenarian hopes and anxieties. The concept of the constellation was developed by the Marxist philosopher and historian Walter Benjamin. A constellation is the technique of arranging historical materials from different points of time (and possibly space) in order to construct miniature 'flashes' or illuminations of historical truth. Benjamin utterly rejected a historiography which constructed a seamless continuum between past and present. Such a seamless continuum is precisely what myth constructs. Myth turns what is historically transitory into a timeless, a-historical story. For example, *Elizabeth* depicts the Queen's successful consolidation of Protestantism as the embodiment of Englishness, thus retrospectively imposing the closure of Protestant victory onto what was an open-ended and volatile situation. Benjamin saw his aim as:

> the dissolution of 'mythology' into the space of history. That, of course, can happen only through the awakening of a not-yet conscious knowledge of what has been.[55]

We have a knowledge of what has been because the present is linked to the past, but that knowledge needs awakening from the slumber of myth. One way in which we can awaken our knowledge is by avoiding representations of history which are designed to construct seamless continuities between the past and the present. Such continuities, as in *Elizabeth*, are premised on speaking from a position in which the social order and stability of the present is guaranteed. *Century* by contrast, constellates past and present; finding modernity in the past the film is able to depict it as relatively open-ended, permanently in transition. Politically, this is a very different strategy from the *modernisation* of the heritage genre which *Elizabeth* effects with its intertextual links to conspiracy films (the rapid editing around court intrigues), spy thrillers (elaborate assassination attempts involving poisoned dresses), gangster films and so on. *Century* not only finds the modern within the past, but it works, as Benjamin did, 'to recognise today's life, today's forms'[56] in the past, so that our present, our 'modern' period of change and transformation, is actually in some ways, rather old and long in the tooth. What we discover in the past is a very contemporary bourgeois fear of the masses, mediated through the science of eugenics and crossed with racism and suspicion of cultural difference.

Finally *Century* subverts the myth of British identity which turns on the notion of the stiff upper lip and sexual repression. The internalisation of polite manners which check the expression of desire in countless British films, the individual's obligation to duty which calls for sacrifice or better, resignation (a word which has less redemptive qualities) are the familiar terms of the battle between individual and society in British cinema. Poliakoff's characters are, by contrast, casually sexual creatures: doctors hire prostitutes; the central female lead, Clara, enjoys having sex. The film finds that what is problematic is not desire (this is expressed easily enough) but the difficulty of sustaining relationships in a class divided society. It is not quiet fortitude which the film celebrates, since this slides all too easily into conformism, but passion which fires conviction and is the guardian of personal integrity. Such themes, as we shall see in the next section, place *Century* rather closer to the French historical dramas which have emerged since the mid-1990s, than it does to the British history films of recent times.

The film opens in 1899. Our narrator is Paul Reisner (Clive Owen) who introduces himself and his father. His family background as a Romanian Jew brought up in Scotland before his father relocated his building contractor business to the south-east of England, immediately locates the Reisners (a family with German origins) in a contradictory social position. They are at once members of the prosperous upper-middle class but culturally and temperamentally they sit askance British conservatism, insularity and conformism. The town outside London where the Reisners have settled is, we are told, 'a horrible town full of suspicious, nosy people'. The film opens with a conflict between Mr Reisner, who has set up a large electric bulb sign welcoming in the new century, and local dignitaries who protest that the sign is on council owned land and that, anyway, the new century is being counted in the following year. Thus in this film, it is not the English who appear as the eccentric individuals, on the contrary, they are conformists, but those with more mixed or hybrid cultural identities. The electric bulb sign is also an example of the eagerness with which Reisner's progressive mind embraces technological modernity. Paul Reisner leaves for London to join a new medical research institute in the National Telephone Company van which has just delivered his father's new phone. The fact that the van is horse-drawn is an appropriate image in miniature of the film's sensitivity to the combination of the old and the new which marks a social order in permanent transition.

Paul settles into life at the institute, an unorthodox place where women work as laboratory assistants; James, the doctors' assistant, is black; and, where the doctors' dormitory has a special room to entertain female prostitutes. The institute is funded by a rich widow, Mrs Whiteweather, whose husband set it up. Paul is invited to lunch with Mrs Whiteweather where he discovers that she is most concerned that the institute does not carry out experiments on the 'higher' animal species such as dogs and monkeys. Their conversation is intercut with a speech taking place in an adjoining room where someone is giving a lecture on eugenics, the science by which the 'higher' genetic pools of the human race (invariably the dominant classes) must protect themselves from the lower genetic pools (often the working classes and the poor). The institute is run by the brilliant Professor Mandry (Charles Dance). Paul rapidly distinguishes himself and becomes a favourite of the Professor who asks him to become his assistant. Together they attend the destitute and homeless who have gathered on some common land in makeshift huts. Returning from one of their trips, the Professor sounds Paul out about his views on the poor producing children which they cannot afford to keep. But when Paul expresses his opinion that the medical world can have no power over this, the Professor suggests that perhaps they should not return to the commons for a while.

At the same time, Paul becomes increasingly attracted to Clara (Miranda Richardson), one of the women who works in the laboratory. One evening, Clara and Paul's fellow doctor and friend, Felix, go to a scientific exhibition dedicated to the technology of the future. The trio discuss the possibility of a visual telephone in the future, the sort of discussion about modernity which rarely surfaces in the heritage film for fear of disrupting their aura of nostalgia. *Century* however is all about historical progress, or the hopes of progress, as well as regression. Felix tells Paul of a possible breakthrough he has made to combat diabetes. Despite the fact that it was Paul who is supposed to be the star pupil, Paul is tremendously excited by the ideas and together they go to the Professor and submit Felix's proposals, asking for the institute to fund further research. Although arrogant and vain, Paul is not small-minded and is sufficiently committed to scientific progress to swallow his pride and back Felix's ideas. Yet the Professor responds by sitting on the research and stalling in his response to it. Paul's direct and passionate character gets him into trouble when he challenges the slow pace with which the Professor is assessing Felix's ideas. Expelled from the institute for one month, he goes to stay with Clara where their relationship now develops sexually, although tensions remain surrounding their different class backgrounds. Clara later suggests that when his troubles are over, Paul will leave her and return fully to his class.

Paul's fortunes spiral downwards when his father arrives in London unexpectedly and insists on being shown the institute. Paul takes him and runs into Professor Mandry. The Professor offers Paul a pardon if he agrees to drop pressing for Felix's idea. Once again, Paul explodes with anger at this apparently irrational blocking of scientific progress (a blocking which Felix, more securely embedded in his upper-class English identity, has quietly accepted and conformed to). This time the Professor expels him from the institute permanently. Fearing that Paul will stir up the other doctors, the Professor has the police harass Paul who pick him up and question his 'foreignness'. Throughout the film, the racial question has been represented by various little scenes at Mr Reisner's house. Here we see him being spied on by the distrusting locals, and receiving racist phone calls from his neighbours after he tells the local newspaper that the town is being run by vegetables.

Paul returns to the commons with Clara to practice, only to discover that many of the women have been sterilised, often very clumsily by the Professor. Some have even died. Paul and Clara research into eugenics literature and find that it has a growing presence in political and medical circles. Here we see modernity taking the fork in the road that will lead to the horrors of the Nazi concentration camps. Determined to bring the Professor to account, Paul turns up at a public lecture with one of the women who he has sterilised. Our expectations of the conventional classical narrative tell us that a big public unmasking scene is about to take place. But *Century* is too subtle for this. Paul in fact fails to confront the Professor who displays the confidence of public speaking, the wit, the charm and erudition of his class. And Paul is still too much a member of that class to stand up and denounce the Professor, whose charisma, he freely confesses afterwards, kept him sitting in his seat.

Yet still determined to stop the Professor's experiments on the poor, Paul meets Mrs Whiteweather who shows not the slightest concern that people have died. As a last throw of the dice, Paul informs her that the institute is experimenting with dogs and monkeys, the 'higher' species. This proves decisive. The next scene we see the institute closing and it is New Year's Eve, 1900. Paul invites Felix to his father's party, but when Clara asks him if she can come, he hesitates before agreeing. The difficulty in his mind is introducing her to his father, to whom he lies fairly frequently (writing to him at one point to say that he is seeing the daughter of a Russian Count). Clara sees his hesitation and explodes with anger, believing that he is already withdrawing back into his class. But Paul does manage to persuade her to come to the party. He then discovers that the Professor has also accepted his father's invitation, where they will meet for their final confrontation.

At the party, Paul discovers that his father is planning to leave the town since his business is being boycotted by the racist locals. Once again Mr Reisner's troubles run in parallel with the main narrative strand concerning eugenics. At the party, Professor Mandry begs Paul to retract his accusations so that the institute can begin working again. Paul is firm, reminding the Professor of how he tried to get the police to have him deported. Yet even now, there is still a quotient of respect and admiration between the two men. It is Clara, who does not share their class background who confirms to Mandry that there is no way back for him when she throws her drink in his face and tells him to leave.

The film ends at the stroke of midnight. Paul has persuaded Clara to stay with him at his father's house. We learn in Paul's closing words as the narrator that they did spend the rest of their lives together (she as his common-law wife) although not without battles. We learn that Felix went on to make great contributions to the study of diabetes, but Paul is convinced that had things gone differently that year, he would have been the first to discover insulin. As for Mandry, he fades from the medical scene, his fate subject to rumour but no hard knowledge. A brilliant doctor who took a 'dark path', he is a precursor to some of the terrible political and social projects that science will become tied to. The film has been bookended by two New Year's Eve parties: in-between the narrative that has unfolded has shown that hope and fear, progress and barbarism and a struggle over the meaning and politics of modernity, will characterise (as we know, watching from the closing years of the twentieth century) subsequent decades.

Century stands in a very different tradition of historical drama than the one which dominates British cinema. It demonstrates that British filmmakers can tackle the past in ways which do not succumb to a cloying nostalgia, to myth and to an affirmation of the social order. Yet at the same time, *Century*'s fate at the box-office also suggests that while such films can occasionally get made, the wider culture in which audience expectations get formed, is hardly conducive to fostering such films and providing them with anything but the most negligible profile in the marketplace. The film, funded by the BBC as part of a small slate of productions intended for theatrical release, opened in three central London cinemas and took a mere £6296 in three days.[57] It had a three week run in central London, but was down to one cinema in the final week. Compare this with a star-driven vehicle such as *The Remains of the Day* (James Ivory 1993), also, co-incidentally, an examination of fascism, which opened in central London a few weeks earlier in four cinemas and took £70196 over the first three days.[58] The different marketing and organisational powers behind the two films (*The Remains of the Day* was distributed by Columbia Pictures) only partly accounts for the films' respective box-office performance. Equally significant is the cultural pattern of expectations as to what constitutes a British historical drama. *The Remains of the Day* fits very comfortably into the traditional iconography of the historical drama, with its country-house setting, rural life, upstairs-downstairs scenario and narrative of sexual repression, albeit with a critique of the link between the repression of emotions and feelings and the conformism of the butler Stevens (Anthony Hopkins) to his fascist leaning Lord (James Fox). However as a metaphor for investigating fascism, the country-house domain hardly taps into some of the *modern* dynamics of fascism, not least that it is a political response on the part of the ruling classes to contain the emancipatory desires of the industrial working class. Although it is impossible to prove, my hunch is that if *Century* had been a French film it would have had a more receptive audience in its domestic market and possibly abroad as well.

French Politics and Cinema in the 1990s

In her influential study of French cinema, Susan Hayward reads the 1980s and early 1990s as a period of artistic decline, when the cinema rushed into a headlong embrace of postmodern cynicism and indifference. Although Hayward does allow for a critical, subversive strand to postmodern film practice, the dominant tone in French cinema during this period is an obsession with the image for and of itself. 'All is style, be it retro-nostalgic or hi-tech.'[59] Hayward is obviously not enamoured by this trend but following many other writers, notably Fredric Jameson,[60] Hayward's historical and political framework entrenches the postmodern as a substantive epochal phenomenon. But what if the postmodern is more shallowly rooted in a set of political defeats for the left in the 1970s and 1980s ?[61] Postmodernism can be viewed not so much as the permanent 'death of ideology' (that is, substantive political disagreements) as the temporary unchallenged ascendency of a particular ideology: neo-liberalism. But even the drift towards neo-liberalism was contradictory and uneven. The left won office under Francois Mitterand in 1981 on a programme of reflation, nationalisation and the redistribution of wealth. It was not the 'death of ideology' which destroyed this attempt to build social democracy in one country, but big business. The money markets sold French francs like there was no tomorrow, forcing three devaluations of the currency. Within two years Mitterand's Keynesian policies were in tatters. Economic power, not a lack of general political will among the population, foistered a tight neo-liberal monetary policy on France. Indeed, in many ways, the recognition that national governments no longer had the autonomy to pursue the policies for which they were elected, laid the ground for increasing Franco-German co-operation and beyond that, European integration, in subsequent years.[62] Yet, as we shall see, this integration has hardly rescued social democracy from the neo-liberal agenda.

The importance of not overestimating the entrenched nature of the postmodern becomes clear when critics are confronted with a new political conjuncture. Ginette Vincendeau's discussion of *La Haine* is fissured between a residual commitment to the postmodern paradigm and an emergent sense of a new historical conjuncture that the film is anticipating. The first half of the discussion is obviously working within the postmodern paradigm. Vincendeau critiques what she sees as the film's aestheticisation of poverty. The use of black and white film stock, for example, 'signals distance from 'normal' (colour) documentary and from the naturalistic beur films' although quite why that is a problem is unclear. Black and white we are told ' "looks cool" like postmodern music videos; it establishes a link with *film noir* and recalls Scorcese's *Raging Bull* (1980) and Spike Lee's *She's Gotta Have It*.'[63] Again, despite the vague tone of disapproval, it is not clear why these intertextual links are 'bad'. If avoiding aestheticism means avoiding all intertextuality there would be no film. The unstated argument here is that French cinema is all image and no substance. An authentic engagement for Vincendeau, at least in the first half of the analysis, seems to require aesthetic purity. The second half of the analysis appears to be written by another Ginette Vincendeau who now appreciates the film's successful aesthetic strategies, its critique of the limited options for working-class masculinity and its intertextual references to American culture which subverts a French tendency towards a simple anti-Americanism.[64]

Once we relinquish the postmodern paradigm which absorbs all forms of resistance back into the image, we can see that the second half of Vincendeau's discussion fits rather better with the new political context of resistance which was developing in 1995. When in the autumn of 1995, Alain Juppe, the conservative prime minister put forward a programme of massive cuts in social security, public sector workers responded with a wave of strikes and demonstrations. Two million workers brought much of France to a standstill, protesters carried placards making the link between December 1995 and the (arguably) revolutionary moment of May 1968. Yet, in an indication of how deep the postmodern paradigm has penetrated the intellectuals, despite this return to collective political struggle, two prominent French sociologists published a book in 1996 which declared that in an era of individualism and defensive protection of established gains, 'the generalisation of demands, that go with a class logic, [is] impossible.'[65]

Yet the strikes did mark a watershed in French political life, destroying the Juppe Plan and eviscerating Chirac's conservative presidency. In 1997 the huge conservative majority of the RPR was swept from office. The Socialist Party, in coalition with the Greens and the Communist Party, returned, committed to a number of progressive social changes, such as the 35-hour week – the central issue in the 1999 film *Ressources humaines* (*Human resources*). But beyond the merely revolving door of electoral change, a deeper and more fundamental sea-change had occurred. Intellectual debate had shifted decisively to the left. Viviane Forrester's attack on neo-liberal policies, *The*

Economic Horror, became a best seller in France while Pierre Bourdieu, the left wing sociologist, became the most prominent intellectual in France. His book (a collaboration) *The Weight of the World* charted the experiences of people living at the sharp end of an unequal and divided society. Over a 1000 pages long the book sold nearly 100,000 copies by the late 1990s.[66] In numerous speeches and articles, Bourdieu has intervened in the struggle to overturn the 'inculcation' of the neo-liberal agenda and legitimise the on-going struggles of the new social movements, as they have been called.

Bourdieu argues that the French state has been abandoning its commitments to social welfare and that in America, that neo-liberal paradise, the state's main relationship to the poor is one of coercion and repression (a key theme, as we shall see, of *La Veuve de Saint-Pierre* (1999)). This regression to a 'penal state' is now on the agenda within Europe.[67] For Bourdieu, the notion of 'globalisation' is in part an ideological discourse with which to undermine the gains of the welfare state by pitching the working class in the advanced industrialised world in competition with the poorest, cheapest most exploited labour force in the Third World. The law of the market which globalisation 'ratifies and glories' unleashes an 'unfettered capitalism' on the population.[68] Bourdieu notes that this new conservative revolution has little in common with the archaic nostalgia for rural times which characterised older conservative ideologies. Its main thrust is to dress up its nostrums with appeals to progress, reason, science, technology and economic efficiency. It presents itself as the discourse of modernity. This is one reason why historical drama is so potentially important, since it reminds viewers that the struggles of today have long historical roots and that there are other political traditions which have a better claim to represent modernity than neo-liberalism. This question of contemporary progress being checked by irrational elites is implicitly posed by a historical drama such as *Ridicule* (Patrice Leconte, 1996).

Although the concept of globalisation functions primarily as 'a justificatory myth', Bourdieu does concede that the international financial markets do severely reduce the autonomy of national capital markets and limits any national governments' ability to manipulate exchange and interest rates.[69] Thus he calls for European-wide organisations to defend 'the social dimension of the European institutions.'[70] December 1995 'outlined a genuine project for a society, collectively affirmed'[71] but it was not merely a French affair. Instead it marked the beginnings of a 'rotating struggle' around Europe.

Bourdieu writes of the violence which economic decisions and calculations inflict in the form of unemployment, loss of security, rising crime and suicides. The neo-liberal agenda has been helped immeasurably by the complicity and complacency of the intelligentsia. Bourdieu identifies the postmodern 'condemnation of the great explanatory narratives or the nihilist denunciations of science' as a key reason for the rise and celebration of the 'uncommitted intellectual.'[72] Bourdieu attacks the 'passive complicity' of intellectuals, especially those in the media, when confronted by the neo-liberal ideology. Their receptivity to it has helped shape the 'horizon of expectations' which has made the neo-liberal doctrine so unquestioned and widely circulated.[73] This discourse has a kind of 'authority effect' which 'runs from the mathematician to the banker, from the banker to the philosopher-journalist, from the essayist to the journalist.'[74] Combatting the legitimacy of the neo-liberal authority is the key role of the committed intellectual. Bourdieu identifies that their central contribution is to engage in symbolic and cultural struggles. Cultural workers in cinema are part of that process and it is clear in a number of films that have come out since the mid-1990s, that they have been connecting their artistic work with the broader social movements of the times and intervening in the consciousness struggle.

Five French Films From The 1990s

Julianne Pidduck notes that after Francois Truffaut's attack on the 'Tradition of Quality' in the late 1950s[75] and the subsequent New Wave, historical costume drama went into decline until the mid-1980s when Claude Berri's *Jean de Florette* (1986) and *Manon des Sources* (1986) became international successes. *Cyrano de Bergerac* (Jean-Paul Rappeneau,1990) consolidated the new found commercial viability of the costume/historical drama and laid the ground for subsequent films such as *Germinal* (Claude Berri, 1993) *La Reine Margot* (Patrice Chéreau,1994) *Ridicule* (Patrice Leconte, 1996), *The Horseman On The Roof* (Jean-Paul Rappeneau, 1995) and *D'Artagnan's Daughter* (Bertrand Tavernier, 1994).[76] I have argued, however, that the French cultural scene can accommodate critical historical dramas alongside mythic affirmations of national identity such as *Cyrano de Bergerac* or *D'Artagnan's Daughter*, and it is important to distinguish between these ideological currents. Yet even *Cyrano de Bergerac* has a gritty *mise-en-scene*, full of poverty and misery,[77] which would be unusual in an equivalent big budget British heritage film. Nevertheless, the production of such large-scale historical dramas – the French equivalent to the disembedded films discussed earlier – is one strand of a consciously planned French film policy that has increasingly sought to encourage globally orientated productions.[78]

Martine Danan has suggested that the other strand to French film policy, encourages an alternative cinema rooted in the 'concrete realities' of the nation and not completely subordinated to the profit motive. For Danan this cinema, sensitive to French particularity, is *not* in contradiction with the homogenising films dedicated to maximum profitability on the international market. Instead, Danan suggests, this cinema plays an analogous role to the state generally, which attempts to bind citizens into a national unity even as it opens their lives up to the competitive dynamics of global capitalism.[79] Yet this seems to me to be an overly functionalist account, good at situating auteur national films with little political ambition (apart from uncritically affirming French national life and culture) but less attuned to the possibility of films developing what I have called an anti-national national cinema.

Such a cinema has been developing in tandem with the altered political context of the mid-1990s. I want to discuss five films which can, to varying degrees, be understood as examples of an anti-national national cinema. They are three historical dramas: *La Reine Margot* (Patrice Chéreau, 1994), *Ridicule* (Patrice Leconte, 1996) and *La Veuve de Saint-Pierre/The Widow of Saint-Pierre* (Patrice Leconte, 1999); and two contemporary set films: *It All Starts Today* (Bertrand Tavernier, 1998) and *Ressources humaines/Human Resources* (Laurent Cantet, 1999).

Historical Drama

It is interesting to compare *La Reine Margot* (a French-German-Italian co-production supported by Eurimages) with *Elizabeth*. The French film is set in 1572 and like the British film, tells a story about conflict between Catholics and Protestants in France. Specifically the film explores the events leading up to and the aftermath of the St Bartholomew's Day massacre when an estimated 25000 Protestant Huguenots were killed by the Catholic forces of King Charles IX. Yet while *Elizabeth*, as we have seen, mythologises the young Queen as the Protestant embodiment of the nation, *La Reine Margot* is by contrast exploring what one writer described as 'a collective admission of French guilt'. In examining a mass slaughter, the French national past is opened up and questioned, rather than affirmed.

> 'It's a serious malaise for the French' says Pascal Greggory, who plays the murderous Duke of Anjou, Catherine's favourite son. 'We have never come to terms with this massacre as we have never come to terms with the second world war. But Patrice has decided to wade into this mire right up to his neck.'[80]

Like *Elizabeth*, the French film is clearly influenced by conspiracy thrillers and gangster films, with the director reportedly spending hours watching the *Godfather* films. But where such intertextual influences are the limits of the British film's 'modernisation' of the costume drama, the French film constructs a more substantial modernisation, or, as with *Century*, a Benjaminian *constellation* between the past and the present. The massacre in Paris, both within and outside the Royal quarters, is distinctly evocative of twentieth-century genocide. There is the organised manner with which it is carried out, with hordes of people being funnelled towards soldiers with long pikes; there is the mass scale on which it is carried out, with the corridors of the Royal quarters and the streets of Paris strewn with corpses; there is the way the corpses are rapidly stripped of their clothes, loaded onto wagons and dumped into mass graves the next morning, scenes which evoke the Holocaust. At the centre of the film is Margot, a Catholic and sister to the King. By falling in love with a Protestant, she makes a political journey which it is hard to see an aristocratic heroine making in a British film. 'I have joined you among the oppressed,' she tells her lover. 'I never want to be an oppressor again.' It's just not a position one can imagine Helena Bonham Carter espousing in a British film.

This is a film which clearly does not seek to affirm contemporary elites but to establish some continuities in their rule across the ages. Martin Bright, for example, notes a connection between 'an over-zealous immigration policy and a bribery scandal surrounding Edouard Balladur's RPR party' and the depiction of the past in *La Reine Margot* where French audiences 'may well have discovered where their present batch of politicians got their inspiration.'[81]

With hindsight, *La Reine Margot* is tapping into the emerging political forces which would explode so abruptly and decisively barely a year after its release. *Ridicule*

(Patrice Leconte,1996) was produced and released right in the middle of the public-sector strikes which checked the advance of neo-liberalism in France. The film is a celebration of the French Enlightenment and rationalist ideas which flowed into another historic popular uprising: the French Revolution of 1789.

The story concerns Grégoire Ponceludon de Malavoy, a landowner from the mosquito infested provinces whose peasants are afflicted with malaria. Malavoy wants to drain the swamp, build dikes and canals, plant trees and sow seed. This perfectly embodies the progressive strain of rationalism, which sought to use science and technology to cure humanity of the various afflictions caused it by poverty and subordination to nature. However, to do this, he must travel to Versailles and seek an audience with the King to win financial backing for the drainage scheme. He soon learns that access to the King is jealously guarded and that it is not reason or compassion which opens doors at Versailles, but the cruel deployment of wit. Aided by the Marquis de Bellegarde, he is introduced to the court where he must avoid the intrigues of the Countess Blayac and her favourite, the Abbé, whose barbed wit has destroyed reputations and lives. Malavoy proves himself to be a most able verbal jouster which makes the Countess fear and desire him in equal measure. At the same time, Malavoy falls in love with Bellegarde's daughter, Mathilde. As with *Century*, *Ridicule* identifies the seeds of modernity in the past. Just as Malavoy represents rationalist Enlightenment values, so too does Mathilde who is conducting scientific experiments with a prototype diving suit. With its metal bulbous helmet and attached pipes through which air is pumped from dry land, the wet suit is the kind of emblem of modernity which rarely gets acknowledged in British period drama. However, both Malavoy and Mathilde are in danger of compromising their integrity and frustrating their love for each other. Mathilde plans to marry a rich lecherous old man so that she can fund her research, while Malavoy eventually finds that he must seek access to the King via the Countess's bedroom.

Although Malavoy gets to meet the King with the Countess's aid, the means is so corrupt that it undermines the end which Malavoy seeks. He becomes estranged from Mathilde when he sleeps with the Countess, not realising that Mathilde has herself called off her marriage of convenience. Not only that, but to get to impress the King, Malavoy has to make one of his officers look foolish. Insults are traded and a duel planned. Malavoy kills the officer and leaves the Countess Blayac for Mathilde, believing that he has secured access to the King. But his personal reception with the King is then delayed because he has killed one of his officers. This leaves time for Blayac to plan her revenge. At a masked ball, she arranges for Malavoy to be tripped and publically ridiculed. This is the kind of character assassination that destroys all his chances of winning the King's favour. Beaten, he returns to the provinces with Mathilde.

But then there is the wonderful postscript. It is now 1794 and Mathilde's father is on the English cliffs overlooking the English Channel with another Frenchman and lamenting his exile from France. We learn that Mathilde and Malavoy are still there and the closing titles tell us that the drainage of the swamps started in 1793 under the guidance of 'Citizen' Grégoire Ponceludon de Malavoy. Thus it is the Revolution, a collective, social eruption, which sweeps away the corrupt rule of Versailles and which lays the basis for Malavoy's engineering plans. The fact that the film has ignored the impending signs of revolutionary change merely confirms the utter isolation and remoteness of the regime at Versailles. However, the unanswered question which hangs over the film is this: who today are the irrational elites whose rule must be swept away if there is to be human progress? If it is the bourgeoisie, then the mythologisation of the 1789 Revolution as the pinnacle of human progress, must be challenged.

If *Ridicule* can be criticised for being insufficiently sensitive to the different social forces at play *within* the French Revolutionary forces and therefore being overly optimistic concerning the benefits which bourgeois rational modernity would bring to the poor, *La Veuve de Saint-Pierre* (Patrice Leconte, 1999) articulates a deeper political awareness of the conflicting class interests at work within French society and therefore the conflicting visions and versions of rationality and modernity thereby generated. Thus *La Veuve de Saint-Pierre* should be read as a response to the maturing and spreading political opposition to neo-liberalism and globalisation which has characterised French society since the mid-1990s.

Set in 1850 on a small French island off the coast of Canada, the story is bookended by the narration of the Madame La. As with *Century*, this narrational strategy helps sharpen the film's analytical qualities by presenting its story as the product of retrospective reflection where judgment and assessment take precedence over naturalistic immediacy. Indeed the film is centrally about the question and nature of judgment. It begins with the drunken murder by two sailors of their captain. Louis Oliver is sentenced to hard labour while Neel Auguste is sentenced to death. But when the sentenced men are transported back to the prison, an angry mob hurls stones at them. The horses bolt in fright and the wagon overturns where upon Louis Oliver is killed when his head is smashed on the cobblestones. This community outrage is important because of the transformation they will undergo during the course of the film. And this transformation in a sense also redeems the community as much as the individual. The immediate problem for the authorities however is that having sentenced Neel in accordance with the law, they lack the proper machinery for carrying out the death sentence. They cannot shoot him or hang him, because in post-revolutionary France, the guillotine is the proper official mode for carrying out the death sentence from a civilian court. The guillotine – famously much used during the Revolution of course – symbolises rational efficiency and even 'humane' execution, since it was designed to deliver an instantaneous death. The trouble is that the island of Saint-Pierre does not have one. The island's governors request that one be dispatched from Paris.

Saint-Pierre's geographical distance from the metropolitan centre is also reproduced in the spatial lay-out of the Captain's quarters, which house the island's prison cells. The modern divisions of space which would substantially separate the cells from the Captain's living quarters have not yet been constructed. The Captain, Jean-Pierre, has newly arrived on the island with his wife, Madame La. Her proximity to Neel's cell facilitates a relationship between them in which she seeks to rehabilitate the prisoner.

Madame La is compassionate and independent; she too represents 'modernity', but it is a very different modernity to the one embodied in the governors of the island, who believe that the Captain indulges his wife. However, Jean-Pierre lets her will set the course of events because he loves and respects her and he shares her values. Through various forms of community service, Neel comes to be seen as a valuable member of the community, and even a hero when he saves a woman's life and the island's only drinking house from destruction.

At first the viewer may be skeptical that such a woman as Madame La (or her husband) would give Neel a second glance or chance. Gradually, however, we become convinced by the film's historical acuteness that, in such a time and (importantly) such a peripheral place, these two non-conformists could exist. The machinery of administration and careerism has yet to be fully in place which would later weed out two such people, but here, caught between the two competing visions and versions of modernity -one based on abstract law and one on the belief in secular redemption – Madame La and Jean-Pierre can exist, albeit precariously and on borrowed time.

On the surface,the film is an almost Foucauldian story about crime and punishment; about justice being dispensed by an administrative machine, formally rational, scientific and 'fair'.[82] Yet the film is more *marxisant* than Foucauldian. For Marx the problem with bourgeois political rights and their embodiment in the state, is that they are *abstract*. While they claim to be universal, fair, rational and open to scientific evidence, rights, the law, justice, is embedded in a class society which means that such claims exist only in the abstract while *in practice* the law, justice and the state, shore up the partial and particular interests of the bourgeoisie.[83] Thus the film has an eye for the political machinations of the governors and how the fates of Jean-Pierre, Madame La and Neel are bound up with the ascendancy of reactionary political forces in Paris (Napolean III's *coup d'etat* of December 1851, the subject of Marx's famous satirical analysis).[84] The film also has an eye for the divisions between the political elites and the ordinary inhabitants of the island. The elites are embarrassed by the discrepancy between the sentence handed down, the initial inability to carry it out and then later, as Neel becomes a hero while the island awaits the guillotine, the discrepancy between his dual status as prisoner and hero. At best, the island's governors wish this embarrassment, this odd cog in their administrative machine, to simply disappear. But they do not warm to Neel as a human being in the way that the island's inhabitants do because in truth there are two communities on the island – the ruling elite (increasingly angered by Madame La's personal interventions in Neel's case) and the rest.

When the ship finally arrives with the guillotine, the tension between the administrative centre of the nation (Paris) and its far-flung peripheral domains, burst into the open as the local community protest at the dockside, chanting that they do not want this machine on their island. Jean-Pierre refuses the governors' instructions to carry out the execution personally and refuses to suppress the dockside dissent. In doing so, Jean-Pierre seals his own fate. Meanwhile the governors find an executioner in the form of a migrant, Chevassus, who arrives with his family on the same boat which carries the guillotine. Chevassus, a tragic figure himself, will disappear mysteriously shortly after he carries out the execution. Arriving on the island penniless and with no local loyalties, he is easy to bully into the job which no one else wants. He does not enter into it enthusiastically, but neither does he have the integrity to refuse the material rewards it offers. A combination of circumstance and lack of moral fibre leads him to do the job his masters set him. He is a very modern figure. As with *Century*, this is a film which is very much about preserving integrity in the context of powerful conformist pressures.

Jean-Pierre, played by the French star Daniel Auteuil, may be said to represent an 'embattled, noble masculinity'[85] which is a very deeply rooted French cultural myth. His relationship with his wife, played by Juliette Binoche, represents an ideal of equality and mutual love which makes us a little shamefacedly readjust our narrative expectations when the growing relationship between Madame La and Neel does not – as the gossip amongst the ruling elites suggest – turn out to be of a sexual kind.

What saves *La Veuve de Saint-Pierre* from succumbing to myth, is its precise sensitivity to the historical moment in which this embattled masculinity can, for the last time, exist. Juliane Pidduck notes how such figures, which stretch back into nineteenth-century French literature 'stand in for the burden of social suffering'.[86] This embattled masculinity, like Jean Gabin's proletarian heroes in the 1930s, is doomed because it is 'a symbol of a time of greater glory'.[87] Leconte's film however reworks the conservative myth since the 'greater glory' here is, in fact, the radical ideals generated by the French Revolution – the ideals (including female emancipation) that are being snuffed out by the French bourgeoisie and the petty dictator Napolean.

The denouement of the film sees the Captain relieved of his post on the island and transferred back to Paris. It sees Neel die under the guillotine, but Madame La tells the audience that because it was an old one, second hand from the French colony of Martinique, it does not work properly and so Neel has to be finished off with an axe. Thus the guillotine, symbol of efficiency and rational justice, stands revealed as the agent of a brutal class machinery. Even as we watch Madame La come to the end of her story, staring offscreen out of a window, we hear the gunshots that kill her faithful husband who has been court marshalled and sentenced to death.

Contemporary Stories

The underfunding of education has been a key grievance amongst the progressive social forces which have flowered in France since the mid-1990s. Thus students and teachers have frequently been at the fore in the attempts to delegitimise the neo-liberal agenda. In this context, Bertrand Tavernier's decision to make *It All Starts Today* is inescapably making a conscious intervention into the legitimation struggle. The film is centred around a primary school in a poor region of Northern France. It is 'Germinal' territory as a local politician says, before exhorting an audience of dignitaries that the region's future lies in embracing tourism and the 'laws of the market'. The social effect of those laws, the violence of neo-liberal economics which Bourdieu reminded us of, is evident everywhere. The film opens crosscutting between the school's director, Daniel Lefebvre, the film's main character, and Samia, a new paediatric nurse. Lefebvre is left in charge with a five-year-old child and a baby when the mother arrives drunk to pick up her elder child from school. Embarrassed and confused, she runs away leaving the kids with Lefebvre. This narrative strand is run in parallel with Samia arriving at a home to weigh a baby and finding the mother unsure and indifferent to her baby's whereabouts. Samia searches through the rubbish and litter scattered about and finds the undernourished baby too weak even to cry.

Such cases of neglect (and worse, abuse) are repeated throughout the film's episodic, loose narrative. In a typically naturalistic strategy, the cycle of similar incidents produces a gradual drip-drip effect in which the enormous social disadvantages with which people are struggling is felt as a pervasive and dominating reality. Lefebvre struggles to keep the school together as the problems accumulate and staff morale erodes. There are tensions between the school and social services when the latter fails to help endangered children. Levebvre kicks up a stink about the lack of support and wins some concessionary visits from social services, but in general, the political apparatus is concerned to contain dissent rather than address causes. Indeed the political apparatus continues to implement the consequences of a structural underfunding of social provision. The 'Communist' mayor is responsible for cutting free school meals to the poor.

Once more the question of personal integrity within the apparatus is posed when Daniel's teaching is assessed by an inspector, who makes it clear that his average mark is punishment for his misconception of his role as an 'agitator' instead of 'mediator'. Other victories, such as the financial help he manages to arrange for Mrs Lucie Henry, the drunk woman at the beginning of the film, are short lived. Having lived through the winter without power in her flat, the final straw comes when she receives bailiff fees on top of her rent arrears. She commits suicide and kills the children as well. The film documents what happens when the self-worth of individuals is eroded by the conditions of their lives. Their capacity to look after themselves and their children is undermined. In one telling instance, a couple explain that their child often misses school because they are now unemployed and so do not have anything to get up for in the morning.

The problems in Daniel's professional life are mirrored by problems in his personal life. He lives with Valéria and her son, Remi, with whom he has a strained relationship. When Remi is involved with other children who break into and vandalise the school, Daniel confronts him and slaps the unapologetic Remi. This he finds agonising, not only because of his own professional involvement with children, but because we learn that his father, a retired miner, used to beat him unconscious. The film is interspersed with Daniel's poetic, narrator's voice. These are strongly metaphorical reflections. 'A story can unfold like a dream' Daniel tells the audience. 'You want to be caring, help your character, take him by the hand. But you just stand there doing nothing.' This voice-over allows the film to access his subjectivity which the otherwise naturalistic mode would be unable to reach. Thus the film combines a naturalistic attention to the social grind of the external world with an awareness of its impact on the interior, subjective life of the individual as Daniel struggles to make sense of the world. This subjective life is important because *It All Starts Today* is a testament to the capacity and necessity of people to keep on keeping on, albeit collecting casualties and scars along the way. Pushed to the edge of resigning after Mrs Henry's family suicide, Daniel rediscovers his commitment to the children and the job during a final sequence when his partner, a sculptor, organises a major arts and craft project at school. The film ends on a note of collective affirmation.

Although *It All Starts Today* is clearly responding to the newly radicalised context of the late 1990s, it is important to bear in mind that films do not in any way simply *reflect* this context. The strategies which they choose to adopt constructs a *particular* intervention into the political struggle. And it has to be said, that for all its strengths, *It All Starts Today*, retains some familiar weaknesses of the naturalistic aesthetic. For the Hungarian literary critic, Georg Lukacs, one of the fundamental problems of naturalism was that it presented social problems 'as social facts, as results, as *caput mortuum* of a social process.'[88] The progressive side of naturalism is that the world which it reconstructs in such detail, is often evidently harsh and unjust, but the regressive side is that that world is already understood as fixed, given, and unamenable to change. This accounts for the pessimism of many naturalistic texts and also for their lack of understanding of the historical dynamics which have led to the moment in time with which the naturalistic fiction is concerned. (It is significant that the title of Tavernier's film suggests a temporal immediacy and historical *tabula rasa*). As a Marxist, Lukacs argued that the presentation of the world as a thing external to human involvement and resistant to human change, was itself an example of our alienation. In consciousness and to some extent in a range of interrelated social practices such as the operation of capital, wage labour, divisions of labour and the market, the world becomes 'alien' to us; it escapes collective democratic control; it is no longer a product of social relationships, social priorities and social conflicts, but a thing that is external, given, appearing to be almost a fact of nature, which, like the weather, you can complain about but not actually do anything to change. Yet Marxism also reminds us that human beings *produce* their own alienation, that they individually and collectively shape the world they live in and so, while there are powerful impediments, both material and ideological, to changing that world, there is no ontological reason why change cannot be brought about. To realise this aesthetically, Lukacs argued, required developing narrative strategies which could represent 'the complicated intercatenation of varied acts and passions'[89] which constituted the lives of characters. The emphasis on *intercatenation* is significant because for Lukacs society is a web of conflicting social relations, a social *totality* in which practices, institutions, relationships exist not in isolation from one another, but in mutual and dynamic interaction. It follows from this that a narrative structure composed around discrete, only loosely or thematically related events (as *It All Starts Today* is) is going to struggle to grasp the deeper social dynamics at work in a situation. It also follows that for Lukacs, one key aesthetic necessity is to construct stories in which characters and events signify wider social forces and struggles -without simply being reducible to them. Thus Lukacs called for *typicality* in art (the capacity to invest individual characters and situations with more general social significance) but, as a Marxist humanist, he also called for there to be an appropriate level of *individuation* to characters and situations so that they were not simply crude 'reflections' or 'stand-ins' for larger social forces. Bringing typical characters and situations together, within a set of narrative *intercatenations,* creates a social microcosm, what Lukacs described as an intensively worked fictional totality.

This digression into the politics of naturalist aesthetics is worthwhile because it helps us understand the significant differences between *It All Starts Today* and *Ressources humaines*, the last film I want to discuss in this chapter. This is despite the fact that in both its look and its production methods, *Ressources humaines* has been influenced by naturalistic aesthetic strategies. The director Laurent Cantet gathered together a team of unemployed factory workers to work for months developing a screenplay and coaching them into acting out the roles they had helped to create. The $1.2 million production (which was developed with support from the MEDIA programme, and also has BBC money in it) was shot on location in a real factory during working hours. Working with non-professional actors whose real lives bear some similarity to their fictional counterparts and shooting the story in real locations, are familiar strategies of the naturalistic aesthetic. However, the film's deeper claim to realism resides less in the production methods themselves and still less in the documentary quality of the film's *mise-en-scene*, than in the way the production process and visual look of the film have fed into a structural arrangement of the story that brings out the social *intercatenation* and general significance of the action.

At the centre of the film is Franck, a business college graduate who returns home from Paris having landed an internship at the metalwork plant that dominates the small town he grew up in. The film opens with Franck's train journey back home which in classic narrative style, immediately tells us that an established situation is going to be changed by the arrival of an 'outsider'. In fact Franck's ambiguous status as both an insider (his working-class background) and an outsider (education has lifted him out of his class and he has joined the ranks of management) is a constant source of tension and confusion both for him and others. One route which this film might have taken is the more familiar one in which Franck has to relearn from his authentic blue collar father the values of working-class solidarity which his class trajectory has removed him from. But the film does not opt for the simplicities of a *Wall Street* (Oliver Stone 1987), instead exploring a more complex father-son relationship.

Franck finds his father's deference to him, his awed respect for his formal education and profession, painfully embarrassing. At work, his father, Jean-Claude, is a passive and unquestioning cog in the factory machine. When his father takes him onto the shop floor to show him, with glowing pride, the machine he has worked on routinely and uncreatively for years, a foreman orders him to get back to work; and wordlessly, in front of Franck, he obeys. This deference to social hierarchy (a deference which he urges Franck to emulate in his relations with the boss) passes seamlessly into private life, where Franck's parents whisper on the couch in their living room so as not to disturb Franck while he is working. Yet while embarrassed by his father's downtrodden attitude to life, Franck is no class-warrior. He dreams instead of reconciling bosses and workers from his position within the human resource department of the factory. The term 'human resources' has emerged relatively recently from management theory and is supposed to indicate a benevolent interest in and recognition of the value of the work force. The title is ironically deployed within this film, however, for under capitalism, resources, whether human, raw or plant, are mere factors of production to be shunted around to achieve optimal efficiency (that is, profits). It is this fundamental lesson – which goes to the core of the social structure – that Franck (and thus the audience) will have to learn.

Franck's uncertain class position generates much of the tension and drama in the film. His father tells him not to eat lunch with him or his old school friends who work in the factory since he has got to earn their 'respect'. But neither does he fit in with his fellow managers who discuss their ski holidays (Franck, needless to say, has not had the class opportunities to have gone skiing). There are also tensions between Franck and his friends. He has an argument with one of them who is talking ignorantly and with a small-town mentality about Paris. But behind this lies a deeper rift concerning the life opportunities or limitations which are shaped by an individual's class position.

The wider context in which this personal drama is played out is the whole question of implementing the 35-hour week. The introduction of the 35-hour week has been a key union demand in the struggles of the mid-1990s and, indeed, the whole issue of increasing workers' leisure time has been an important strand of French socialism. The 40-hour week was introduced by Leon Blum's 1936 Popular Front government, while the nineteenth-century French/Cuban writer Paul Lafargue (Marx's son-in-law) popularised the importance of leisure, pleasure and non-work.[90] By explicitly locating such a contemporary social issue within its narrative, *Ressources humaines* is clearly asking itself to be read as an intervention into the political struggles of the late 1990s. Needless to say, business has been resistant to attempts to limit the working week, a measure which has been designed to create more employment. Within the film, Franck sits in on the negotiations between workers and management on the implementation of the 35-hour week. Franck of course sits on the management side while he listens to the unions voice their concerns that management will use this to cut overtime. There are three trade unions involved in the talks, but the most formidable figure is Mrs Arnoux, who represents the Communist led CGT. A measure of the film's overall political sympathies can be gleaned from the fact that while Mrs Arnoux's militancy makes her a little insensitive to the personal nuances of the lives of individuals (she upbraids Franck as a management flunkey), her assessment of the factory boss and her argument for class solidarity, proves to be essentially correct.

We have then all the Lukacian primers in place for a successfully realist narrative. We have typical characters (workers, union representatives, bosses, middle management), individuated with their own personal qualities and characteristics (Franck's ambition mixed with idealism, his father's pride and deference) in a typical situation (the negotiations over the 35-hour week) drawn together around the factory and the town (the social microcosm) in a narrative structure sufficiently integrated to draw the events together into a series of climaxes (threatened redundancies and a strike) in which the nature of the social world is revealed to characters and audience alike.

Franck comes up with the idea of asking the workers to fill out a questionnaire on the 35-hour week. Getting a lift from his boss, listening to the classical music on the tape, Franck catches a whiff of ambition and sells this idea as a means of circumventing Mrs Arnoux. His boss agrees – although the idea is initially spiked by Franck's personnel manager who tells him to first submit the idea to him (that is, respect the chain of command). But Franck does see it as a way of genuinely consulting the workers. However, his personnel manager transforms the questionnaire into a series of multiple-choice questions, thus eliminating the opportunity for the workers to express their thoughts and opinions. But this is only the start of Franck's problems. Using the personnel manager's computer one day, he comes across a redundancy plan which has been drawn up with the help of the information the workers provided via Franck's questionnaire. And his own father is one of those listed for termination. This knowledge places Franck in a position where once again, personal integrity vies with towing the line and slotting into the apparatus of control and conformity. Franck chooses integrity. With one of the black workers, Alain, who has been friendly towards him, he breaks into the factory one night, photocopies the redundancy plan, pastes them on the doors to the factory which they then weld shut just for good measure.

Led by Mrs Arnoux, most of the workers immediately strike and picket the factory gates. But some of the workers continue to go in, including Franck's father, timorous to the end, even though he knows of his imminent sacking. Franck is sacked for his class treachery and he joins the workers on the picket line. The striking workers invade the factory calling the remaining workers out to support them. In an emotional encounter, Franck confronts his father who continues to work diligently on his machine. He tells him how ashamed he is and it is clear that he means it in two, diametrically opposed ways. On the one hand, he is ashamed of his father's lack of solidarity towards his own class, but he also admits that he is ashamed because of his father's class. In other words, his father has passed onto him his own sense of inferiority which has motivated him to leave his class. Thus at the heart of Franck is a glaring contradiction which is now revealed to him and us, just as a broader social contradiction, between capital and labour, has been revealed.

The final scene of the film takes place outside the gates of the factory, where the strike has taken on the quality of a united community, with families picnicking and children playing. The ending is a curious mix of upbeat collective unity and downbeat personal tragedy. Franck is leaving the next day. His friend Alain tells Franck that he does not belong in this 'rotten place'. But it is clear that Franck does not belong anywhere. He has left his class but does not have anywhere else to belong to. The film has wisely and deliberately avoided giving Franck a romantic relationship to act as a palliative. He sits to one side watching his father, who has now joined the strikers, play with his grandchildren. His father looks at him. There has been no reconciliation between them and the outcome of the strike is undecided. The future is open. The present is one of struggle. The past is marked – as it always is, for both individuals and collectives – by unhealed wounds.

I began this chapter by identifying some of the contradictions and tensions by which national identity is lived and represented. The loss of national autonomy within a global economy, the nation's internal divisions, its continual renegotiation (and disavowal of that renegotiation) of the tensions between modernity and tradition, are key fissures within national identity. Historically, the UK film industry has been largely locked into producing for the American market, increasingly skewing its self-representations towards the archaic and tradition-bound. There have been recent attempts, such as by PolyGram, to chime with a concerted and broader UK business strategy to broaden and diversify the brand of 'Britishness'. In the case of *Elizabeth*, I argued that this involved the *reinvention* of tradition, a thematic and stylistic modernisation which is in fact a pseudo-modernisation concealing a deeply conservative and ideological trajectory. I juxtaposed this strategy with a more progressive one exemplified within British cinema by *Century*. Rather than affecting a superficial modernisation of the heritage genre, this film, in Benjaminian fashion, constellates the past and the present, finding in the past the struggles still resonating in our own time and thus simultaneously calling the 'modernity' of today into radical question. The narrowness of British cinema (typified by the marginal fate of *Century*) is not solely a product of its relation to the international market. I consolidated the argument that the *internal* social and political dynamics of the nation also crucially determine the national cinema by focusing on examples of recent French cinema. These I held up as exemplifying the category of critical films I have called anti-national, national films. These are films whose critical powers have been fed over the long term by the relatively progressive legacy of the French Revolution (particularly important when it comes to historical dramas) and more immediately by the radicalised political conjuncture of the mid-to-late 1990s.

References

1 P. Schlesinger, 'The Sociological Scope of National Cinema' *Cinema and Nation*, (eds) M. Hjort & S. Mackenzie, Routledge, 2000, p. 22–3.

2 B. Anderson, *Imagined Communities: Reflections on the Origin and Spread of Nationalism*, Verso, 1986, p. 15.

3 B. Anderson, *Imagined Communities*, p. 25.

4 B. Anderson, *Imagined Communities*, p. 16.

5 E. Gellner, *Nationalism*, Phoenix, London,1997, p. 3.

6 E. Gellner, *Nationalism*, pp. 6-7.

7 B. Anderson, *Imagined Communities*, p. 16.

8 A. Higson, 'The Limiting Imagination of National Cinema' *Cinema and Nation*, (eds) M.Hjort & S.Mackenzie, Routledge, 2000, p. 66.

9 E. Hobsbawm and T. Ranger (eds), *The Invention of Tradition*, Cambridge University Press, Cambridge,1983.

10 S. Hall, 'The Local and The Global: Globalization and Ethnicity', *Culture, Globalization and the World System* (ed.) A.D.King, Macmillan, Basingstoke, 1991, pp. 20–1.

11 T. H.Guback, 'Hollywood's Foreign Markets',*The American Film Industry* (ed.) Tino Balio, University of Wisconsin Press, Wisconsin, 1985, p. 466.

12 N.Klein, *No Logo*, Flamingo Press, London, 2000, pp. 195–229.

13 J. Finch, *The Guardian*, June 14, 1997, p. 30.

14 J.Meikle, *The Guardian*, September 18, 1997, p. 3.

15 T. Blair, *The Guardian*, July 22, 1997, p. 17.

16 A. Elwes, *Nations For Sale*, BMP DDB Needham, 1994, p. 19.

17   A. Elwes, *Nations For Sale*, p. 23.

18   A. Elwes, *Nations For Sale*, p. 23.

19   A. Elwes, *Nations For Sale*, p. 27.

20   A. Elwes, *Nations For Sale*, p. 29.

21   A. Elwes, *Nations For Sale*, p. 29.

22   A. Elwes, *Nations For Sale*, p. 31.

23   A. Elwes, *Nations For Sale*, p. 28.

24   A. Elwes, *Nations For Sale*, p. 28.

25   P. Fussell, *Abroad, British literary travelling between the wars*, Oxford University Press, Oxford, 1980, p. 38.

26   A.Jackel, 'Les Visiteurs': a popular form of cinema for Europe?', *European Identity in Cinema* (ed.) W. Everett, Intellect Books, Exeter, 1996, pp. 35–44.

27   So called 'quota-quickies' emerged for a few years after the 1927 Cinematograph Films Act which required distributors and exhibitors to handle a minimum quota of British films.

28   J. Perotti, *The Guardian*, May 26, 2000, p. 2.

29   A.Rawsthorn, *Financial Times*, Aug 30, 1997, p. 7.

30   A.Rawsthorn, *Financial Times*, Aug 30, 1997, p. 7.

31   A.Rawsthorn, *Financial Times*, Aug 30, 1997, p. 7.

32   A. Rawsthorn, *Financial Times*, July 26, 1997, p. 7.

33   A. Rawsthorn, *Financial Times*, Mar 26, 1999, p. 13.

34   Murray Smith, 'Transnational Trainspotting', *The Media In Britain*, (eds) J. Stokes and A. Reading, Macmillan Press, Ltd, 1999, p. 219.

35   Murray Smith, 'Transnational Trainspotting', *The Media In Britain*, p. 220.

36   A. Rawsthorn, *Financial Times*, July 26, 1997, p. 7.

37   A. Finney, *The State of European Cinema*, p. 217.

38   T. Wollen, 'Over our shoulders: Nostalgic screen fictions for the 1980s', *Enterprise and Heritage, Crosscurrents of National Culture* (eds) J. Corner and S. Harvey, Routledge, 1991, p. 192.

39   T. Wollen, 'Over our shoulders', *Enterprise and Heritage*, p. 181.

40   A. Higson, 'Re-presenting the National Past: Nostalgia and Pastiche in the Heritage Film', *British Cinema and Thatcherism* (ed.) L. Friedman, University College Press, London, 1993, p. 128.

41   A. Higson, 'Re-presenting the National Past', *British Cinema and Thatcherism*, p. 119.

42   S. Street, *British National Cinema*, Routledge, London, 1997, p. 105.

43   C. Monk, 'Heritage films and the British cinema audience in the 1990s', *Journal of Popular British Cinema*, no. 2, 1999, pp. 22–38.

44   B. Manning, *The Far Left in the English Revolution 1640–1660*, Bookmarks, London, 1999, p. 33.

45   E. P. Thompson, *The Making of the English Working Class*, Penguin Books, 1980, p. 26.

46   P. Anderson, 'Origins of the Present Crisis', *Towards Socialism* (eds) P. Anderson and R. Blackburn, Cornell University Press, New York, 1965, p. 21.

47   N. Cohen, *The Observer*, 22 October, 2000, p. 31.

48   *Time Out*, Penguin Books, 1999, p. 304.

49   R. Barthes, *Mythologies*, Paladin, London, 1986, p. 131.

50   R. Strong, *The Story Of Britain*, Hutchinson, London, 1996, p. 197.

51   H. Hackett,*Virgin Mother, Maiden Queen Elizabeth I and the Cult of the Virgin Mary*, Macmillan Press, 1995, p. 63.

52   H. Hackett, *Virgin Mother, Maiden Queen*, p. 7

53 H. Hackett, *Virgin Mother, Maiden Queen*, p. 10.

54 M. Wayne, 'Constellating Walter Benjamin and British Cinema: a study of *The Private Life of Henry VIII* (1933)', *Quarterly Review of Film and Video*, vol. 19. no. 2, 2002.

55 W. Benjamin, *the Arcades Project*, (translated by H.Eiland & K.McLaughlin, Massachusetts, Harvard University Press,p. 458.

56 W. Benjamin, *the Arcades Project*, p. 458.

57 *Screen International*, no. 939, Jan 7–14, 1994, p. 32.

58 *Screen International*, no. 934, Nov 19–25, 1993, p. 22.

59 S. Hayward, *French National Cinema*, Routledge, London, 1993, p. 284.

60 F. Jameson, 'The Cultural Logic of Late Capitalism', *Postmodernism or, The Cultural Logic of Late Capitalism*, Verso, London, 1991.

61 A. Callinicos, *Against Postmodernism, A Marxist Critique*, Polity Press, Cambridge, 1989, pp. 162–71.

62 W. Hutton, *The Guardian*, May 3, 1991, p. 26.

63 G. Vincendeau, 'Designs On The Banlieue, Mattieu Kassovitz's *La Haine* (1995)' *French Film Texts and Contexts*, (eds) S. Hayward and G. Vincendeau Routledge, 2000, p. 316.

64 G. Vincendeau, 'Designs On The Banlieue', *French Film*, p. 322.

65 Quoted in J. Wolfreys, 'Class struggles in France', *International Socialism*, 1999, 84, p. 35.

66 J. Wolfreys, 'In perspective: Pierre Bourdieu', *International Socialism*,2000, no. 87, p. 96.

67 P. Bourdieu, *Acts of Resistance*, Polity Press, Cambridge, 1988, p. 34.

68 P. Bourdieu, *Acts of Resistance*, p. 35.

69 P. Bourdieu, *Acts of Resistance*, pp. 38–9.

70 P. Bourdieu, *Acts of Resistance*, p. 41.

71 P. Bourdieu, *Acts of Resistance*, p. 53.

72 P. Bourdieu, *Acts of Resistance*, p. 42.

73 P. Bourdieu, *Acts of Resistance*, p. 49.

74 P. Bourdieu, *Acts of Resistance*, p. 54.

75 F. Truffaut, 'A Certain Tendency of the French Cinema', *Movies and Methods Vol. 1* (ed.) B. Nichols,University of California, London, 1976, pp. 224–36.

76 J. Pidduck, 'Versions, Verse and Verve, Jean-Paul Rappeneau's *Cyrano de Bergerac*', *French Film: Texts and Contexts* (eds) S. Hayward and G. Vincendeau, Routledge, 2000, p. 282.

77 J. Pidduck, 'Versions, Verse and Verve', *French Film*, p. 285.

78 M. Danan, 'French cinema in the era of media capitalism', *Media, Culture & Society*, vol. 22, no. 3, 2000, p. 356.

79 M. Danan, 'French cinema in the era of media capitalism', *Media, Culture & Society*, p. 362.

80 M. Bright, the *Guardian 2*, January 12, 1995, p. 12.

81 M. Bright, the *Guardian 2*, January 12, 1995, p. 12.

82 M. Foucault, *Discipline and Punish, The Birth of the Prison*, Penguin, London, 1991.

83 D. Sayer, *Capitalism & Modernity, An excursus on Marx and Weber*, Routledge, London, p. 83.

84 K. Marx,*The Eighteenth Brumaire of Louis Bonaparte*, Lawrence and Wishart, London, 1984.

85 J. Pidduck, 'Versions, Verse and Verve', *French Film*, p. 291.

86 J. Pidduck, 'Versions, Verse and Verve' op.cit., *French Film*, p. 291.

87 J. Pidduck, 'Versions, Verse and Verve' op.cit. ,*French Film*, p. 292.

88 G. Lukacs,*Writer and Critic*, Merlin Press, London, p. 113–14.

88 G. Lukacs,*Writer and Critic*, p. 128.

90 P. Webster, the *Guardian*, August 9, 1999, p. 14.

3 Pan-European Cinema

The films discussed in this chapter testify to the emergence – still in its early phase – of a pan-European cinema. This means that the films are multi-national in terms of funding and usually talent and that they articulate in their subject matter and theme, a shared (if often conflictual) European history, culture and politics. A new cinematic sense of Europeanness is in the process of construction from the mid-1980s onwards, with perhaps *The Name of the Rose* (Jean-Jacques Annaud, 1986) being the first major example of a filmmaker responding to the political and economic ambitions of the European Union. The other films discussed here, *Land and Freedom* (Ken Loach, 1995), *The Disappearance of Finbar* (Sue Clayton, 1996), *Europa* (Lars von Trier,1991) and *Three Colours Blue* (Krzysztof Kieslowski, 1993) testify to the quite diverse positions which European films will take up in relation to the present historical conjuncture. They also testify to the diverse positions which European cinema takes up in relation to Hollywood. As well as dialoguing with Hollywood, European cinema must also engage with national histories and inter-nation conflicts which have shaped Europe. The question of the nation is not superseded by pan-Europeanism anymore than the local and the regional is abolished by the national. Pan-Europeanism, in my view, will construct social relationships operating at another scale to nations and regions below nations, without absorbing or displacing them. However, we will need to retain a critical perspective on many aspects of the new Europe being forged and I will use the work of the nationalist philosopher Anthony Smith to suggest why. At the same time, many of the objections that Smith holds against pan-Europeanism, are equally valid objections against the nation-state which Smith holds dear. This mutual critique of pan-Europeanism and nationalist resistance, will imply that we must look elsewhere for a critical position from which to understand the politics of European cinema.

Pan-European Cinema

Trying to define a pan-European cinema means differentiating it from other cultural sources. Clearly, Hollywood remains a key interlocutor in an unavoidable, unequal but, nonetheless, often productive cultural dialogue. We can identify three modes in that dialogue which individual films and a pan-European cinema might operationalise. They are: emulation; translation; and rejection. Hollywood cinema has become the dominant paradigm by which films engage with popular culture. Thus when a European film articulates some relationship to popular culture, it at one and the same time strikes up a dialogue with Hollywood. But there are two types of engagement possible. The first is that of *emulation*, where European cinema adopts the cultural model of the Hollywood film, its narrative strategies, its generic markers, its use of stars, and so on. A film like *The Name of The Rose* might be said to be largely working within this mode of emulation. The second mode, *translation*, also seeks some engagement with popular culture as defined by Hollywood, but here emulation gives way to a reworking of such cultural materials, making them 'other' to what they once were and thus claiming them as in some way distinctly European. This strategy was pioneered by the French New Wave in the late 1950s and early 1960s and it was evident too in the work of some of the German filmmakers that achieved prominence in the 1970s, such as Fassbinder and Wim Wenders.[1] Despite being primarily an example of emulation, *The Name of The Rose*, also, as we shall see later, displays some translation of film strategies associated with Hollywood. Finally there is rejection. Here European cinema adopts a mode of film practice that rejects dialogue with Hollywood, favouring instead filmic models, which appear to be embedded in European culture and untouched by American cultural influence. This of course has been the favoured mode of the art film such as *Three Colours Blue* and *Europa*, although *Land and Freedom* would also be an example of this rejection of the Hollywood model even though its political lucidity does not sit very comfortably within the art cinema category. *The Disappearance of Finbar* meanwhile is shot through with translated elements of popular culture while largely rejecting the clear generic markers of the Hollywood paradigm.

The option of 'rejection' has often been criticised for its elitism. The Hungarian director Istvan Svabo has recently adopted a slightly different objection, criticising European cinema for representing 'losers', while Hollywood has an optimistic philosophy of the future. 'Every European hero' Svabo argues, 'carries inside him [sic] the experience of collapsed empire, lost wars, revolution [...]'[2] Yet it could be argued (ironically using Svabo's films as an example) that a sensitivity to historical context and the manner in which its tragedies are inscribed into the actions and values of the central protagonists, is one of European cinema's contributions to world cinema.

The other main cultural source for a pan-European cinema is going to be national cinemas and cultures. As Bill Grantham notes:

> 'Europe', and the idea of a European culture, may have emerged in the sixteenth century
> as a humanist successor to the idea of Christendom,[5] but there is not yet, despite the
> efforts of the past half century, a 'European' identity as strong as that of any of the
> continent's many nation-states.[3]

Thus a pan-European cinema will need to construct itself out of elements of national cinemas in much the same way as national cultures constructed themselves out of the local and regional cultural materials to hand within the territorial boundaries of the nation-state. One of the main narrative strategies for achieving this is to build co-productions around tales of travel, where national borders are crossed and where contact between different nationals is established so as to explore the similarities and differences within Europe.

Nationalism and Pan-Europeanism

I want to contextualise the discussion of pan-European films by exploring some of the processes, implications and problems involved in the formation of a pan-European cultural identity. It has long been a liberal and socialist dream that historical progress would involve progressively more extensive links between peoples over increasingly greater geographical spaces. These links would transcend localism and see the dissolution of national boundaries and a certain insularity that goes with those boundaries. Capitalism, Marx noted, draws nations into the global market: 'In place of the old local and national seclusion and self-sufficiency, we have intercourse in every direction, universal inter-dependence of nations.'⁴ Where liberals argued that it would be the market that would transcend narrow national seclusion, the left has looked ultimately not towards capital (although it was recognised that capital laid the basis for internationalism), but the international solidarity of labour as the means to transcend what Marx called national one-sidedness. This contest between socialist and liberal visions of pan-national intercourse, is still very much with us and lies, as we shall see, in the competing visions of Europe articulated in *The Name of the Rose* and *Land and Freedom* and at the centre of contemporary debates concerning the future nature and direction of the European Union. As we saw in the last chapter, that future could be shaped by the neo-liberal drive to let the market be the final arbiter of all economic and cultural decisions, or, as Bourdieu argues, the left should look to international modes of organisation to preserve and extend the social and cultural gains of past labour struggles.

Either way, the economic integration and political co-ordination going on within the European Union is the most substantial and ambitious attempt in the modern era to renegotiate the relations between nations. For a nationalist philosopher like Anthony Smith, the project of European integration amounts to what he calls cultural imperialism. Whether this is political, ideological or economically based it is always driven by powerful minority groups using administrative and communication apparatuses to impose from above identities onto the majority 'with little or no reference to the cultural traditions of the people incorporated in their domain.'⁵

Yet many of the objections which nationalists have to the pan-European project, while in themselves valid, are also equally applicable to the nationalist project itself. It seems that what often offends nationalists is the sheer *visibility* of the process of identity formation underpinning attempts to construct a new integrated European Union. This process is evidently being driven from the top down by political and economic elites. Yet nationalists like to think this is qualitatively different from the organic popular roots which they imagine characterises the formation of national identity in general and their own national identity in particular. It is for this reason that the new European identity strikes nationalists as a bloodless, anaemic affair, technical and rationalist, as Anthony Smith complains, mobilising modern means of communication that are global in their reach and operated from places quite removed from the national and local cultures they speak to and/or represent.

Smith argues that past nationalists constructed national motifs and styles out of popular cultures, working within the 'cultural traditions and popular, vernacular repertoires of myth, memory, symbol and value' to be found at hand.⁶ If they were to some extent 'invented' and therefore new, they nevertheless evoked older cultural traditions and memories. Yet if this is an argument against constructing a new European identity, it seems particularly weak since any such 'new' identity will also, as we shall see, have to draw on older traditions and memories, hence once more, the importance of the historical drama in European culture. And speaking of history, past nationalists were not averse to practicing cultural imperialism. In Peter Watkins' *Culloden* (1964) the final subjugation of Scotland in 1746 is dramatised using the novel conceit that it is being filmed as if a documentary camera crew had been there to cover the events at the time. Aside from the anachronism of a modern media apparatus transplanted to the 18th century, *Culloden* scrupulously details how English imperialism in Scotland succeeded through superior military force subsequently backed up with substantial cultural terrorism designed to root out Scottish cultural forms (language, dress codes) and attachments.

Another example of projecting onto supranational projects the same problems that also pertain to the nation-state, can be found in Smith's suggestion that the decontextualised symbolism of worldwide telecommunications networks conceals particular histories and cultures which have divided social groups.[7] Quite so, and this was part of my critique of the international image market structuring British film production in the previous chapter. But then, as we have seen, one of the characteristics of national identity is its effacement of the internal fissures of class, gender and ethnicity which fracture national 'unity'. Indeed, one of the problems which postmodernist critics have with the European Union is not that it is doing something *different* from the nationalist formulation of culture and state, but that it is exactly reproducing nationalism's blindness or even hostility to cultural plurality.[8] There is something to this critique. Take for example a EU- backed web-site that has been set up. This wraps European news and information around a cartoon character called Captain Europe. This superhero, we are told, defends a Union 'of prosperity and innovation'. Born Adam Andros, he grew up travelling the world (and learning numerous languages) with his father, a famous European ambassador. Today his most persistent adversary is the evil Dr. D.Vider.[9] The website is run by Twelve Star Communications, a group specialising in helping organisations to define their brand image. The question we have to ask though of Captain Euro, is why this figure, who is supposed to embody the new European identity, is white, male and middle class?

Such narrowly defined versions of what constitutes social life has of course been absolutely characteristic of nation-states. Yet much of Smith's position recycles the nationalist perspective that elites and 'the people' come together in some common project of identity formation. It is true, as Smith argues, that 'images and cultural traditions do not derive from, or descend upon, mute and passive populations on whose *tabula rasa* they inscribe themselves.'[10] But what is missing from Smith's account is any sense that national identity is the outcome of negotiations between *different* groups with *conflicting material* interests and unequal powers. In fact what is missing is something like Gramsci's concept of hegemony. For Gramsci, the direction of social life is a struggle, between different classes, for intellectual and moral leadership. One gloss on Gramsci's concept of hegemony, defines it thus:

> *Negotiation* and *consent* are key terms for understanding the concept of hegemony. Whereas some interpretations of society insist that ideas are somehow 'imposed from above' and others argue that ideas, beliefs and so on are 'free floating', hegemony

involves an understanding of the ways in which, through a series of struggles and conflicts, a certain 'compromise equilibrium' is formed between competing classes. Hegemony therefore designates an *active* process, a constant struggle for leadership conducted on many fronts.[11]

Smith, like many nationalists, has a rather more organic conception of the nation which draws on the cultural resources of Romanticism, with its emphasis on sentiment (rather than rationality) and rootedness (rather than cosmopolitanism).[12] He identifies three components of what he calls an 'ethno-community' which form the basis of the nation-state: 1) a sense of continuity between the experiences of succeeding generations; 2) shared memories of specific events/personages; 3) a sense of a common destiny. Smith argues that pan-national projects such as the new Europe cannot be organised around these characteristics precisely because of the national divisions into which humanity has been organised. To be sure, the history of Europe has been one of division and war, with strong national rivalries and conflicts. A film like *Europa* is, as we shall see, deeply pessimistic about overcoming such divisions, while *Three Colours Blue* offers, albeit tentatively, the prospect of recovery from disaster. The idea that national conflicts are insurmountable, or that reflecting on past divisions cannot be the basis for a new set of identities determined to surmount past divisiveness, seems odd. After all, the nationalist project often required surmounting local and regional loyalties and attachments. Here again lies the importance of historical drama in reconstructing the past in such a way as to tell the European story from a pan-European, not merely national, perspective. Indeed a conviction that returning to the past is important, is a feature shared across European cinema, as Everett notes:

> European film is fascinated by time, and shaped by a desire to return to the past, by an almost obsessive need to explore and interrogate memory and the process of remembering, apparently convinced that therein may be found the key to present identity.[13]

Smith however does perform something of a u-turn by the end of his essay, 'Towards a Global Culture?' Recognising that with minority ethnic nationalisms threatening the 'integrity' of already existing nation-states and the potential for territorial rivalries between nation-states, Smith, reluctantly one feels, meets the proponents of a new pan-European identity half-way. He concedes the need for some *loose* pan-national contacts/links and identifies some common cultural patterns within Western Europe which provide the basis for this. These include: Roman Law, Renaissance humanism, Enlightenment rationalism, romanticism, democracy, parliamentary institutions, civil rights and legal codes, Judea-Christian traditions of ethics, scientific enquiry, artistic traditions of realism, humanism and individualism.[14] There are two significant absences from Smith's list. Firstly, Europe also shares a history of colonialism and subsequently, a post-colonial history which has seen significant immigration from outside Western Europe, often from former colonies. Secondly, Europe has had, for over a hundred and fifty years, various strands of socialist politics which have informed the cultures and institutions of the Continent.

The Name of the Rose

In production terms *The Name Of The Rose* is a German, French and Italian co-production (the latter two have a history of cinematic collaboration) and based on the now famous novel by Italian semiotician, Umberto Eco. Visually, the film has a European aesthetic, its picture of the past is full of mud, its gallery of characters have a grotesque quality reminiscent of Bruegel's paintings. In narrative terms, however, the film, borrowing strongly from the Hollywood paradigm, is a classically structured mystery story with elements of the romance genre. The film also draws on images of Britishness which are quite crucial to its ideological operations. Firstly, Sean Connery's Holmesian detective Brother William of Baskerville, travels into Europe (with an intertextual hint of Scottish Enlightenment traditions via the star image?) to provide the reference point for the film's valorisation of proto-scientific, Enlightenment rationality. While the monks at the monastery interpret various mysterious deaths as signs of the work of the devil, Brother William, a figure who anticipates a more modern age, tries to use reason to read the clues or signs which have been left around the various bodies. Secondly, Brother William provides the film with its moderate politics. Drawing on associations of moderation and evolution in British politics, Brother William is the mid-point between the extremes at war in the film. On the one hand there is the Church hierarchy, with its attempts to legitimise its wealth and riches; and on the other side there is the proto-socialist monastic order, the Dolcenites, attempting to bring the Church closer to the poor by eliminating its wealth – and prepared to engage in political violence to achieve its goal. Of the Dolcenites, Brother William remarks to Adso, his protégé, that 'the step between ecstatic vision and sinful frenzy is all too brief.' At the same time, his pursuit of knowledge and his rational outlook brings him into conflict with the Church establishment. This conflict (rationalism vs. superstition) is distinctly less explosive politically for the contemporary audience than the class politics engaged in by the Dolcenites and which Brother William's discourse attempts (not all that convincingly) to define and contain.

The Name Of The Rose fits very nicely into the supranational project of pan-Europeanism which globalisation has encouraged. But it has all the weaknesses already identified with just such an attempt to construct a new European identity. It exemplifies many of the weaknesses which the big budget, 'big picture', commercial and 'popular' cinema suffers from. '[H]istory' notes Vincent Porter, 'is a resource which can be plundered at will for subjects and themes which can be mapped onto the consciousness of the spectator of today.'[15] There are, however, particular political and cultural pressures at work around *The Name Of The Rose* which help produce a rather problematic plundering of history. The conservative cultural unity conjured up in the language of official Euro-culture is often found in mythical pasts. '[T]he fundamental European belief that we are our past,' as Everett puts it,[16] has been accentuated by the European project. As Collins notes, one has to go back to the Middle Ages for:

> the last moment in European history when the horizontal stratifications were more important than vertical ones. When religious, political, military and cultural elites circulated freely across the continent sharing language, religion, ethnicity, in short the attributes of a

nation. After the Middle Ages the European nation-states formed themselves on a vertical basis, through exacerbating differences with neighbours (war) and accentuating similarities within the national community by expulsion and suppression of minorities.[17]

Collins is describing a complex historical context within which *The Name of the Rose* must operate. The film returns to the past by-passing the 'moment' of national formation and rediscovering an image from the past more complimentary to dreams of European integration *now*. At the same time, this return to the past is governed by the same ideological assumptions which the formation of nation-states has made common-sensical and habitual. For example, Ien Ang has argued that it is precisely Europe's 'historically sedimented 'identity' and its habits of thought and action'[18] which needs to change, particularly its racist and patriarchal underpinnings. Instead, however, European culture is 'characterised by smug complacency on the one hand and by unrecognised nostalgia on the other.'[19]

The Name Of The Rose is certainly open to this double critique of complacency and nostalgia. Its vision of European civilisation stemming from ancient Greece as the source of all progress and democracy is a familiar Eurocentrism. The ethnic bias of this vision is hardly questioned by the presence of Venantius, the one black monk who has no dialogue and dies halfway through. *The Name Of The Rose* is problematic at the level of gender as well. The focus on monastic orders which equate women with the devil is not in fact the main problem. The film's narrational perspective, particularly as it is mediated through the key protagonist, William, does not align itself with *this* view, yet elsewhere it is in gender terms, a profoundly compromised text. The only female character is a peasant woman whose name we do not learn, who appears to have no language, and who can only whimper as she seduces the young monk Adso (Christian Slater). At the film's conclusion, the voice-over of Adso, now as an *old man* remembering his brief dalliance with the peasant wench, only adds to one's unease. This representation chimes in with Ang's rebuke that, 'the legitimisation of male authority is one of the most persistent dominant values by which European greatness has been celebrated and commemorated.'[20]

Towards the end of the film, the narrative splits along two parallel lines. In the library, Brother William is surrounded by flames. The books are burning and he is desperately trying to save himself and some of these printed testaments to human knowledge. The cathedral to this knowledge, the library, ironically, had been in the charge of Jorge who detested everything it stood for, who restricted access to this knowledge and who even committed murder to prevent the books undermining the Church's authority. In a Europe which has seen the burning of books and the political tyranny and scapegoating which was Fascism, the image of Brother William in the library, strikes a profound chord.

In the other narrative strand, outside, the Spanish Inquisition is preparing to burn the scapegoats it has found to explain the murders which have been committed in the name of the Church by Jorge. The Spanish Inquisition, led by Bernardo Gui, prepare to burn the former Dolcenites and the peasant girl Adso has fallen in love with. The other peasants look on, angry but cowed. And then everyone outside turns to see the flames leaping from the towers of the library. Far from this being a disaster, as it is for Brother William, the peasants take this as a sign that the old order is vulnerable and that the moment of revolt and of an albeit momentary rupture with the past, has presented itself. The leading Dolcenite, Remigio de Varagine, dies at the stake, but not before he senses what is about to happen. Remigio and Brother William represent two rather different positions which the intelligentsia can take in relation to the exploited class. I suggested above that the film's attempt to use Brother William's discourse to call the radical discourse of the Dolcenites into question was not entirely successful. For it is not Brother William who saves the peasant girl from the stake, but the peasants themselves. It is not Brother William who dispenses justice, but the peasants who push Bernardo Gui's wagon over the cliff. In the Hollywood model, parallelism was devised to show two events happening simultaneously, in which the villain generally is about to do something unspeakably bad and the hero is struggling to get to the scene to save the day. Thus parallelism works to reinforce the causal agency of the hero and intensify spectator identification with him (it is usually a he). But here, in *The Name of The Rose*, emulation gives way to translation: parallelism turns Brother William into something of a mock-heroic character who does not, in the crucial denouement, control the causal chain of events. It is for this reason that we are invited (perhaps against the grain of the film) at the narrative's conclusion (rather than just the beginning, as is typical with the Hollywood protagonist who must 'learn' something) to adopt a critical stance to William's priorities and ineffectualness. Whatever its inadequacies, we can extract from *The Name Of The Rose* something of the 'big story' of class conflict and emancipation and (in the figure of Brother William and Remigio) of the problematic position of the 'intelligentsia' in that story.

Land and Freedom

If *The Name of the Rose* does its best to marginalise and contain the proto-socialist tradition of the Dolcenites, *Land and Freedom,* a British/Spanish/French/German co-production, is that rare European film which makes socialist politics its explicit and passionate moral and dramatic centre. The film announces itself as 'a story from the Spanish Revolution'. In July 1936, backed by big business and military aid from Hitler and Mussolini, General Franco led an armed revolt against the left-wing Spanish government. A variety of left-wing forces sought to defend the Spanish Republic and some wanted to build on the worker occupations in cities like Barcelona and turn the fight from a defence of social democracy into a full-scale socialist revolution. This indeed was to be the major debate within the left during the Civil War: whether, as the Communist Party argued, the first task was to defend bourgeois democracy against Franco's fascism, or whether, as other groups were arguing, such as the POUM (Workers Marxist Unity Party), the fight against fascism was inextricably tied up with the fight for a new form of direct, bottom-up democracy. As George Orwell wrote in *Homage To Catalonia*, arriving in Barcelona in December 1936 he found:

> something startling and overwhelming. It was the first time that I had ever been in a
> town where the working class was in the saddle. Practically every building of any size

had been seized by the workers and was draped with red flags or with the red and black flag of the Anarchists; every wall was scrawled with the hammer and sickle and with the initials of the revolutionary parties; almost every church had been gutted and its images burnt [...] Every shop and café had an inscription saying that it had been collectivised [...] Waiters and shop-workers looked you in the face and treated you as an equal. Servile and even ceremonial forms of speech had temporarily disappeared.[21]

The conflict in Spain was not merely an internal national situation but had important implications for everyone in Europe and perhaps beyond. This was the last chance to turn the tide against the forces of fascism which had already been successful in Italy, and most alarmingly of all, as Europe's major industrial power, Germany. For this reason Spain became the destination for thousands of young men and a number of women from across Europe and even America, who came to help the Spanish left fight against Franco. Establishment figures and financiers tried to obstruct the Spanish left at every turn (the Midland bank in Britain held up a £6 million check for six months saying that the name on it was incorrectly spelt)[22] while many ordinary people, mostly working class with no military experience risked their lives and lost them for what has been described as 'the last good cause.' Today, the International Brigades as they were known, exert an enduring fascination as an image of idealism, heroism, sacrifice and international solidarity. Television programmes and newspaper features regularly retell stories of the Spanish Civil War and the International Brigades. One historian tries to account for the popular nostalgia in these terms:

> Migration, instantaneous media communication and loneliness has left people in the nineties filled with a sense of powerlessness, the impotency of the individual. We are much lonelier people now.'[23]

This is certainly not the full story. The European context has seen, however sporadically, significant revivals of collectivism and solidarity. But it is the dominant narrative within a British context, especially since the defeat of the miners strike in the mid-1980s. Capturing that sense of isolation and weakness, *Land and Freedom* opens in contemporary Britain with a young woman, Kim, finding her grandfather collapsed in his Liverpool council flat. She calls an ambulance but he dies on his way to hospital. The run-down council estate, daubed with National Front insignia, tells the story of decline, the triumph of fear over hope, of fracture over community. Back at the flat, Kim finds a suitcase that contains her grandfather's mementos from Spain – newspaper cuttings, letters to his girlfriend, a red scarf containing Spanish earth. In a politicised example of Proust's theory of involuntary memory, this collection of objects triggers historical memory. In an almost Benjaminian constellation, we are transported back in time, via film footage from Spain, to 1936. And it is clear that in the context of EU integration and debates about the 'values' of Europe, this juxtaposition of the 1990s and the late 1930s, represents, as Ian Christie notes in his discussion of the film, 'a reminder that there could be a workers' as well as bosses' Europe.'[24]

The political narrative which *Land and Freedom* charts follows George Orwell's trajectory . When he joined the International Brigades he was initially little concerned with politics, thinking that the conflict was a straight forward one between the left and the Fascists. Only later, did he gradually come to political consciousness, concluding that 'official Communism must be regarded, at any rate for the time being, as an anti-revolutionary force.'[25] Unlike Orwell, the film's central protagonist, David Carr, is a working-class member of the Communist Party, but like Orwell, he ends up joining the POUM almost by accident. Through his experiences with the POUM, both military, political and personal (he falls in love with Blanca, a Spanish revolutionary), Dave moves gradually leftwards, tearing up his Communist Party card as they become increasingly oppressive towards left revolutionaries.

Land and Freedom was filmed using Loach's trademark naturalistic production techniques. There are no stars, the professional actors he uses have had low-key success at best (Ian Hart who plays Dave Carr was best known for his portrayal of John Lennon in the low budget British film *Backbeat* (Iain Softly, 1993)) and they are mixed in with non-professionals. Moreover, the actors do not get to see the script (by Loach's long-term collaborator, Jim Allen); there is no storyboard, and actors usually have little idea what will happen to their character. Some actors may receive a few lines just prior to shooting, others are encouraged to respond as they believe their character would to the situations confronting them.[26] This in turn means that the story must be shot in chronological sequence, so that the actors can build up their characters in a coherent manner. Loach sometimes takes this naturalistic authenticity to extremes:

> When he needs to film Hart looking into the distance at some soldiers coming over the brow of the hill at dawn, he gets the other actors up at dawn to come over the brow of the hill. They're not in shot, No one else would bother.[27]

Loach undoubtedly achieves an authenticity of performance from his actors with such techniques. There is however the question of transcending the limitations often attached to naturalism: principally its tendency towards a certain environmental determinism in which individuals are crushed by their social circumstances while the broader social dynamics of a situation are lost in a welter of minutely observed quotidian details. But *Land and Freedom* draws on the historical resonance of a real revolution which makes it emphatically a collective story and one which celebrates the potential of human agency, to change, as individuals and as collectives, the social order around them.

The key scene in the film, much commented on, is the one which takes place after the POUM militia have liberated a small village from the control of the Fascists. After the military victory there is a moving burial scene in which villagers and the militia pay their respects to those who died in the fighting. Some brief speeches, the singing of a revolutionary song, combined with an urgent drum roll and the cutting between the past and the present (Kim reading Dave's letters) builds the emotions, which, as Ian Christie notes, 'spills directly into the following scene, which is a full-scale political debate convened by the POUM, on whether or not the liberated village should collectivise.'[28]

Here the debate about whether the fight against fascism can be separated from the fight for a revolution flares up passionately. It is strikingly reminiscent of a similar debate between union radicals and moderates recorded in Patricio Guzman's documentary *The Battle of Chile* (1973). In cinematic terms, the debate is long, around twelve minutes of screen time. This may stand as a key signifier of the film's difference from the Hollywood model of filmmaking. A twelve minute political debate would be seen as box-office death within the Hollywood model today, although once upon a time, political debates were seen as an important component of the Roman epic. Today, a political debate in Hollywood is always likely to be brief and strongly integrated with a strand of narrative action, as in the case of *Panther* (Mario Van Peebles, 1995) where a political speech is cross-cut with a chase sequence happening nearby. Similarly, the political debate concerning the relationship between Christianity and wealth in *The Name of the Rose* is cut short in screen time when Brother William is pulled out of the debate by new developments in the murder mystery.

In *Land and Freedom*, Loach films the debate with a minimal sense of ellipsis. There is cutting, but the camera almost always with two, three or more people in shot, frequently pans around the room, trying to catch up with what then feels like a very spontaneous debate as each new speaker commands the floor. Sometimes, many voices are speaking at once, and the chair struggles to keep control. The language switches from Spanish to English, with some speakers switching between the two even as they speak, and others, among the POUM for whom English is not their first language, struggling nervously, while one speaker gets in a muddle over the word 'socialism' providing what appears to be a very spontaneous moment of humour. Yet despite the naturalistic qualities of the performances, the dialogue is typical, in the Lukacian sense of representing broader social and political positions, rather than being merely ordinary, mundane or inconsequential. Lawrence, the American POUM member who argues for moderation, is, at one level politically sophisticated, talking in terms of international political strategy and the need to keep the 'neutral' capitalist powers happy. Dave Carr's intervention veers towards Lawrence's position at this stage, but as befits a working-class protagonist, still quite politically naive, he talks in more down-to-earth terms of the need to keep people alive (that is, win the war against fascism first) in order to sustain socialism which exists, not in textbooks but in real physical people. It is significant that as the central protagonist, Carr makes the kind of small-scale contribution that would be inconceivable in a bigger budget, star-driven film with Hollywood as its paradigm. Although he does speak, Dave has fewer lines than anyone else and his position loses the debate (and the vote) to those arguing for full-scale collectivisation. Here in this image of different language speakers debating and communicating around life and death issues, the European co-production and socialist internationalism converge. As Christie notes, the film represents 'a sharp new historicism in action – and a timely argument for pan-European funding in the post-GATT era.'[29]

The Disappearance of Finbar

If *The Name of the Rose* and *Land and Freedom* offer different pan-European visions operating 'above' the nation-state, a number of European films are beginning to articulate a geo-cultural awareness of the segmentations and subdivisions which are going on 'below' the nation-state.[30] Bigas Luna's *The Tit and the Moon* (1994) was largely marketed and received by critics as a tale of a young boy at that transitional moment between childhood and the burgeoning sexuality of adolescence.[31] Yet the film can also be read as an allegory of a Europe in transition. The boy, Tete, is growing up in Catalonia, which has retained a strong separatist culture within a Castilian dominated Spain. Tete is an 'anxaneta', the young boy who must climb to the top of the human tower which is built during street festivals. As he climbs, he is harangued from the pavement by his fiercely Catalan father, who urges him up the tower, citing that Catalan pride and Tete's own masculinity is at stake. The tit of the film's title is Tete's mother's breast which has been commandeered by Tete's newly arrived baby brother (the baby is first seen amongst a row of other babies in the hospital, but he is differentiated by the black and red Catalan cap he is wearing). Within Europe there are increasing pressures from regions and nations (such as Scotland) that have historically been welded into nation-states, to wean a new autonomy within the emergent institutional and cultural European space. The emblematic image from *The Tit and the Moon* which articulates this comes when Tete has a fantasy in which he imagines himself on the moon, dressed in a silver space suit, planting the Catalan and European Union flag. The moon as a metaphor of a new frontier becomes the site where a linkage is made between Catalonia and the EU which by-passes the Spanish state.

The Disappearance Of Finbar (Sue Clayton, 1996) is also about the marginalised spaces within nations, as Danny's search for his friend Finbar Flynn takes him from the peripheral space of a Dublin housing estate to the freezing, depopulated landscape of Lapland. We saw in chapter one that the director Sue Clayton was looking for an 'anywhere in Europe' feel for the Irish housing estate. The social exclusions of the housing estate was made most spectacularly visible in the mid-1990s by *La Haine* (Mathieu Kassovitz, 1995), with its depiction of the Parisian suburbs or *les banlieues*, which literally means place of exile. *The Disappearance Of Finbar* takes up this theme of the struggle to expand the narrow horizons that society has imposed. The film has a white diasporic structure of feeling, an atunement to the sort of hybridities of identity and culture usually associated with Black and Asian cinema in the UK, but here drawing, no doubt, on the Irish experience of emigration (one of the few routes to better opportunities), which has been so central to the history of the country for nearly two hundred years.

The film opens with Finbar and Danny as children singing along with Finbar's dad in his country-and-western band, the Rosscommon Cowboys. This indigenisation of cultural material from other countries -predicated on the idea that culture travels as well as people – is a common motif in the film. The songs which the band sing are full of images of wandering, of journeys in wide open spaces, of nights by the camp-fires under open skies. Yet as Danny, who narrates the story, tells us, the hopes which Finbar's father had to make it big with the Rosscommon Cowboys, turned to nothing. If there was no escape for Finbar's father, then it seems in the following scene that Finbar, now in his late teens, has got his big chance. He is leaving the community a minor hero having secured a place in the Zurich-based football team Grasshopper FC.

But he is soon back, having blown his chance, much to his father's frustration. So he seems trapped with Danny, on the housing estate, which is full of squats, desolate urban spaces with open fires on them, and abandoned flats. But one night, after arguing with his girlfriend Katie -who he is barely interested in – and Danny (who fancies Katie), Finbar climbs atop the half-built flyover which is the very symbol of the estate's disconnection from the main arteries of Europe. Below, the lorries and cars flash by, the motorway's orange lights blur into the distance. And then Finbar disappears. We will find out later that he dropped off the precipice onto a lorry loaded with sugar-beet heading to Stockholm.

What is interesting about Finbar's disappearance is the way the community reacts to it. While his mother is unhinged by it, the community rediscovers itself, forming a 'Finbar Flynn Action Committee' and launching a campaign to find him. People cannot forget Finbar even though he has forgotten about them. Three years later, on the anniversary of his disappearance, Katie sleeps the night under the flyover. The community holds onto Finbar as tenaciously as Danny's slightly deranged grandfather holds onto the memory of Thorsten, a Swedish friend he met many years ago, while working on the docks. The mythologisation of Finbar reaches its high-tech, mass media pinnacle when a music impresario produces a pop video based on Finbar's mysterious disappearance, casting the people from the housing estate. The technological and cultural construction of community is nicely revealed in the scene where Danny walks from the Chinese take-away (more evidence of cultural hybridity) where the video song is starting, out into the streets, where the video is playing on the multiple television sets in a shop window, and then along past the houses where the glow of the TV screens in the front rooms can be seen, and finally to his own home where the song is just ending. The community thus rediscovers itself in and around Finbar's absence (voluntary as it turns out) in an attempt to negate its own negation (the hole in the concept of 'togetherness' which Finbar's disappearance represents).

Significantly it is the music video as an example of travelling culture which prompts Finbar to phone Danny one night advising him and the community to forget about him. But having discovered that he is alive and in Stockholm, Danny sets out on a quest to find Finbar, funded by his grandad's savings. Arriving in Stockholm, Danny traces Finbar using the telephone book, but discovers that Finbar has moved on, up north. And so Danny follows him into a snowy frontier culture with many generic hints towards the western (the drinking bar, community dancing – although here, in hybrid fashion, the dance is the Argentinean tango, snow mobiles and reindeer instead of horses and cows). But when Danny finds Finbar, it is only to see him move on again, further north, and this time definitively into myth. This time Danny will not follow him, but neither does he go home, choosing instead to stay in Lapland.

We can allegorise Danny and Finbar to some extent, seeing in them two contradictory pulls which are very evident in the contemporary world. Danny represents community, which, as Anthony Smith tells us, has huge investments in continuity and memory and rootedness (Danny's new Lapland community immediately expects him to stay there). Finbar on the other hand represents a wandering, restless spirit. For him, Lapland is not a community at all, but, as Sue

Clayton has expressed it, an image of oblivion, a '*tabula rasa* on which to start out all over again.'[32] Danny and Finbar represent two sides of modernity which do not add up: community and separation, continuity and rupture.

Europa

As a Danish, French, German and Swedish co-production with additional funding coming from Eurimages, *Europa* (Lars von Trier, 1991) is a reminder of precisely the kind of divisions and conflicts which the European Union is being constructed, in part, to transcend. *Europa* opens with the camera moving along the railway tracks in the pitch black of night. As the film's 'overdetermined' symbolic centre, the train condenses travel, sleep, the past and the future in a single image. In a playful self-conscious move, *Europa* has veteran actor Max Von Sydow's voice hypnotically speaking to the spectator, counting them down as they go 'deeper and deeper' into the past, which is not just Germany immediately after the Second World War, but Europe itself. Von Sydow's voice is addressed both to the spectator who is being drawn into the 'spell' of cinema, and the film's central character, Leopold Kessler, whose helplessness amid the events he barely understands and has even less control over, is underlined by the way Von Sydow's narration operates like the voice of fate. (This self-reflexive analogy between life and the act of watching a film is not uncommon in European films. *It All Starts Today*, discussed in the previous chapter, made a similar comparison).

Kessler is American born, but via his German father he feels an affinity with a country which he neither knows nor understands. Politically he is a naive idealist who has returned to Germany to 'show a little kindness' to it. Despite this symbolic act of reconciliation he is abused and manipulated by all around him as Germany struggles to escape its fascist past while being dominated by the Americans. The latter seek commercial advantage for American companies while at the same time reconstructing Germany, even if that means working with people who operated successfully under the Nazi regime. One such group is the Hartmann family who own the Zentropa railway, where Kessler's uncle has secured him a job as a sleeping car conductor. (The name of the railway alludes to the primitive moving image device of the Zoetrope, thus connecting the theme of travel with the imaginative journey that the cinema spectator undertakes). Despite the devastation all around and the lowly status of his job, Kessler's uncle clings absurdly to an unreconstructed mentality obsessed with rules, discipline and hierarchy. The figure of Uncle Kessler is an almost archetypal German cinematic character, which can be traced back to the Weimar Cinema. In *The Last Laugh* (F. W. Murnau,1924) Emile Jannings plays the officious hotel doorman who compensates for his lowly status by investing massively in his uniform and job until he is crushingly demoted to lavatory attendant. Of course, such economic insecurities were to feed into building support for the Nazis in the following decade. *Europa*'s recycling of this ur-figure in the film's post-war setting is part of the film's insistence on the iron grip of history. This is developed as Leopold is drawn into the affairs of the Hartmann family by Katharina, a femme fatale figure whose wartime involvement in a secret fascist organisation calling themselves the Werewolves, may or may not be a thing of the past. In the post war situation, the Werewolves are still very active, carrying out assassinations of Germans who co-operate with the Americans.

The film mobilises a surreal aesthetic. Its black and white film stock gives a dream-like quality to the *mise-en-scene*, although at certain dramatic moments, individual characters or objects may suddenly turn into colour. With its strange superimpositions (for example, Kessler's eyes top half of the screen, mixed in with a shot of the train on the bottom half moving left to right), its periodic anti-illusionistic use of back projections, its bizarre temporal and spatial logic (in one scene, Kessler is led down the travelling train into carriages where he discovers emaciated Jews in prison camp uniforms) *Europa* evokes history as a nightmare from which neither the spectator nor Leopold can awake.

In the classical Hollywood narrative, dramatic conflicts are usually resolved by the character who occupies an in-between position *vis-a-vis* the conflicting 'extremes' which the film constructs. Such characters are mediating figures, enabling a dominant social order and value system to engage with 'disruptive' elements and come to some negotiated resolution which may modify but not fundamentally challenge the social order depicted. Thus in *The Name of the Rose*, which emulates the classical Hollywood narrative to a large degree, we saw that Brother William functioned as the mediating character between the Church elites and the proto-socialist Dolcenites. If *Europa* were to adopt this model, then clearly Leopold would be the mediating figure. He is 'in-between' in terms of his national identity, being both American and German. Yet the film translates this model into a distinctly un-Hollywood pessimism concerning the possibility of mediation. In fact, Leopold is crushed by his 'in-betweeness'. Such hybridity, as we shall see in the final chapter, has become a key concept within cultural theory amongst an intelligentsia, which has become increasingly enamoured of a cultural cosmopolitanism. Rosi Braidotti, for example, the feminist philosopher born in Italy, raised in Australia, and educated in Paris, argues that the formation of an 'ethnocentric fortress', derives from an unhealthy attachment to 'the concept of the mother tongue':

> It feeds into the renewed and exacerbated sense of nationalism, regionalism, localism, which marks this particular moment of our history. The polyglot surveys this situation with the greatest critical distance; a person who is in-transit between languages, neither here nor there, knows better than to believe in steady identities and mother tongues.[33]

For the intelligentsia, migrancy is both a metaphor for cultural theory and an articulation of their own cosmopolitan social being as they move around the global conference circuit and job market. As Jonathan Friedman notes, the idea that strong cultural attachments can be viewed as a dreadful intellectual mistake by the 'uneducated' tells us much about the (middle) class position of the new advocates for a remorseless hybridity which constantly dissolves 'steady identities'.[34]

As we shall see in the final chapter, hybridity has become an important motif in some European films. *Europa* however is at the opposite end of this spectrum and utterly rejects any possibility of something productive coming out of hybridity. The advocates of hybrid identities tend to downplay history as they promote the productive possibilities of remaking the self. Conversely, and no less problematically, *Europa*'s hostility to crossing boundaries and mixing categories and mother tongues leads it to presenting history as inescapable fate and the self as permanently fixed by the past.

At the end of the film, Leopold is manipulated into planting a bomb on the train to kill a high ranking American officer. Thinking that Katharina, now his wife, has been kidnapped by the Werewolves (in fact she is still a member of the organisation) he initially plans to carry out the task, then changes his mind, only to then detonate the bomb accidentally. The film runs a comedic strand throughout. The night he plants the bomb is also the night of his examination as a sleeping-car conductor by two examiners who are as officious as his uncle. This combination of tragedy with farce is a distinctly European, particularly Eastern European aesthetic sensibility, almost as if the nightmare of history is so burdensome, that it must be leavened with an absurdist streak. The bomb detonates over a bridge and the train topples into the river below. Trapped in one of the cars, Leopold drowns, the omniscient narrator even counting down to his death ('on ten, you will be dead'). As the current frees his body from the car and drifts towards the open sea, Von Sydow's voice-over declares, to the spectator as much to us as to the corpse, 'You want to wake up, to free yourself of the image of Europa. But it is not possible.'

Three Colours Blue

If *Europa* ends with a train crash and the big sleep from which Leopold can never awake, then *Three Colours Blue* (Krzysztof Kieslowski, 1993) begins with a car crash in which Julie's husband and young daughter die. While in *Europa* the train *is* Germany, the car is a rather more private mode of transport and the crash, at one level, is intensely personal in its effects. However, one of the sub-texts of the film, is that the distinction between the private and the public is not in fact absolute. The film is also part of Kieslowski's Colours trilogy (*Three Colours White* (1993) will be discussed in the next chapter), with each colour symbolising the three ideals of the French Revolution. Blue signifies freedom, although for much of the film it also signifies, in the empty blue pool she swims in or the way the film frequently lights her face, Julie's profound and utter loneliness. After the crash Julie (Juliette Binoche) regains consciousness slowly in hospital to hear the doctor, reflected in an extreme close-up of her pupil, telling her that her husband Patrice and daughter, Anna, are dead. The film is full of such close-ups, magnifying the small details of life because the large and important things have been snatched away and left Julie with nothing, a word Julie repeats a number of times. Yet despite the scale of the disaster for Julie, *Three Colours Blue* will affirm, in a way that *Europa* does not, the possibility of recovery.

Julie attempts to withdraw from life, moving to a new apartment, trying to keep herself to herself. The film is thus very quiet, the dialogue sparse, in keeping with her solitude. We find out that her husband was a famous composer who was in the middle of writing a concerto on the theme of the Unification of Europe. Here then is the film's European and public dimension in which Julie's personal disaster interweaves with the ambitions to reunite a European continent which has had its own fair share of unnecessary conflict, death and disaster. There is a question mark however over the extent to which Patrice actually wrote the music. A television journalist visits Julie and asks if she is the true author of this great composer's works.

The fact that *Three Colours Blue* has a female lead is striking for its unusualness. Much pan-European cinema is still dominated by male journeys, transformations and crises. In part this is because pan-European cinema is so orientated towards history where the patriarchal closure on female opportunities can be used to collude with contemporary cinema's male-dominated narratives. *Land and Freedom* shows some understanding of how the Spanish Revolution transformed gender relations with women fighting alongside the men. Significantly, as the Revolution starts to lose impetus and the Communist Party strengthens its grip, women at the front are pushed back into the more traditional roles of nurses and cooks.

In raising the question of Julie's contribution to her husband's music, *Three Colours Blue* questions the domination of institutional and public life by men within Europe, both old and new. Julie's personal life then required her to subordinate her talents and hide them behind her husband's public acclaim. Thus despite the pain and ambiguities of her situation, she does, in fact, by the end of the film, grope towards a new life with a newfound freedom of expression. Just as the private and the public are entwined, so her attempts to withdraw into a life of absolute solitude, to wipe the slate clean in the same way that Finbar (also unsuccessfully) attempts to do, is only temporarily possible. For the world around her keeps drawing her out, keeps knocking at her door, keeps requiring her to engage with it. When a neighbour knocks and asks her to sign a petition to evict a prostitute living in the flats, she refuses because she does not want to get involved. Yet the refusal means that the prostitute, Lucille, is not evicted, and so the grateful Lucille comes around to thank her and strike up a friendship.

The individual is thus tied by numerous threads to others around them and one night, called out to a strip club to comfort Lucille who has seen her father in the audience, Julie in turn, is unexpectedly reminded of a life lived in relation to others. There, on the television, is a programme about her husband (the private made public once again) whose work his friend, Olivier, is desperately trying to complete under commission by the European Council. Olivier has already declared his love for Julie and, indeed, after the crash and just before her disappearance, Julie and Olivier make love. She then disappears, cruelly inflicting on him the sort of presence/absence of loved ones that she herself has suffered. The television programme also shows pictures of Patrice with an unknown woman who Julie discovers was his lover. Finding out that he had an alternative life seems to help Julie try and establish her own new life. She makes contact with Olivier and looks over his attempts to complete the concerto. She then finishes the job herself. Phoning Olivier up, she asks him if he wants to collect the music, but he insists that the world must know that she is the author of the composition. She agrees and when he confirms that he still loves her, she goes round to him. The film ends with the concerto playing over a series of dissolves from Julie and Olivier making love to various people Julie knows or has met, including her husband's lover, now pregnant with Patrice's baby (more evidence of life as a web of interconnections).

For *Three Colours Blue*, it is neither possible nor desirable to abolish the past or a memory of it, but it is possible to come to terms with it. *Three Colours Blue* suggests that European culture may be redeemed by those who it has traditionally excluded (women, in this case). This is a rather different attitude to history than the pessimistic and fatalistic one of *Europa*. This film offers a negation of the pan-European dream, insisting on the temporal and spatial untranscendable quality of national culture, no matter how absurd or discrepant it is in relation to new contexts. We shall see in the next chapter that this theme of the nation-state as untranscendable also characterises a number of Serbian films made during the Balkan wars of the 1990s.

In meditating on Europe from diverse proto-European perspectives, the films that I have discussed have all (except for *Three Colours Blue*) mobilised the motif of cross-border travel and conjured with meetings and places and times in which national borders disappear (*The Name of the Rose*), or are relativised (by internationalism in *Land and Freedom*) or compared (*The Disappearance of Finbar*) or reaffirmed (*Europa*). The films all demonstrate to varying degrees precisely what is productive and interesting about European cinematic characters, those 'losers' which Svabo criticised. For they explore the links between the individual and the social world around them, the internalisation of that world and also the struggles (with varying degrees of success) to change themselves, a change which has incremental public consequences. While at a political and economic level the bourgeoisie have dominated the remaking of Europe as a politically and economically integrated territory;[35] culturally, what is striking about the films which I have discussed, is their disparate diversity. Political and economic hegemony gives way in the cultural sector to a much more fragmented and contradictory field. These pan-European films offer different visions of what Europe has been, what it is and what it could be, and they offer different takes on those borders that divide and exclude: those of class, gender, nation and ethnicity. These historically sedimented fractures in the European 'community' continue to operate and continue to call into question Europe's self-image as the cultural pinnacle of all that has been said and thought. Indeed, these fractures are being extended eastwards as the European Union enlarges.

References

1 T. Elsaesser, 'American Friends: Hollywood echoes in the New German CInema', *Hollywood and Europe, Economics, Culture, National Identity, 1945-1995* (eds) G. Nowell-Smith and S. Ricci.

2 Quoted in A. Finney *The State of European Cinema: A New Dose of Reality, A New Dose of Reality*, Cassell, 1996, p. 54.

3 B. Grantham, *'Some Big Bourgeois Brothel' Contexts for France's Culture Wars with Hollywood*, University of Luton Press, Luton,2000, p. 3.

4 K. Marx and F. Engels, *The Communist Manifesto*, Penguin Books, Harmondsworth, 1985,p. 84.

5 A. D. Smith, 'Towards a Global Culture?',*Theory, Culture and Society*, Sage, London, vol. 7, 1990, p. 176.

6 A. D. Smith, 'Towards a Global Culture?', *Theory, Culture and Society*, p. 181.

7 A. D. Smith, Towards a Global Culture?', *Theory, Culture and Society*, p. 179.

8. D. Morley and K. Robbins, *Spaces of Identity: global media, electronic landscapes and cultural boundaries*, Routledge, London, 1995.

9 Captain Euro online at http://www.captaineuro.com.

10 A. D. Smith, 'Towards a Global Culture?', *Theory, Culture and Society*, p. 179.

11 Open University Popular Culture Course, quoted by G. Hurd, *National Fictions, World War Two in British Film and Television*, BFI, London, 1984, p. 19.

12 E. Gellner, *Nationalism*, Phoenix, London, 1997, p. 67.

13 W. Everett, 'Timetravel and European film', *European Identity In Cinema* (ed.) W. Everett, Intellect Books, Exeter, 1996, p. 103.

14 A. D. Smith, 'Towards a Global Culture?', *Theory, Culture and Society*, p. 188.

15 V. Porter, 'European Co-Production: Aesthetic and Cultural Implications', *European Cinema Conference* (ed.) S. Hayward, AMLC/Aston University, 1985, p. 13.

16 W. Everett, 'Timetravel and European film', *European Identity In Cinema*, p. 103.

17 R. Collins, 'National Culture: A Contradiction In Terms?', *Television: Policy and Culture* Unwin Hyman, London,1990, p. 209.

18 I. Ang, 'Hegemony -In-Trouble, Nostalgia and the Ideology of the Impossible in European Cinema',*Screening Europe, Image and Identity in Contemporary European Cinema* (ed.) D.Petrie, BFI, London, 1992, p. 22.

19 I . Ang, 'Hegemony -In-Trouble', *Screening Europe,* p. 21.

20 I. Ang, 'Hegemony -In-Trouble', *Screening Europe,* p. 24.

21 G. Orwell, *Homage To Catalonia*, Penguin Books, London, 1989, pp. 2–3.

22 L. Manning and M. O'Kane, *The Guardian* 2, July 15, 1996, p. 2.

23 L. Manning and M. O'Kane, *The Guardian* 2, July 15, 1996, p. 2.

24 I. Christie, 'Film For A Spanish Republic', *Sight and Sound*, October 1995, p. 36.

25 G. Orwell, *Homage To Catalonia*, p. 199.

26 R. Butler, *The Independent on Sunday*, July 24 1994, p. 14.

27 R. Butler, *The Independent on Sunday*, July 24 1994, p. 14.

28 I. Christie,'Film For A Spanish Republic', *Sight and Sound*, p. 37.

29 I. Christie, 'Film For A Spanish Republic', *Sight and Sound*, p. 36.

30 I. Aitkin, 'Current problems in the study of European cinema and the role of questions on cultural identity',*European Identity In Cinema* (ed.) W. Everett, p. 78.

31 My thanks to Helen Lane for recommending this film to me.

32 M. McFadyean, *The Guardian* 2, October 14, 1998, pp. 14–15.

33 Quoted in P. Van Der Veer, ' 'The Enigma of Arrival': Hybridity and Authenticity in the Global Space', *Debating Cultural Hybridity* (eds) P. Werbner and T. Modood, Zed Books, London, 1997, p. 94.

34 J. Freidman, 'Global Crises, The Struggle for Cultural Identity and Intellectual Porkbarrelling: Cosmopolitans Versus Locals, Ethnic and nationals in an Era of De-Hegemonisation', *Debating Cultural Hybridity*, p. 79.

35 B. Balanya, et.al.,*Europe Inc. Regional and Global Restructuring and the Rise of Corporate Power*, Pluto Press, London, 2000.

4   After The Fall: Cinema and Central and Eastern Europe

We have seen that the project of political and economic integration within the European Union is in part an attempt to lay to rest the historic divisions within Europe that have generated numerous wars in the modern era. War, with all its technological potentialities for mass destruction, is perhaps the starkest counterpoint to Europe's cultivated self-image as civilised, prosperous, tolerant and culturally diverse. And yet the strategies to remedy the fault lines which have opened up so disastrously in the past are being directed by European and American corporations operating within the parameters of a global system which is structurally geared towards intensifying competition between peoples, regions and nations and increasing socio-economic inequalities.[1] Since these forces are powerful motors for conflict, the European project must be considered a deeply contradictory one.

With the fall of the Berlin Wall in 1989 and the subsequent collapse of the Soviet Empire in 1991, the relations between Western and Central and Eastern Europe (CEE) have been transformed. Many of the films that I discuss in this chapter continue the trend of pan-Europeanism explored in the previous chapter; thus cross-border travel and displacement are key themes within the narratives, but even when they are not, the films display, to varying degrees, an awareness of Europe as a *determining context* (in a way that is quite new) for the events which take place. There are two key inter-related events in recent European history which the films I have selected are concerned with: the integration of CEE into Western market capitalism and the re-emergence of war in Europe with the implosion of the former Yugoslav federation into small ethnically exclusive nation-states in military conflict with one another. Once again we will see films adopting a variety of political perspectives and aesthetic strategies in representing these major transformations. This chapter will also examine the politics of the critical discourses deployed to discuss CEE. At one level, CEE has been constructed as the 'new black' subject, recycling Europe's old colonial mentality but now redirected towards the Eastern part of the same continent. Another discourse has in turn offered a critique of this representation of Eastern Europe along the same lines as the critique which post-colonial scholars launched against Europe's historic tendency to exoticise, marginalise or demonize the 'Other' in its visual arts, anthropology and historiography. However, while this post-colonial discourse has its merits and uses, I will also suggest that as a critical discourse it is insufficiently sensitive, indeed, it actively represses, the historical, political and, above all, socio-economic dynamics in play across Europe. The extent to which socio-economic relations are figured (or not) in political, cultural and cinematic representations, is a key theme in this chapter.

After The Fall
The fall of the Berlin Wall in 1989 was the practical and symbolic confirmation that Western market capitalism had triumphed in the Cold War against the Soviet Empire.

The Soviet Union consolidated itself after the First World War and extended its sphere of influence into CEE countries after the Second World War (East Germany, Czechoslovakia, Hungary, Bulgaria, Poland, Romania, Albania, and, more ambiguously, Yugoslavia). After the fall, Western triumphalism quickly achieved canonical form in Francis Fukuyama's essay (later expanded into a book) 'The End of History?'[2] which argued that with the collapse of the Sovietised bloc, 'history', at least as a contest between fundamentally antagonistic political philosophies, had come to an end. We could all now agree, Fukuyama suggested, that liberal capitalism was the only socio-economic system that 'worked'.

The full force of this closure can be felt in Dusan Makavejev's *Gorilla Bathes At Noon* (Germany 1993). The protagonist is the ironically named Victor, a Russian soldier left behind in Berlin after his platoon goes home after the collapse of the Soviet Union. The film is a kind of reversal of Kuleshov's *The Extraordinary Adventures of Mister West in the Land of the Bolsheviks* (1924). Here it is Mister East's picaresque adventures around Berlin, with Victor, the naive and bemused soldier pledging loyalty in his dreams to a woman dressed up as Lenin even as documentary footage shows a Lenin statue being ceremoniously dismembered. Interestingly, a German woman gives a speech hailing the destruction of the Lenin statue, but her main concern appears to be that Lenin was not even German! To add to the historical ironies, the film intercuts sequences from the 1949 Stalinist epic *The Fall of Berlin*, a Second World War film which shows heroic Soviet soldiers fighting to raise the red flag over the rubble of Berlin in the last days of the conflict. Yet while this lampooning of the delusions fostered by Stalinism are fair enough, the film is utterly lacking any satirical intent as regards the delusions of consumer capitalism. There is no sense in the film of the gap between rhetoric and reality which exists in Western capitalism and no indication of any scepticism concerning the likely future of Eastern Europe under the hegemony of the West.

Prior to the fall of Soviet communism, the lack of political democracy and consumer goods within the CEE bloc was to some extent compensated by a degree of social and welfare securities. With the coming of the market, various (sometimes very constricted) degrees of political democracy have been introduced alongside the jostle of new consumer goods. But the integration of the Eastern bloc countries into the world market has also brought with it some familiar problems. As capital has flowed across the borders of CEE looking to exploit a wealth of natural resources, set up new zones of tourism, exploit labour markets (fewer people working harder) and search for new consumer markets, so unemployment across the CEE bloc rose and familiar patterns of social stratification began to assert themselves very quickly. By the mid-1990s in Russia, the top 10% were earning 14 times the income of the poorest 10% compared with a ratio of 5.4 at the beginning of the 1990s.[3] Thus access to the new consumer cornucopia was highly differentiated according to the unequal distribution of wealth.

To varying degrees, the integration of the post-Soviet nations into Western capitalism has been painful and in the case of the former Yugoslavia, it has been, as a character is fond of saying in Kusturica's *Underground* (1995), 'a catastrophe'. Western journalists who had predicted that the introduction of market capitalism in CEE would rapidly improve the lives of the population, seemed bemused by the failure, most notably in Russia, to develop a proper civil society and democratic politics. They saw no link between the destruction wrought on the socio-economic fabric by IMF structural adjustment programmes and the rise of a 'gangster capitalism' staffed by political demagogues. John Lloyd, writing for the *Financial Times* could only blame the Russians as he surveyed the disaster:

> The belief was -it was not subjected to much analysis – that the Soviet system had been a prison of belief, of nations, of free thought and association, of enterprise. It had: but the prisoners had in many cases known nothing else but prison life. Like old trusties, many liked it, or at least found it impossible to adapt to the loss of confinement.[4]

This superior Western attitude recycles the old colonial mentality which saw the West civilising the natives who were as yet not ready for 'independence'. It also conveniently glosses over the complicity of Western institutions, advisors and the structural logics of market capitalism in the implosion of living standards for the majority, a familiar trope which we will need to return to in relation to cultural theory and film practice. However, many on the left were equally disorientated by the collapse of 'actually existing socialism'. The editor of *New Left Review*, Perry Anderson, reluctantly concluded that while the traditional critique of the inequities of capitalism remain demonstrably valid, any prospect for fundamental social change has vanished in the 1990s.[5]

It is clear that discussing films which are engaging with the new political and economic realities of an altered landscape, will inevitably be a commentary on this larger narrative. A critical as opposed to merely acquiescent commentary must radically prise open the political closure which Western triumphalism, of which Fukuyama is merely a representative example, has tried to impose on the events of the 1990s. For one thing, we do not have to accept the labels which the major actors of the Cold War accorded themselves and others. Ever since Trotsky there has been a long tradition of Left thinking that has had few illusions about the Soviet Union or its satellites as standard bearers for an alternative social formation to capitalism. In his *magnum opus, Beyond Capital*, the Hungarian born, British-based political philosopher, István Mészáros, makes a very useful distinction between capitalism, which he associates with the market system and the legal protection of private property (abolished by the Sovietised regimes) and *capital*, as a socio-economic order founded on the 'explosive structural antagonisms'[6] between labour and those who are placed in controlling positions (insofar as capital can be controlled) *over* the direct producers.

The 'post capitalist' regimes of the Soviet bloc were not, in this view, *post capital*. They abolished the market and the legal right to privately own productive capital, but they were still based on exploitation, although here this was regulated not by economic agents (the private capitalist) but by political agents (the Party). These agents are for Mészáros, the 'personifications of capital'. Mészáros notes how political revolutions, from capitalism to postcapitalist states, such as happened in the aftermath of the First and Second World War, or back again, from postcapitalist to capitalist states, such as happened in the aftermath of the collapse of the Soviet Empire in 1989, essentially leave:

> the edifice of the capital system standing [...] This is because the three fundamental dimensions of the system – CAPITAL, LABOUR and the STATE – are *materially* constituted and linked to one another, and not simply on a legal/political basis.[7]

Mészáros thus provides us with a radical, and in terms of mainstream political discussions, deeply unfashionable, alternative perspective with which to approach the whole issue of the nature of the regimes in the Sovietised bloc, their relationship to Western capitalism and how we are to read, politically, the 'triumph' of the market after the fall of the Berlin Wall and the Soviet Empire. In Mészáros' narrative, the Eastern bloc was not a qualitatively different social system, but one part of the World system and the alter ego of Western capitalism. What Mészáros provides us with is an unfinished narrative, one which refuses the temptation to close the book on history as a struggle between what is and what could be. The importance of such an unfinished narrative can be gleaned by recalling the discussion in chapter two on the way the postmodern paradigm had effected a closure on how to read contemporary French cinema, a closure incompatible with the substantial political and cultural openings from the mid-1990s onwards.

Mészáros' account is also consistent with the sceptical stance I have taken on the question of the state throughout this book. Whatever the ideological colouration or affiliations of the political class who staff the state apparatus, and whatever scale at which the state is constructed (small nation-state, large nation-state with a history of imperial conquest or supranational, pan-European polity), Mészáros reminds us that the state is inescapably a product of the need to manage a conflictual and contradictory social formation. As Mulhern notes, the nation-state is 'superintendent of an economy,' seeking 'to optimise the internal and external conditions of capital accumulation.'[8] It is the 'external' conditions, that of the European and beyond that, global economic context which is becoming increasingly pertinent to life *within* the nation state. Thus the economic base of capital increasingly conflicts with the myth of the nation as autonomous and sovereign. The appeal to the supposed cultural unity of the nation – the central plank of nationalism – is one response to its diminished autonomy within global capital and the internal fractures, which this can produce. Mészáros also provides us with a resolutely *materialist* framework with which to approach CEE after the fall, in contrast to the cultural bias of much cultural theory, which, while it is certainly alive to geo-cultural dynamics that transcend the nation, has had the effect of repressing the vital question of *socio-economic* relations from its understanding of the world.

Prometheus

Prometheus (Tony Harrison, 1999) is an angry rebuke to the neo-liberal market order which has triumphed across Europe, including the former Soviet bloc. This British film is a kind of throw-back to the 1980s political filmmaking that came out of the largely Channel Four backed, workshop movement.[9] However, *Prometheus* lacks the kind of self-reflexive examination of film that characterised such workshop films as *So That You Can Live* (Cinema Action, 1981) *Territories* (Sankofa, 1984), *Handsworth Songs* (Black Audio, 1986), and *Time and Judgement* (Ceddo, 1988). The poetry of Tony Harrison's film resides entirely at the level of the spoken word leaving the image track, music and sound effects to verge on the plodding.

Yet if the film's audio-visual execution is disappointingly unimaginative, its subversive use of myth intriguingly recalls the rhetorical strategies of the Marxist philosopher Walter Benjamin. He used myth and nature to articulate the pervasive tug of historical forces in contrast to the dominant tendency, which routinely uses myth and nature to de-historicise social relationships. Thus in his discussion of the late-nineteenth-century Paris metro, Benjamin uses myth for the purposes of historical critique and to question the nature of *progress* (a key trope in Western celebrations of the fall of the Soviet bloc regimes). Here, underground, 'in the lightning-scored, whistle-resounding darkness', we find 'not one but a dozen blind raging bulls, into whose jaws not one Thebian virgin once a year but thousands of anaemic young dressmakers and drowsy clerks every morning must hurl themselves.'[10] The new sacrificial god is capital to which labour must daily spill its life blood.

Prometheus has a similar strategy in grafting the mythic figure of Prometheus and his conflict with Zeus, onto the contemporary political and economic landscape of Europe. Prometheus gave humankind fire by stealing it from the gods, a theft for which Zeus has never forgiven Prometheus nor humankind. For his troubles, Prometheus (celebrated by Aeschylus and P. B. Shelley) was chained to a rock and had his liver fed on by a vulture everyday until rescued by Hercules. The mythic conflict between humankind and the gods is here reconfigured as part of the class conflict on earth. By beginning with the closure of the last Yorkshire mining colliery, the film aligns the figure of Prometheus with socialism. Zeus's henchman, Hermes, has come down to Earth to gloat over the closure and scheme to further demote Prometheus in the eyes of humankind. The original theft of fire is seen by the gods as an overturning of the natural hierarchy. Hermes tells us that Prometheus' 'theft of fire first blurred the line/dividing mankind and divine/letting lower challenge higher/by giving mere men, Zeus's fire.' The film is structured as a journey from Britain to CEE. Mobilising once more the symbolic resonance of the statue, the film has Hermes cast a giant gold statue of Prometheus out of some real miners from the closed colliery, and on the back of a lorry he travels through Europe in a kind of victory parade for Zeus, trying to encourage humanity to turn against the captured, humiliated and apparently vanquished figure of human aspiration, rebellion and socialism. But the film's position is that the statue of Prometheus reaffirms to some extent what all those images from the early 1990s of the dismembering of the Lenin statues tried to crush. As Judith Williamson notes, 'in our muddled cultural jargon', the falling Lenin statues conflated 'a regime, a person, an event, a movement, an organisation, a small group of bureaucrats and a country.'[11] The alternative figure of Prometheus helps the film cut through this muddled, and it should be said, deeply ideological cultural jargon, and articulate the 'morality' of communism: that labour should have full access to (and, therefore, control over) the social wealth it generates.

This, of course, is not how Hermes/capital sees things. Hermes travels to Dresden. Infamously firebombed to destruction during the Second World War, Dresden was the scene for the technological implementation of fire against humanity by humanity. Here in this 'city of destructive flames/the best for blackening his good name/those 35,000 fire flayed/won't cheer Prometheus on parade.' Hermes articulates for us the eternal hostility and aggression of 'fuhrer Zeus' for human kind as we pass a former concentration camp. 'Every human rights abuse/had its proud origins in Zeus/ who deemed that man was only fit/for dumping in a mass pit.' Zeus endorses all destruction of humanity, including war and the holocaust. He is a kind of death drive who finds his latest incarnation in the triumph of market capitalism. Crossing the border into Czechoslovakia, the new economic order is clear. The border is a place of exploitation and division as queues of prostitutes service Western clients: 'A man drives from Dresden in his new free market BMW, finds a quiet place and parks/and gets sucked off for fifty marks.'

The Czech filmmaker Wiktor Grodecki has explored how the rise of the money dominated society has led to the growth of prostitution, male and female. In his documentary *Not Angels, But Angels* (1994) Grodecki enters the world of adolescent prostitution, where young boys sell their bodies to gain access to the consumer life after the fall of Communism. Grodecki continues the theme in his feature film *Mandragora* (1997). The film opens at night in a small Czech village. Panning around, the camera is drawn to a small, brightly lit window which stands out in the drab gloom. The shop window – a metonym of consumer capitalism – is a modest grotto of consumer goods (clothes, in this instance), lit with golden lights and displayed against a cardboard background of a glittering, exciting cityscape. Suddenly a brick smashes the window and a gang of boys raid the display. Before long, one of the boys, Marek, has arrived in Prague, hoping to escape his diminished social horizons (his father wants him to be a welder). Before long he has been drawn into a nightmare world of bars, pimps,whorehouses, violence and exploitation, lit in garish blues and reds, in which the only thing he has to sell is his sexual labour power to middle-class clients, many of them from the West.

This is the wreckage of CEE into which Hermes takes his statue of Prometheus. At a Polish smelting factory he is angered to find that the workers salute 'Golden Balls' rather than turn against him. But in Romania he finds enough dereliction and desperation among the significantly 'jobless carbon workers' to persuade them to smear the statue with dirt: 'How they converted/to bombard one they'd worshipped?/It's not hard. Hard Currency is all I need/some greenbacks and their human greed.' The triumphal procession is watched not only by the film's audience, but by an old British miner from a crumbling, disused cinema back in Yorkshire. (The town also appears to have a scrapyard for buses, a symbol of the death of public services). The film acknowledges the ambiguous benefits which the original theft of fire has culminated in. The wars and destruction of twentieth century Europe testify to this on a continental scale. But it is an ambiguity which is grounded right down in a very personal level, with the old man, an unrepentant life long smoker, puffing away on the fire stick which is both pleasurable and destructive. As he says: 'Fire that

brought man close to brink/ Were first to help him dream and think.' The cultural
expressions of that dreaming and thinking, of course, include poetry, which *Prometheus*
is most dedicated to. We have to look elsewhere, however, for a film which reflects on
the role of film itself in the contemporary European situation.

Ulysses' Gaze

Ulysses' Gaze is constructed around a journey by boat, car and train, through Greece,
Albania, Romania, Bulgaria and within the former Yugoslavia, from Belgrade in Serbia
to Sarajevo in Bosnia. It is a film which subordinates narrative drive to episodes on a
journey or rather a quest, in which the main character, known only as A. (Harvey
Keitel) searches for the first footage shot in the Balkans by the legendary Manakis
Brothers. Having lived in the US for thirty-five years, A. has returned to Greece, where
he was brought up, for a retrospective of his work (he is a filmmaker). The art film is in
some ways as conventional as any genre film. *Ulysses' Gaze* has the classic features
adumbrated by David Bordwell: it has a fractured narrative, loosely organised and
shifting back and forth in time; it has its drifting protagonist who has a goal but little
sense of clear motivation or direction;[12] and the film is steadfast in its refusal to engage
with popular culture, making it a good example of the European film which rejects any
taint of association or dialogue with Hollywood. Above all the film rejects classical
decoupage and privileges the long shot, which since Italian neo-realism has been a
favourite means of demarcating the art film from Hollywood and popular cinema
generally. But the meaning of the long shot in *Ulysses' Gaze*, although reaching back to
preexisting theories and practices, is mobilised within a quite specific set of meanings
and responses to the film's current historical moment.

Having rejected any strong narrative causal agency or tight narrative structure, it is
left to the image, unfolding through the long shot, to evoke in *Ulysses' Gaze*, a sense of
historical change and dramatic conflict. This is indeed a film of striking images, at the
centre of which is once again a Lenin statue as the symbol of the transformed
geopolitics of the 1990s. In his search for the lost film, A. hitches a ride down the
Danube on a boat which is transporting a huge statue of Lenin to a 'buyer' in Germany
(shades here of Zeus's 'victory' parade in *Prometheus*) now that even Lenin's image has
become a commodity. We have already seen the statue being loaded by crane onto the
boat, dwarfing the crew who perform the operation. Now, as A. travels down the
Danube, the Lenin statue is placed in a reclining position, strapped down like Gulliver
by the Lilliputians, his arm raised and gesturing into a future no longer assuredly red.
It is an awesome sequence (in long shot and close-up, and with an almost 360 degree
pan around the statue) which conjures up the huge historical transformations wrought
by the collapse of the Soviet bloc. It raises the question of what will fill the vacuum left
by the implosion of the Soviet Empire.

In another sequence historical time unfolds within the shot without any cuts or
dissolves or other cliche signifiers for the passing of time. A. has seamlessly slipped
back in time to his family home in Romania. It is the end of the Second World War and
the communist partisans are marching in the street. A. comes from a middle-class
family and rejoins them in the large house where the other members of the family are

celebrating the return of loved ones separated by the war. Through a dance sequence in which the family call out 'Happy New Year' periodically, the post-war years are rapidly charted. One year, a member of the family is led away by the communist authorities; another year, members of the family (including A.) emigrate to Greece; then another year the confiscation committee arrives and takes various objects, including the piano they are dancing to. The years pass *within* the single shot/scene.

The theoretical justification for the long shot was, of course, given its classic formulation by the French theorist Andre Bazin. Bazin celebrated the quality of experiencing duration (as well as spatial continuity) within the shot and keeping intrusive editing, whether Hollywood's classical decoupage, or the 1920s Soviet style montage of Eisenstein, Pudovkin or Vertov, to an absolute minimum. Bazin rooted this formal strategy in the supposed ontology of the camera, which he suggested had the ability to objectively record what was placed in front of it. Editing, of course, drew attention to the filmmakers' subjectivity and disrupted this apparent objectivity.[13]

Similarly, the camera of *Ulysses' Gaze* watches and observes, its own gaze aspiring to a Bazinian conception of 'pure cinema', an objectivity which is aligned with the proposed 'purity' of the gaze which A. imputes to the Manakis brothers' lost film footage. The meaning of this footage is ambiguous and is never pinned down by A. except that it seems to have some redemptive powers. In fact, we see the lost footage at the beginning of *Ulysses' Gaze*, thus confirming that A. will be successful in his quest. The content of the footage, women handweaving, is doubly significant. For against the massive historical transformations which the film records at the level of the image, the undeveloped film which A. seeks is like a still point in this fast changing world. But there is also an alignment between the artisanal craft skill of handweaving, and what was at that time, the primitive film medium itself. The artisanal mode of production (the Manakis brothers were themselves itinerant filmmakers) is one which art cinema – the tradition which *Ulysses' Gaze* unambiguously locates itself in – often sees itself as inheriting, along with its connotations of authenticity against the advanced industrial production (and inauthenticity) of commercial cinema. But if the Manakis brothers' footage inscribes the film with a historical and aesthetic identity, there is an aching fissure in the film around the politics and ethics of A.'s search.

What is the role of culture in a world of change, much of it horrible? This is the central question which troubles *Ulysses' Gaze*. The film comes to a climax in Sarajevo where A. has tracked down the lost footage. The Bosnian war is underway and the Bosnian Serbs are shelling the city. In a striking image we see a multicultural orchestra defiantly performing in no-man's-land during the cease fires. The camera cranes up from street level, over the barricades which have been set up, and there, half shrouded by the mist, is the orchestra. It is a hugely powerful moment amidst the rubble and destruction of Sarajevo by ethnic nationalism. It asks what culture can do in the fate of such barbarism and if the answer is not much in any immediate practical sense, the orchestra nevertheless holds out an alternative set of values to the ones of separatism, ethnic division and hatred. The image leaves the spectator wondering what the contribution of film is to humanity in this desperate time. It is, or so *this* film would have us believe, A.'s search for the undeveloped lost film of the Manakis brothers. And yet although the film is developed, this success is dwarfed by the scale of the horrors of war which impacts directly on A. when the woman he has fallen in love with and her father (a refugee from the Nazi holocaust, who has developed the film), are murdered.

But A.'s search, a personal obsession for a fragment of historical visual documentation, is hardly equivalent to the kind of intervention which the orchestra makes – one that is collective, public and politically meaningful to its audience. There seems to be a contradiction between the film and the acts of cultural intervention that occur *within* the film. *Ulysses' Gaze* opens with A.'s film causing a civil disturbance in a small Greek town, having apparently done the same all over Greece. Once again, change and conflict are primarily conveyed at the level of mise en scene. Those watching the film or (in the overspill) listening to it in the streets on outside speakers, standing under black umbrellas or sheltering from the rain, are ranged against the 'religious fanatics', according to one man, who march in protest around the town holding candles. But it is hard to see *this* film, *Ulysses' Gaze*, causing a similar disturbance. It is devoid of criticism, satire or any overt commentary, almost as if the film itself does not want to contribute to any more conflict by becoming *part of* the disputes and changes which it records. The ethics of the long shot in *Ulysses' Gaze* attempts to heal the wounds of history by adopting objective distance. Thus the film aspires to the purity and innocence which it confers, with incredible naivete, on the Manakis brothers' footage (even though we later fleetingly learn that they were involved in anarchist politics, thus calling into question the 'purity' of their gaze). Yet having followed A. for three hours of screen time, the spectator discovers that this is not enough in Sarajevo. The film is positioned in a classic art cinema ambiguity: caught between the purity conferred on the lost/undeveloped film and aspired to by the film we are watching via its own formal composition (the long shot), but haunted by doubt that this quest and by extension the film's own modus operandi, has the redeeming powers wished for.

A film so worried about being drawn into the conflicts which it records finds in the character of A. the perfect point of focalisation, an outsider to the region who is uninvolved and largely uncomprehending (as uncomprehending as Kessler in *Europa*) of the events around him (despite apparently being an old 'lefty' from 1968). This focalisation is as open to critique[14] as those Hollywood films which locate a Westerner in an exotic setting, using them as the perceptual grid with which to guide the (Western) spectator through the terrain and its inhabitants with a minimum of self-questioning or engagement with the social and cultural specificity of the people whose land is being visited.[15] Thus despite the film's *formal* differentiation from Hollywood, it has some familiar ideological gambits.

Three Colours White

Jonathan Romney described Angelopoulos's film as 'a monumental attempt to tackle questions about the state of central Europe and about the state of cinema in its centenary year.'[16] Certainly the film is monumental, self-consciously so, but it is rather less successful in tackling the state of central Europe than *Three Colours White*.

Popularly regarded as the slightest of Kieslowski's trilogy films, it is in many ways, the most politically acute of the three.

Allegory is a recurrent modus operandi for European cinema. Allegory works by converting a large story with a scale unrepresentable within the finite boundaries of a cultural artifact, into a smaller, more manageable story, with, for example, fewer protagonists. Thus the struggle between Prometheus and Zeus becomes the means for spanning the Second World War and post-war years in twentieth-century Europe right up to the contested triumph of neo-liberal capitalism. In *Three Colours White*, this last part of the European story, the fall of the Berlin Wall and the integration of Poland into market capitalism, is allegorised as a very personal story of love and betrayal between two people.

The white of the film's title refers to equality of which there is precious little. The story concerns Karol, a Polish man (Zbigniew Zamachowski) and Dominique (Julie Delphy), a French woman. The film begins with Karol nervously arriving at a French court (where ominously a pigeon shits on him from a great height) where his wife is demanding a divorce on the grounds that their marriage has not been consummated. As in Kiéslowski's *Three Colours Blue* (1993) the private is constantly being catapulted into the public realm and here, Karol suffers the humiliation of having to explain (through an interpreter) how, since he arrived in France, he has suffered from impotence. The court grants Dominique her divorce and Karol (despite his pleas of 'where is the equality?') rapidly becomes a non-person. Dominique unceremoniously dumps his suitcase on the pavement outside the court and drives off. We have already seen an image of suitcases on an airport conveyor belt in the credit sequence and this is subsequently intercut with Karol's arrival at the court. This cross cutting functions as a symbol of Karol's geographical displacement, his reduction to mere baggage and a narrative anticipation of later events. Karol's utter dependence on Dominique becomes evident when he finds out that his access to the shared bank account has been blocked. Out on the streets without money, he finds the keys to the hair salon which Dominique owns (Karol is himself a hairdresser) and lets himself in. When Dominique arrives in the morning they try once more to make love, but again Karol's problem manifests itself. Now his ex-wife throws him out, framing him for setting fire to the curtains in the window for good measure.

It should be clear that we are not just dealing with two people here, not even two countries, France and Poland, but the whole question of Western Europe's relationship to the prostrate 'communist' failures of CEE. Karol's impotence and Dominique's cold indifference to him is explicable only within this larger historical context. The contempt with which she holds him (her name is clearly a play on the word *dominant*), her lack of sympathy, derives precisely because he is dependent on her, precisely because she senses his weakness and he, in a self-fulfilling prophesy confirms the weakness which he feels most keenly once in France, by developing impotence. Does this not exactly sum up much of Western Europe's ambivalent relationship with its new CEE 'partners'? As with Dominique and Karol, East and West desire each other, but the relationship is not sustainable because there is no equality between them.

Humming a Polish song on the Paris metro, the destitute Karol meets fellow national, Mikolaj. A card player, Mikolaj is returning to Poland. Karol wishes to join him, but he has no passport and is on the run from the police, so Mikolaj smuggles him back in the only thing Karol has left: his suitcase. Thus his reduction to something less than human is complete. The Poland he returns to however has been transformed by the fall of Soviet communism. It is a country which has embraced capitalism, doing business, entrepreneurialism, both legal and illegal, is rife. Thus the suitcase Karol arrives in is promptly stolen by thieves. When they discover him in the suitcase they try to rob him, but discover to their disgust that although he has arrived from Paris, he is penniless, while his watch, even worse, is Russian! After taking a beating from the thieves, Karol staggers to his brother's place. The first thing he notices as he embraces his brother, who is also a hairdresser, is that the shop now has a bright neon sign, to which his brother replies, 'This is Europe now.'

In this context, where Poland seeks to integrate itself into the Western European economy and culture, Karol will reinvent himself in the image of that which is desired by both himself and Dominique: he will reinvent himself as a successful businessman. The entrepreneurial opportunities are certainly there. Karol gets a job guarding a local criminal involved in the black market economy. He starts to learn French by audio-tape and he saves his money. One day on a trip to the countryside with his boss and a client, he discovers that large European companies such as Hartwig and IKEA want to build warehouses on the land and it is his boss's job to get the small peasant farmers to sell up cheap. Karol sees his chance and persuades several farmers to sell up their plots to him, before selling them onto his enraged boss for ten times the amount. With the capital he then sets up an import/export business: his triumphant rise to the top of the new business elite in Warsaw is complete.

The film then is structured around a series of reversals, one of which concerns his relationship with Mikolaj. When they first meet in Paris, Mikolaj makes it clear that he is looking for someone to kill him. Although he has a wife and children who love him, and although he has no financial problems, he is weighed down by a deep, inexplicable and unarticulated sadness. The lack of fulfilment in Mikolaj's life of course mirrors the unfulfilled lives of both Dominique and Karol, but its mysterious nature pulls the film towards the metaphysical or a general humanist ideology which is certainly typical of the way the film and the Trilogy generally was received by Western critics. But this cuts against the film's more precise sense of historical tragedy embodied allegorically in the relationship between Karol and Dominique.

Having written his will and left everything to his ex-wife, Karol, with Mikolaj's help, fakes his own death. Dominique arrives for the funeral, genuinely upset. Back in her hotel room, Karol is waiting for her. Now when they make love, Karol is no longer impotent. The screen goes white as Dominique reaches orgasm, representing their sexual equality. But this equilibrium in their relationship is temporary and transitory. For Karol has a larger plan. The next morning the police arrive and arrest Dominique for plotting her ex-husband's death. Although he subsequently regrets this turn of events, it is too late. It is Dominique's turn for her fortunes to now suffer a reversal and she ends up in a Polish prison. Karol, now effectively a non-person as well since he is officially dead, watches her from the courtyard of the prison and she him. Together they have brought about their own downfall and an irrevocable separation. The film can be read as a parable about the impossibility of equality in the context of the business society. And there were periods in the 1990s, when the gulf between the West and East, seemed likewise to be presaging a similar ruin for all as war in the former Yugoslavia threatened for a time to draw in all of the Balkans, and beyond that Western Europe itself.

Cultural Theory and The Death of Yugoslavia

Nowhere has the integration of CEE into Western market capitalism proved more disastrous than in the former Yugoslavia which during the 1990s imploded into a series of brutal wars between competing nationalisms. The passage from a multi-cultural federation to nationalist rivalry and ethnic cleansing of places with mixed populations was also profoundly traumatic for Western Europeans. The implosion of Yugoslavia raises questions in terms of how such an event and its consequences gets represented, not only in films, but more broadly, in cultural and political theory as well. It is the politics of such representations, both East and West, which I want to draw out now by broadening the discussion beyond specific films. For one of the curious features of discussions and representations around the wars that broke out in the 1990s, is the way the socio-economic relations between East and West, disappeared. As we have seen, some films did acknowledge the detrimental impact that Western market capitalism made on Eastern Europe. But when it came to the question of war, the likely outcome of the socio-economic crisis that plagued much of CEE, particularly Yugoslavia and Russia, analysts and cultural workers failed to make the imaginative and political links that pointed to the surprisingly rapid failure of what US President George Bush (senior) declared to be the New World Order. With the outbreak of war, the nation-state, its people and its political elites are pushed to the fore in the *mise-en-scene* of the news media. The key agents and actors become the people on the ground and the political elites locked in negotiations and/or belligerent declarations. Although global capital does have its agents and institutions, the immediacy of the war dominated media coverage at the expense of an investigation into causes. Film, of course, may escape this tyranny of the now and give some historical perspective, but generally, films on the Balkan wars found that it was immeasurably easier to represent, to concretize the war in terms of the political leader, the burning village, men with guns, victims and so forth, than represent the field of transnational flows and pressures, which make up global capital today. These dynamics are, as Fredric Jameson would say, our culture's political unconscious.

The Cultural Turn

It is not only media representations for whom the figuring of capital's dynamics have become the greatest challenge, but cultural theory as well. The triumph of the 'cultural question' in the former Yugoslavia, albeit in the form of cultural rivalry and hatreds, has a peculiar analogy in the triumph of culture as the ultimate frame of reference within cultural theory in Western Europe. Within the humanities and even the social sciences, socio-economic relations have been displaced by the so called cultural or linguistic 'turn'. So central in fact has culture become for the advocates of the cultural turn, that it has reconstructed the very categories of thought that we use to generate knowledge and comprehension of the world. The cultural turn is profoundly *epistemological* in its implications. It is a position that argues that the *generation* of meanings and signifying practices, become the central object of enquiry for the social sciences and humanities.[17]

A representative figure advocating this new orientation towards the centrality of culture is Stuart Hall. He is well aware that the cultural turn is open to a materialist critique and denies that this emphasis on the cultural means that 'everything is 'culture' and that 'culture' is everything'.[18] He recognises that social practices cannot be simply absorbed into or reduced to culture. His argument instead is that 'every social practice has a cultural dimension. Not that there is nothing but discourse, but that every social practice *has a discursive character.*'[19] This is entirely unobjectionable in my view, but in practice, Hall represents a trend within cultural theory in which the 'discursive dimension' of social practices becomes *the* dominant focus of enquiry while the impact of social practices on culture, meaning and discourse, largely disappears. The sort of questions which *do not* get asked within this discursively orientated theory are well illustrated by Hall's own example of the relation between the material and cultural world.

> Similarly, the distribution of economic wealth and resources has real and tangible *material* effects for rich and poor people in society. However, the question of whether the present distribution of wealth is 'fair' or 'unjust' is a matter of meaning – that is to say, it depends on how 'justice' and 'fairness' are defined.[20]

But how definitions and meanings around 'fairness' and 'justice' get forged, the weight and profile they have in circulation, the degree of acceptance they achieve within and across social groups, none of this can be accounted for simply by focusing on the discursive dimension, on the rhetorical effectiveness and sensitivity to cultural struggle that the various combatants have. It is not in other words just a struggle over definitions and signifying practices, it is not just a matter of *debate*; it is also a question of the social practices and struggles in play at any one time and the material resources and strategies, which different collective agents can muster. It is precisely such real world, material dynamics that have been sidelined across the curriculum. The historian Bryan D. Palmer, for example, argues that while the concept of discourse,

> is clearly vital to any historical practice […] what I refuse, what I mark out as my own differentiation from the linguistic turn, is all that is lost in the tendency to reify language, objectifying it as unmediated discourse, placing it beyond social, economic and political relations, and in the process displacing essential structures and formations to the historical sidelines.[21]

Similarly, the social anthropologist Jonathan Friedman complains that even when categories other than cultural identity are invoked, they tend to become 'cultural constructs' rather than 'phenomena produced by social realities.'[22] This tendency to dissolve the material world into the cultural is powerfully operative across the majority of social and cultural theory today, with the effect that theory fails to identify, indeed it actively represses, the deep ontological delineaments of power in our time: namely the socio-economic relations of life within capitalism.

Cultural Theory and the Other

The concept of Otherness has been widely disseminated and deployed within cultural theory. It describes a complex psycho-cultural dynamic between unequal protagonists. A principle characteristic of this dynamic is that those who are subordinate -politically and economically – internalise and reproduce the stereotypical conceptions which powerful others have of them, thus turning the *dominated* into *Others*. Otherness becomes a condition in which the dominated are absolutely different to the dominant, a difference frequently guaranteed by locating the Other as being outside historical change. This Otherness is feared in some representations, desired in others, often fear and desire are uneasily combined simultaneously. The West has been the principle generator of others as Others and so the concept has been particularly useful in post-colonial studies. And certainly it has been fruitful in identifying at a very general level a set of common psycho-cultural patterns well beyond post-colonial studies. Such patterns are evident in my discussion of British cinema's subordination to and desire for the Hollywood/American market, which lock it into producing a dominant set of representations of Britishness which play well across the Atlantic.

Dina Iordanova has deployed the concept of Otherness to good effect in her discussion of the representation of the Balkans by filmmakers from both the East and the West. She argues that the Eurocentric construction of the Balkans as a place of tribal conflicts, backward, undeveloped and prone to irrational violence, has been internalised and reproduced by Balkan filmmakers.[23] This she argues is the price which Balkan intellectuals pay for admission into some sort of European recognition (box-office success, critical acclaim, film festival awards).

The danger, however, with the theory of Otherness is that it can quickly become as a-historical as the psycho-cultural dynamics which it analyses, being content merely to note once again, the dialectics of the master-slave relationship mapped out by the German philosopher Hegel. The other problem is that while it implies that there are realities which are not registered by the stereotypical fantasies that both master and slave, dominant and dominated, feed back to each other in a perpetual loop, the theory of Otherness is often loath to be explicit about what those realities are, since to do so, requires going *beyond* the question of culture and meaning, a 'beyond' which the cultural turn has comprehensively delegitimised. As we shall see, the theory of Otherness tends to suppress the class relations that are *internal* to a situation and the *external* class relations which are impinging on a situation from without: in short, the class relations of the nation and of Western imperialism respectively.[24]

The problems and limitations (as well as strengths) of the theory of Otherness are evident when applied in more directly political analysis. The Slovenian Lacanian philosopher Slavo Zizek brilliantly sums up the way Otherness works in relation to the Balkans. Writing in 1992, after the outbreak of war in Bosnia, Zizek argues that:

> What is effectively at stake in the present crisis of post-socialist states is the struggle for one's place: who will be admitted – integrated into the developed capitalist order – and who will remain excluded […] Every participant in the bloody disintegration tries to legitimise their place "inside" by presenting themselves as the last bastion of European civilisation […] [25]

As with Iordanaova's Balkan intellectuals seeking admission into the European club, so too with whole nations. Although the Balkans can be configured in the arts as a place of 'folkloric diversity', in relation to war, the Balkans has always been seen by Europe as 'the spark threatening to set all of Europe ablaze'. Thus, in terms of geopolitics, admission requires dissociating oneself from the Balkans. Where, asks Zizek, does the Balkans start? The answer depends on who you are. For many Austrians, their country's eastern borders mark the frontier between European civilisation and Balkan irrationality, which begins in neighbouring Slovenia. But for Slovenes, the Balkans begins in Croatia. For Croatia, of course, 'the crucial frontier is the one between them and the Serbs, between western Catholic civilisation and the eastern Orthodox collective spirit.' Serbs however see themselves as the last line of defence of Christian Europe against the fundamentalist danger embodied in Muslim Bosnians and Albanians.[26] And so it goes on. The Balkans is always to the east, to the south, even Austria, for some Germans, 'is tainted with Balkan corruption'. As Zizek notes elsewhere, the Balkans is 'an imaginary cartography' onto which many racist fantasies are projected.[27]

Yet while this theory of Othering nicely captures the attempts to construct firm cultural boundaries between insiders and outsiders, it has virtually nothing to say about the political, social and above all, economic dynamics at play. For while it is possible to be culturally excluded from 'civilised' Europe, one can also be – and this has been the experience of the Third World – politically, socially and above all, economically, *integrated* into the 'developed capitalist order'. But this disjunction and inter-relationship between economic *integration* and cultural *exclusion* is precisely what is missed by a theory which focuses primarily on Otherness, that is, on perceptions, cultural meanings and boundaries. This is crucial because, as Michael Barratt Brown notes, Western accounts of the Yugoslav tragedy, erased the collapse of the economy after the region became integrated into Western and global capitalism.[28] The catastrophic collapse of the Yugoslav economy is the absence, the silence around which a Western discourse of centuries-old ethnic (that is *cultural*) enmities can be built and blamed. Once we understand that the Balkans have been subordinated into Western imperialism *economically*, then it becomes impossible to view the Balkans tragedy as some dreadful return of historical hatreds. As one commentator noted, in the context of global inequality, economic crisis and the centralised, undemocratic exercise of power from the boardrooms of capital's global companies and institutions, *this is the future.*[29]

None of this however can surface within Zizek's account where the repression of the economic determinants of Western capitalism generates contradictions within his argument, at both the level of diagnosis and proposed solution. Zizek's analysis of *why* the region has descended into war boils down to 'one simple answer: the political crisis in Serbia.'[30] Thus the Serbs are to blame. It is a purely *internally* generated problem in his view ('the survival of the old power structure') – and this is the only conclusion which can be drawn once the region's integration into Western capitalism has been made invisible. It is indisputable that Serbian nationalism was a key factor in the slide towards war: but Serbian nationalism (whatever its own fantasies of national autonomy) has causes (as we shall see below) which lie well beyond Serbia and indeed beyond the Balkans. Thus Zizek himself reproduces the strategy of Otherising by projecting onto the Serbs the causes repressed in his own account. Zizek's Serbs are not quite the homogeneous ethnic cleansers found elsewhere in the Western media (he allows for the possibility of a Serbian democratic force extinguishing 'the flames of that nationalist passion') but it is not far off it either (he writes of a 'satisfied Serbia', a Serbia which the West has disreputably allowed 'to save its face').

Having made a diagnosis which reproduces the very strategies which he criticises (essentialising groups) Zizek's proposed cure is equally self-contradictory. Again there is no need to import any evidence or frames of reference beyond the article since an immanent critique reveals the signs of its mutilated logic well enough. For having condemned the West of racist fantasmatic investments in the Balkans, he then proposes (as did many on the left) that they can be trusted to intervene militarily to stop the killing. This unhappy notion that NATO will transcend the Orientalist preconceptions of Europe flows from the repression of the socio-economic dynamics at work and an over reliance on cultural explanations that sever the cultural from its materialist underpinnings.

Post-Yugoslavia: economy and culture

A report from the *Financial Times* in March 1990 gives details of a new IMF loan of 600 million dollars to help pay off Yugoslavia's existing debt of some twenty billion dollars:

> Mr Trbojevic [vice-governor of the Yugoslav central bank] said: 'IMF directors expressed support for Prime Minister Ante Markovic's anti-inflation programme, based on tight control over the money supply and public spending [...] ' The Government will face a serious challenge as their programme begins to bite and over 1m workers face losing their jobs when loss-making companies are forced to go bankrupt.[31]

This report is indicative of the interlocking relations between national elites (Trbojevic and Markovic) and international capital (the IMF directors). An economy orientated towards foreign debt repayments whatever the social costs is unlikely to be fertile soil for democratic politics. And so it proved. In the post-Second World War period, under Josip Tito's authoritarian 'communist' rule, Yugoslavia borrowed Western dollars. The loans were given with preferential conditions in order to keep Yugoslavia semi-autonomous from the Soviet bloc and act as a buffer between East and West in the Cold War. But once the Soviet Union and the Eastern bloc collapsed, financial institutions like the IMF and transnational companies could attach the usual tough stipulations to their loans and investments: slashing public spending, encouraging privatisation, deregulation, Western asset stripping and so on. It was the economic crisis of the late 1980s which laid the basis for the rise of Serbian nationalists such as Milosevic and Croatian nationalists such as Tudjman. Both Balkan and Western representations of the conflict had a vested interest in presenting the implosion of Yugoslavia into rival nation-states as the activation of ancient grievances which had been lying dormant within Tito's Yugoslav federation. For the West, it helped absolve market capitalism from any responsibility for the wars; for Balkan nationalists it was the logical outcome of reconstructing the region as a series of nation-states. For nations, as we have seen, mobilise history and tradition in the context of modern needs, to legitimise the social order.

While historical conflict in the Balkans is a fact, it is also true that there have been periods of peaceful living and cross-ethnic co-operation. While the Yugoslav federation was no paradise and there were certainly tensions within it, particularly as the economic crisis deepened in the 1970s, people were not cutting each others throats on a routine basis. John A. Vincent argues that within the Yugoslav federation patronage networks (fixing jobs, pensions, grants, promotions and so forth) ran implicitly along ethnic lines but within a federal framework (of cross-subsidy support, for example) which held any ethnic tensions in check. But as the federation disintegrated and resources became scarce, there was 'an inevitable progression, patronage politics became nationalist politics.'[32]

Thus (nationalist) culture becomes promoted as a sort of compensation for the disruption to the subject's ontological security in the world of material things. Culture and identity become the defining terms for sociality in the virulent nationalism-cum-racism that emerged in the former Yugoslavia during the 1990s. The material structures of organising life within the framework of the nation-state has usually required the rapid invention of traditions. State builders within Western Europe used the symbolism of national flags, national weights and measures, national currency, national days of celebration and remembrance, national monuments and valorised institutions with which to bind different and unequal classes together.[33] This was the strategy that the nationalist elites used as the Yugoslav federation splintered. Each nationalist side reworked history into a series of myths, which could legitimise or represent inter-ethnic conflict in a calculated repression of the economic determinants, which, of course, the nationalists as the new 'personifications of capital', were in no way going to address. For example, in their conflict with the Bosnian Moslems, Serbian nationalism reached back in time to the Battle of Kosovo in 1389 to legitimise their war. This battle saw Serbs die fighting the Moslem foe of the Turkish Ottoman Empire (in *Pretty Village, Pretty Flame* (Srdan Dragojevic, Serbia, 1996) Serb soldiers call their Moslem enemies 'Turks'). But, even if we accept the nationalist logic that a mediaeval battle should determine events today, what the nationalists conveniently discount is that Kosovar Moslems fought *alongside* Serbs in that battle.[34]

Culture, identity and history have certainly been important in the aftermath of Yugoslavia's bloody disintegration, a means of mobilising people around one set of identifications and accentuating their differences from other groups. Cultural and religious monuments have been deliberately targeted in the various wars that have broken out. Serb nationalists shelled mosques and destroyed the Bosnian national library in Sarajevo (portrayed in *Welcome To Sarajevo* (Michael Winterbottom, 1997)), while Croat nationalists destroyed the Moslem centre of Mostar. In this way 'the warring parties sought to eradicate the cultural treasures of the separate communities.'[35] But as Vincent notes, the rapid invention and heightened prioritisation of symbols of identity can only be explained by terms of reference that go beyond the cultural.[36] Much contemporary cultural theory however can only advocate cultural solutions (like the nationalism with which it has little else in common) based on hybridity, cultural mixing and, as Jonathan Friedman notes, 'a militant attitude against all forms of rootedness.'[37] But in the context of a crisis of the socio-economic proportions faced by the former Yugoslavia, 'there is little room for the hybrid identification discussed and pleaded for by cultural elites. Even hybridity tends to become ethnic, that is bounded and oppositional.'[38]

Films and Film Criticism on the Balkans

Surveying the critical reception of the films, which emerged in the 1990s portraying the war in Bosnia, it is evident that the critics were struck by a certain aesthetic quality, which the films seemed to strive for. Disrupting classical narrative logic, these films, to varying degrees and with diverse methods, attempted to inscribe the dislocation, the loss of normality and reason which war brings, into their very forms. The Serbian film *Pretty Village, Pretty Flame* shifts across time to produce a 'kaleidoscopic picture of lives shattered by war'.[39] Another critic describes the film's temporal switches as an 'anarchic' but 'brilliant piece of storytelling'.[40] *Underground* (Emir Kusturica, Fr/Ger/Hun/ 1995) has been described as 'Alice in Wonderland rewritten by Franz Kafka' and as a 'Hieronymus Bosch movie'.[41] Even *Welcome To Sarajevo* (Michael Winterbottom, GB 1997), a more classically structured film, opens with forty minutes of 'fevered free flowing stuff',[42] while another critic describes the film as 'shot and cut like a heart attack'.[43] *Beautiful People* (Jasmin Disdar,1999) meanwhile, set in London at the time of the Bosnian war, is described by Andrew Horton as a 'documentary fairy-tale', a term borrowed from the Belgrade director Srdjan Karanovic, meaning the fusing of recognisable realities with a 'sense of surprise'.[44] Similarly, Stella Bruzzi locates the film in 'a distinctly European tradition of surrealism, irreverence and anarchic political commentary.'[45] The film links London to the war both by the refugees that have arrived in the city and who impact in various ways on the lives of the British and, more surrealistically, in the fate of Griffen, one of the characters we follow in this ensemble, multiple plotted film. Griffen, late teens and middle class, is on the skids towards football hooliganism and drugs. On his way back from Rotterdam from the England-Holland 1994 World Cup qualifier (England lost 2–0), Griffen is separated from his junkie mates at the airport. Collapsing on a UN aid pallet, he wakes up to find himself being parachuted into Bosnia. This surreal relocation with Griffen still in his England football shirt running around a terrain littered with dead bodies, brilliantly establishes the war not just as temporally simultaneous, but geographically and spatially connected to European lives.

Picked up by a UN convoy, he eventually ends up helping out at a medical facility and after his return to Britain, is watched by his amazed parents when he appears on some BBC news coverage of the war. Griffin's experiences in turn provide the necessary shock, relativising his woes, putting them into their proper perspective and thus transforming his morality and behaviour.

There were two characteristic and unsatisfactory responses to the distinctive aesthetic of these war films. One response separated the films from the political issues at stake in the representation of war, enjoying them primarily for the particular and unusual aesthetic experience which they seemed to offer. Countering this separation of art and politics was another response which argued, rather crudely, that the 'aesthetics of chaos' (as Benjamin Halligan put it) made these films congruent with Serbian propaganda. For Halligan, the collapse of the classical narrative is 'achieved through meandering, chance-filled seemingly inconsequential, absurdist narratives' that he takes as evidence of these films submitting to irrationalism and stereotypes of Balkan 'wild men'.[46] Halligan has a point about 'wild men' but his uncritical attachment to classical narratives smacks of the socialist realism which was instituted as the aesthetic norm within the Eastern bloc and from which CEE film directors struggled to escape from the 1960s onwards.[47]

Emir Kusturica's *Underground* (1995) was cited as a particularly high profile example of Balkan stereotyping after it won the Palme d' Or at the Cannes film festival, ahead of *Land and Freedom* and *Ulysses' Gaze*. Indeed, Dina Iordanova suggests that *Underground* won the prize in part because its purely aesthetic qualities were so radically different from the classical narrative of Hollywood.[48] The award is, thus, a statement of European difference. However, at the festival the Paris-based Montenegran journalist Stanko Cerovic quizzed Kusturica and the French production company that had funded the film, CiBy 2000, on Kusturica's politics and the extent of the role of Belgrade TV in the making of the film.[49] Cerovic argued that Kusturica's characters romanticise the Serbs as people 'who fight and make love better than anyone else in the world' making their violence a natural, even alluring extension of their vitality.[50] Peter Krasztev argued along similar lines that the film recycled Serbian propaganda in presenting the Balkans as a cesspit of tribal and ancient enmities to discourage Western intervention.[51] Slavo Zizek gives a slightly different spin on the issue, suggesting that the film's portrayal of the Balkans is less a product of Serbian propaganda intentions than broader cultural dynamics:

> *Underground* is thus the ultimate ideological product of Western liberal multiculturalism: [...] it offer[s] to the Western liberal gaze [...] precisely what this gaze wants to see in the Balkan war – the spectacle of a timeless, incomprehensible, mythical cycle of passions, in contrast to decadent and anemic Western life.[52]

Certainly the film recycles a vision of Balkan identity that is essentialist and patriarchal, but the film as a whole cannot be reduced either to recycling Serbian propaganda or Western perceptions of the Balkans. Indeed, insofar as the film adopts certain Western aesthetic/philosophical premises associated with postmodernism, it undermines any and all notions of national identity and insofar as it is also recycling *embedded* Balkan cultural traditions – problematic as they may be – one cannot simply account for these self-perceptions as pandering to the Western perception of the Other.

There is, for example, an indigenous tradition within the former Yugoslavia of Native Art, a celebration by (invariably) middle-class artists of primitivism, peasant culture and native mysticism.[53] This *internal* class relation whereby the intelligentsia celebrate the rural, organic, artisanal stratas as part of an authentic tradition, is in fact quite typical of national cultures everywhere. However, in the case of Kusturica's film, it is not quite the *values* of the peasant or folk cultures that are celebrated, since they in fact do not seem to have any. As Dina Iordanova argues, the film's characters operate in a moral vacuum.[54] Rather the film celebrates the raw physicality of these people, their 'passion'. Here we are close to the 'wild, free, prowling men' of Nietzsche's imagination as much as Western stereotypes of the Balkans.[55] In the film, when the Germans begin their bombardment of Belgrade in 1941, both Marko and Blackey demonstrate their resistance by continuing to satisfy their physical desires. Marko is having sex with a prostitute, and when she leaves the quaking building in terror, he finishes off the job himself, while Blackey continues to calmly eat his food while the bombs rain all around him.

Another embedded cultural tradition evident in a number of films about the war is that of the *kumovi*. Misha Glenny explains this as the deep bonding between two men which is cemented by being a witness at one's wedding.

> In northern Greece, Albania, Macedonia and Montenegro, the bonding of *kumovi* until quite recently involved the literal mixing of two men's blood, the basis of a complex set of social relations which led to alliances among clans […] [56]

The unity of the nation and the rivalries which tear it apart are mapped onto the relationship between Blacky and his *kum*, Marko. This cultural tradition, with its roots in pre-capitalist social relations, provides a remarkably strong personal and local filter through which to view the national tragedy of war. Although not literally *kumovi*, a similar model of male bonding between childhood friends now turned deadly enemies, structures Milan (a Serb) and his Muslim friend Halil's relationship in *Pretty Village, Pretty Flame*. This male bonding, boisterous but riven with rivalries is in turn symptomatic of a strongly patriarchal culture. Thus *Cabaret Balkan* despite being set in a modern urban city -Belgrade – does not have the slightest tincture of feminist consciousness to it. The film is episodic, with multiple plot strands crisscrossing (often fairly briefly) with each other and compressed over the course of a single night. This tight temporal duration helps give the film its intense explosive quality, with every character on the verge of hysterical aggression (the film's Serbian title is *Powderkeg*). One episode again recycles the important image of male bonding and rivalry and it is not coincidental that one of the characters is played by Lazar Ristovski, here reprising a similar macho character and male-male relationship to his portrayal of Blacky in *Underground*. The scene is a boxing gym where two life long friends are training. One of the boxers confesses that twenty years ago, he slept with the other's girl. This in turn triggers a slew of confessions in which this life long friendship turns out to have been riven with jealousy and betrayal. The confessions are mixed in with their continued sparring. Finally, in the showers afterwards, one of them tells the other that his son is not in fact his son. This proves too much and whereas before anger turned to reconciliation, now, this final betrayal leads to a fatal retaliation. Once again, the fragmentation of Yugoslavia is filtered through the metaphor of male friendship discovering its riven realities.

Nietzche's celebration of a body unconstrained by conscience was the logical result of a moral relativism which regarded all law, ethics, morality and religion as mere fictions. 'What is a word?' asked Nietzsche. 'The expression of a nerve-stimulus in sounds.'[57] The philosophical tradition which Nietzsche presaged is of course postmodernism, which has also turned in fascination to the sheer physicality of the body as the last realm of authenticity. Thus the earthy primitivism of *Underground,* its celebration of physical exuberance, is in some ways entirely compatible with its cosmopolitan postmodern critique of national identity as no more than a media fabrication. This is really developed in part two of the film which takes place during the Cold War. Marko has risen to the top of the Communist Party; a close aide to Tito, he has reinvented himself as a cultured intellectual, a poet no less. But Marko has tricked Blacky and the rest of the community hiding in the large cellar of a house, into believing that the Second World War is still continuing. This deception is crucially aided by his use of various media. He has, for example, manufactured films of the war's progress; he has his own radio booth above ground which pipes in sounds of the conflict such as air-raid sirens. He has cameras installed so that he can monitor events in the cellar which has now transformed itself into a miniature society, with a Church, a barber shop, a bakery and an extensive arms manufacturing system that produces weapons which Marko sells on the black market. Marko's underground cellar society is of course an allegory for the Yugoslavia above ground. And above ground, the media are pressed into similar myth making duties. A film called *Spring on a White Horse* is being made to celebrate the life of Marko and the apparent death of Blackey who Marko has transformed into a heroic figure of the resistance. Thus the spectator watches the making of a film fictionalising events which have taken place in the fiction. When Blackey finally leaves the cellar to carry the fight directly to the fascists, he runs into the film crew making the film of his life/death and mistakes the actors in costume for real Nazis. Blackey's inability to distinguish between the real and the fictional, and Marko's inability to distinguish between truth and lies, of course mimes the postmodern collapse of the boundary between representation and the real.

The film's portrayal of national identity as something manipulated by political elites is the chief reason why the film can hardly be accused of peddling Serbian propaganda. If Marko is a critique of Titoism, then clearly, a character who dupes and exploits people by fabricating a war through his extensive control of the media, also bears more than a passing similarity with Serbian leader Slobodan Milosevic.

Commenting on the ground/underground divide and the fabrication of a 'national history from above', Dimitris Eleftheriotis argues that, 'although the film seems to criticise this manipulation it does not suggest an unproblematic true/false dichotomy.'[58] This is true, but only because *any* distinction between true and false has been abolished. The film thus presents all representations as essentially false. This homogenising gesture produces a very simplistic relationship between the media and the real and between the political elites and the people. Here the latter are portrayed simply as a *tabula rasa* on which elites inscribe their interpretations, a vision that is then in some contradiction with the film's vision of an irrepressibly energetic people.

But at least there is some acknowledging of the vertical relations that constitute the nation. This is true also of *Pretty Village, Pretty Flame*, another film that was received in some quarters, such as the Venice film festival, as Serbian propaganda. Yet the film satirises Milosevic's destructive nationalism through the figure of Slobo. This critique was recognised by a number of critics. Slobo is a cafe owner turned 'local war profiteer'[59] who whips up nationalist hatred against the Muslims 'providing a most convenient cover for his criminal dreams.'[60] Yet while the very local, small scale and petty nature of Slobo accurately places Milosevic's provincial dreams of a Greater Serbia in perspective, the absence of any external determinants on the rise of nationalism, keeps the film well within the mythology of the nation-state. Viewed from the West, the disappearance of external determinants on the Balkans, leads inexorably towards seeing external intervention in the spirit of European 'humanitarianism', as the answer to internal Balkan conflicts. *Time Out* describes *Welcome To Sarajevo* as taking 'an unapologetically polemical line against Europe's hands-off policy '[61] which, of course, implies that Europe has not already had more than a hand in generating the crisis. From inside the Balkans, the disappearance of external determinants means that nationalism may be regrettable, but its causes seem largely internally generated, often verging on the mythical. Thus *Pretty Village, Pretty Flame* shows Milan and Halil as young boys standing outside an abandoned tunnel fearing to go in because they believe that if they awaken the sleeping ogre inside, he will burn their village. However, the film does portray the Serb fighters trapped in the tunnel during the war as a disparate group, made up of people who had various motivations and beliefs in joining the war. Through these diverse characters, the film demonstrates that there was no single homogeneous dedication towards Serbian nationalism, Milosevic style. At the same time, there is also no question of any character transcending nationalism. The film ridicules the anti-war protesters outside the hospital where Milan is recovering, showing one of their number inexplicably kicking away the crutches of a wounded soldier. (*Cabaret Balkan* meanwhile makes no acknowledgement that there might be political channels into which people could direct their anger and frustrations. There is no sign in the film of the political dissent which was to lead to mass protests against Milosevic, for example, in 1996, as had happened already in 1991). All the characters in *Pretty Village, Pretty Flame*, including Milan and Halil, fall in line behind the nationalist war even though they are often sceptical of its rationale and logic. The temporal shifts, which the film negotiates, allows it to juxtapose scenes from before the war, during the war and during the hospital scenes, which constitute the film's present tense, generating irony, parallels and poignancy in the ruptured lives of the characters. Outside the Balkans, the film could be read as a formally unusual but still strongly generic war film, with the customary 'war is hell' theme. Yet within a Balkans context, the film's position, as with *Underground* and *Cabaret Balkan*, may be succinctly defined as *disillusioned nationalism.* Because these films are disillusioned, they cannot be seen as propagandising on behalf of Milosevic's regime. But because they are operating within the parameters of nationalism, there are limits to their critique of national life; they articulate national myths (some of which are congruent with Western stereotypes, just as British cinema articulates national myths for the American market) and they fail to adequately situate the nation within the international determinants which effect it. For these reasons, the Serbian films cannot be considered examples of the anti-national national films discussed in chapter two. At the same time, their inability to break out of a nationalist mindset, is hardly very unusual.

The nation-state as an untranscendable horizon is even evident in *Underground* despite having proffered national identity as nothing more than a media fabrication manipulated by elites (which is one kind of simplification). For the film concludes with a wishful utopian image of all the characters, most of whom have died, reuniting by the Danube, eating and drinking once more and accompanied by the ubiquitous brass brand that follows Marko and Blacky around throughout most of the film. In a final image that was much debated by the critics, the land they are standing on then splits off and floats down the Danube. On the one hand, this image of the land breaking away, is the ur-image of the formation of national identity through territorial differentiation, but on the other hand, this splitting strikes a discordant note in the utopian image, reintroducing, as Eleftheriotis notes, 'the harsh reality of the painful and horrific dismemberment of the country.'[62]

Beautiful People is significantly different to the other films discussed here that have been made by Balkan filmmakers, insofar as it opts not for disillusioned nationalism, but an optimistic humanist internationalism. Structurally and thematically, the film has similarities with the Belgrade set *Cabaret Balkan* insofar as it weaves multiple story lines of London protagonists, usually loosely interconnected but thematically unified around the idea that everyday life is a kind of low-level war, full of skirmishes, arguments, conflicts and tensions which, in a different context, could in fact germinate into the kind of horrors where friends and neighbours become deadly enemies, or where frustrations are displaced onto convenient scapegoats. However, where *Cabaret Balkan* sets its timeframe over the course of one night, a compression which facilitates its bleak vision of each story line leading to explosive violence, *Beautiful People* stretches the storylines out over a sufficient time period to give each strand the chance to come to some sort of happy conclusion. With its sensitivity to London as multicultural, its storylines involving various Bosnian refugees, its surreal relocation to the Bosnian battle front, the film evinces a transcendence of the nation-state unimaginable for the other Balkan films discussed. Yet just as the utopian tones of *Underground's* conclusion are strikingly at odds with everything that goes before, so in *Beautiful People*, the relentlessly upbeat optimism jars with the more realistic assessment of the frustrations, conflicts and grievances that beset the characters. While many critics seemed to applaud this optimism, the sight of Griffin's violent, racist, drug-taking friends going dewy-eyed over the Bosnian kid Griffen brings home, proved all too much for this writer.

However, *Beautiful People* is a suitable film with which to end this chapter, because it brings us back to Britain. The relationship between ethnicity and national identity and the disruption of a homogeneous fit between a single ethnicity and the nation by the transnational forces of migration and media have been key themes and formal concerns for Asian and Black British cinema. The films generated out of a diasporic experience necessarily transcend the hermetic nationalism of the Serbian films discussed here. I have suggested that nationalism invokes the myth of *autonomy* from external determinants while promoting a mythical *internal* unity, which, in turn, requires conjuring up an ancient historical lineage. Contemporary cultural theory and the Black and Asian British films that have been influenced by it, radically break with such nationalist myths. But as I have indicated in this chapter, the cultural turn, while cosmopolitan and internationalist, shares a secret affinity with nationalism: namely its inability to be properly responsive to the divisions of material life.

References

1　B. Balanya, et.al., *Europe Inc. Regional and Global Restructuring and the Rise of Corporate Power*, Pluto Press, London, 2000, p. 56.

2　F. Fukuyama, the *Guardian*, Sep 7, 1990, p. 23.

3　J. Thornhill, *Financial Times*, December 31, 1994, p. 2.

4　J. Lloyd, *Financial Times*, December 24, 1994, p. 6.

5　G. Elliott, 'Velocities of Change: Perry Anderson's Sense of an Ending', *historical materialism*, no. 2, summer 1998.

6　I. Mészáros, *Beyond Capital*, Merlin Press, London, 1995, p. 143.

7　I. Mészáros, *Beyond Capital*, p. 463.

8　F. Mulhern, 'A European home?', *Mapping the futures, local cultures, global change* (eds) J. Bird, et.al., Routledge, London, 1993, p. 201.

9　*Landmarks, Independent film and video from the British workshop movement*, British Council, London, 1989.

10　W. Benjamin, *the Arcades Project*, (translated by H.Eiland and K.McLaughlin) Harvard University Press, Massachusetts, 1999, p. 84.

11　J. Williamson, 'Communism: Should the mighty ideas be falling with the statues?', *Mapping the futures*, p. 268.

12　D. Bordwell, 'The art cinema as a mode of film practice', *Film Criticism*, vol. 4, no. 1, 1979, pp. 57–8.

13　A. Bazin, *What is Cinema? Vol 1*, University of California Press, Berkeley, 1967, pp. 9–16.

14　D. Iordanova, 'Balkan Film Representations since 1989: the quest for admissibility', *Historical Journal of Film, Radio and Television*, vol. 18, no. 2, 1998, pp. 267–8.

15　E. Shohat and R. Stam, *Unthinking Eurocentrism: multiculturalism and the media*, Routledge, London, 1994, pp. 205–8.

16　J. Romney, the *Guardian* 2, May 25, p. 2.

17　S. Hall, 'The Centrality of Culture', *Media and Cultural Regulation*, (ed.) K. Thompson, Sage/Open University Press, Milton Keynes and London, 1997, pp. 220–1.

18　S. Hall, 'The Centrality of Culture', *Media and Cultural Regulation*, p. 225.

19　S. Hall, 'The Centrality of Culture', *Media and Cultural Regulation*, p. 226.

20　S. Hall, 'The Centrality of Culture', *Media and Cultural Regulation*, p. 226.

21　B. D. Palmer, *Descent into Discourse, The Reification of Language and the Writing of Social History*, Temple University Press, Philadelphia, 1990, p. 5.

22 J. Friedman, 'Global crises, The Struggle For Cultural Identity and Intellectual Porkbarelling: Cosmopolitans versus Locals, Ethnics and Nationals in an Era of De-Hegemonisation', *Debating Cultural Hybridity* (eds) P.Werbner and T. Modood, Zed Books, London, 1997, p. 87.

23 D. Iordanova, 'Balkan Film Representations since 1989: the quest for admissibility', *Historical Journal of Film, Radio and Television*, vol. 18, no. 2, 1998, pp. 263–80.

24 The concept of the Other can articulate questions of class when it is used in relation to the strategies which a bourgeois class adopts to deal with various threats to its values and priorities. See R. Wood, *Hollywood, from Vietnam to Reagan*, Columbia University Press, Oxford, 1986, pp. 73–5.

25 S. Zizek, the *Guardian*, August 28th, 1992, p. 21.

26 S. Zizek, the *Guardian*, August 28th, 1992, p. 21.

27 S. Zizek, *London Review Of Books*, March 18, 1999, p. 3.

28 M. B. Brown, *The Yugoslav Tragedy, Lessons For Socialists*, Spokesman, Nottingham, 1996, p. 22.

29 L. German (ed.), *The Balkans, nationalism & imperialism*, Bookmarks, London, 1999, p. 36.

30 S. Zizek, the *Guardian*, August 28th, 1992, p. 21.

31 L. Silber, *Financial Times*, Mar 20, 1990, p. 4.

32 J. A. Vincent, 'Symbols of Nationalism in Bosnia and Hercegovina', *National Identity* (ed.) K.Cameron, Intellect Books, Exeter, 1999, p. 60.

33 M. B. Brown, *The Yugoslav Tragedy*, p. 3

34 L. German (ed), *The Balkans, nationalism & imperialism*, p. 46.

35 M. B. Brown, *The Yugoslav Tragedy*, pp. 74–5.

36 J. A. Vincent, 'Symbols of Nationalism', *National Identity*, pp. 61–2.

37 J. Friedman, 'Global crises', *Debating Cultural Hybridity*, p. 76.

38 J. Friedman, 'Global crises', *Debating Cultural Hybridity*, p. 84.

39 J. Wrathall, *Sight and Sound*, vol. 8., no. 1, January 1998, p. 51.

40 N. Briggs, *Film Review*, February 1998, p. 25.

41 D. Malcolm, the *Guardian* 2, June 29, 1995, p. 10.

42 X. Brooks, *Sight and Sound*, vol. 7, no. 11, Nov 1997, p. 57.

43 M. Atkinson, *Film Comment*, vol. 34, no. 1, Jan/Feb 1998, p. 45.

44 A. Horton, *Cineaste*, vol. 25, no. 3, June 2000, p. 46.

45 S. Bruzzi, *Sight and Sound*, vol. 9, no. 9, Sep 1999, p. 42.

46 B. Halligan, 'An Aesthetics of Chaos', *The Celluloid Tinderbox, Yugoslav Screen reflections of a turbulent decade*, (ed.) A.J.Horton, Central Europe Review, 2000, online at: WWW.ce-review.mirhouse.com/ p. 65.

47 D. J. Goulding, 'East Central European Cinema' ,*The Oxford Guide to Film Studies* (eds) J. Hill and P. Gibson, Oxford University Press, Oxford, 1998, pp. 471–7.

48 D. Iordanova, 'Kusturica's *Underground* (1995): historical allegory or propaganda?', *Historical Journal of Film, Radio and Television*, vol. 19, no. 1, March 1999, p. 71.

49 R. Yates, the *Guardian* 2, Mar 7, 1996, p. 8

50 D. Iordanova, 'Kusturica's *Underground*', *Historical Journal*, p. 74.

51 P. Krasztev, 'Who Will Take The Blame', *The Celluloid Tinderbox*, p. 23.

52 Quoted in D. Iordanova, 'Kusturica's *Underground* ', *Historical Journal*, p. 80.

53 B. Halligan, 'An Aesthetic of Chaos' *The Celluloid Tinderbox*, pp. 68–9.

54 D. Iordanova, 'Kusturica's *Underground*', *Historical Journal*, p. 74.

55 Quoted in T. Eagleton, *The Ideology of the Aesthetic*, Blackwell, Oxford, 1990, p. 237.

56 M. Glenny, *Sight and Sound*, vol. 7, no. 12, December 1997, p. 12.

57 F. Nietzsche, 'On Truth and Lying in an Extra-Moral Sense', *Literary Theory: An Anthology* (eds) J. Rivkin and M.Ryan, Blackwell Publishers, Oxford, 1999, p. 358.

58 D. Eleftheriotis, 'Cultural difference and exchange: a future for European film', *Screen*, vol. 41, no.1, Spring 2000, p. 98.

59 J. Wrathall, *Sight and Sound*, vol. 8., no. 1, January 1998, p. 51.

60 M. Glenny, *Sight and Sound*, p. 11.

61 *Time Out*, Penguin Books, 1998, p. 950.

62 D. Eleftheriotis, 'Cultural difference and exchange', *Screen*, p. 99.

5 Diasporan Travels: British Asian Cinema

This chapter situates British Asian cinema in the context of the debates around Black film generally which emerged in the 1980s. I will explore how new theorisations of hybridity and diaspora influenced cultural debates and cinematic practices. These theorisations were strongly influenced by the cultural turn discussed in the previous chapter. In discussing films such as *Wild West* (David Attwood, 1992) and *Bhaji on the Beach* (Gurinder Chadha, 1993) I will explore the extent to which they test out in dramatic form, some of the cultural principles (of contingency and mixing) which contemporary theory has advocated as being central to contemporary life. However, the films are more interesting than being simple reflections of the theory: the films are themselves composite and hybrid in their philosophical underpinnings and implications, some of which point to contradictions and limits within a philosophy in which culture becomes the ultimate horizon of all thinking.

The Rise and Rehabilitation of Hybridity

The concept of hybridity has in recent years undergone a remarkable rehabilitation. For much of the nineteenth and twentieth centuries, within racialised theories of identity, hybridity was a perjorative term. Often the concept went under another name: half-breed, half-caste, sambo, mulatto, mestizo, etc., but it essentially meant the same thing: the mixing of 'races' was seen as a sign of 'contamination, failure, or regression.'[1] Traditional concepts of the nation having one rightful and dominant culture have been crucial in rationalising cultural purity and separation, at least in the West. Indeed the term miscegenation, another perjorative word for hybridity, literally means mixed nation.

From the 1980s in particular, however, the notion of mixing, of hybridity, has undergone a substantial re-evaluation. Partly the ground for this has been laid by a shift away from an obsession with a biological definition of 'races' and blood, towards the question of culture. This has opened up the prospect of defining cultural mixing, dialogue, fusions and combinations, as a source of creativity, something to be welcomed and embraced rather than feared. Hybridity thus comes to be articulated with a politics which is opposed to 'borders, boundaries and 'pure' identities.'[2] Such a position is a very long way, theoretically and politically, from the views espoused by the nationalist historian Anthony Smith. As we saw in chapter three, Smith values cultural continuity and insists that within an 'authentic' nation, 'eclectism operates within strict cultural constraints.'[3] Yet it is all too easy to coopt such a position to the kind of nationalist racism which has flourished in the Balkans during the 1990s. Against Smith's nationalism, the liberal cultural internationalism of hybridity theorists is infinitely preferable. Yet the repression of class – not least the class location of hybridity theorists themselves – and the obdurate structural materiality of the social world, raises questions over hybridity theory and the cultural practices influenced by it.

Theorising Diaspora

The changing evaluation of hybridity has been causally effected by the increased opportunities for cultural mixing brought about by post-colonial migration. Diasporas (derived from the term 'dispersion')[4] 'emerge out of migrations of collectivities' usually associated with social, political and/or economic upheaval.[5] These collectivities are, as Avtah Brah notes, internally differentiated in terms of class, gender and generation – all important differentials and potential divisions within the films I will be discussing. The concept of diaspora can be defined in radically different ways, either in relation to an 'ontological essentialist view' of identity (in which cultural mixing is negatively valued) or a libertarian, pluralistic, hybrid identity.[6] Black and Asian cultural producers have been well aware of the tensions between these competing definitions of diaspora[7] and the contesting interpretations of identity which they offer. The contesting interpretations are often associated with a generational split, with the older generation most likely to strongly articulate the ontological essentialist view and the younger generation most likely to be the articulators of the hybrid view.

East Is East (Damien O' Donnell,1999), for example, opens with a scene which dramatises the cultural contradictions within the Khan family. Ella, who is white, with her six sons and one daughter, are joining in a Catholic street procession. Suddenly, warned that her Pakistani husband George has come home early from the mosque and is standing on the next street corner, Ella with family in tow, peel off from the procession, and carrying a large crucifix and other Catholic banners, run round the backstreets circumventing George and joining the procession again further down the road. The film is full of such attempts on the part of George Khan's family, but mostly his sons and daughter, to subvert his attempts to impose a fairly traditional Muslim culture and religion on them. Yet Khan himself is a mass of cultural contradictions with his fish and chip shop and white wife whom he playfully teases when he threatens to bring wife number one over from Pakistan. Despite this, Khan stubbornly tries to impose his will (sending his children to Urdu lessons, for example), most disasterously when he attempts to arrange various marriages for his sons.

This split between generations is reversed in *My Son The Fanatic* (Udayan Prasad, 1997) written by Hanif Kureishi. Here, Om Puri, who plays George Khan in *East Is East*, is Parver, a taxi cab driver who is tolerant towards local prostitutes and determined not to interfere with his son's freedoms. The film opens with his son Farid getting engaged to Madeline, a white women from college whose father is the town's Chief Inspector of police. Madeline's parents are evidently less thrilled by this turn of events than Parver, but this free arrangement breaks down when Farid, fairly inexplicably, turns towards Islam. As with *East is East*, the film shows how characters create their own cultural spaces within the domestic location riven with cultural tensions. Thus, Khan's children eat pork while their father is away (cue desperate attempts to hide the evidence when he arrives home unexpectedly). In *My Son The Fanatic*, Parver listens to jazz in the cellar while upstairs his son listens to tapes for religious instruction. Farid insists that 'our cultures cannot be mixed' when explaining to his father why he broke off his engagement with Madeline, while his father is moving in the opposite direction as he is increasingly drawn to a white prostitute.

In the essentialist position represented by Farid, the diaspora is viewed as a kind of Fall, a weakening of identity, a negative condition, a decline from an original unified home or community and subsequent inability to fit in and be accepted elsewhere. It is an in-between condition that is viewed as unproductively troubling and peculiar to the historical experience of a violent uprooting. The coercive conditions of that uprooting for Black Africa, for example, is then projected throughout all subsequent history so that the Black subject cannot be seen to make anything productive out of circumstances that were not of their choosing. Politically, this position is associated with Black separatism and returns to Africa and are somewhat rare within Western academic discourses. Cinematic examples of this position are also rare but *Welcome II The Terrordome* (Ngozi Onwurah, 1993, UK) would be one example. The film was treated to an excoriating critique by Paul Gilroy, an advocate of hybridity theory.[8]

In the other conceptualisation, whatever the original coercive circumstances for the dispersion, the identities, which are subsequently forged, are seen more positively as a creative adaption and syncretism.[9] In contradistinction to the desire for identity as fixed and timeless essence, this version of diaspora becomes emblematic of the claim 'that identity is always plural, and in process'.[10] Diaspora in this conceptualisation is quintessentially typical of the epoch. 'The chronicles of diasporas' argues Iain Chambers, '-those of the black Atlantic, of metropolitan Jewry, or mass rural displacement – constitute the groundswell of modernity.'[11] As Gillespie notes, the conceptualisation of diaspora will have very different uses and politics depending on whether it tracks cultural *routes* or searches for cultural *roots*.[12]

The liberal emphasis on identity as an ongoing shifting process has made a calculated attempt to rigorously distinguish itself from the ontological essentialist position. However, in doing so, it risks abolishing any sense of continuity and any sense of the past as a coherent, knowable resource. Here the conceptualisation of diaspora merges with the postmodernist insistence that the past is recoverable only as eclectic style and image, thus displacing real history with nostalgia.[13] This risks abandoning the question of the past to the conservative appropriation of it evidenced in the ontological position. (Most of the British Asian films, for example, tend to weigh their cultural preferences towards Britishness, while traditional cultures are seen as largely oppressive and intolerant). *Welcome II The Terrordome*, for example, begins with newly arrived C17th Black slaves walking into the sea rather than live in the land of death which the voice-over tells us, belongs to the whites. The film sees this spiritual return to Africa as the model for the Black inhabitants of the futuristic Babylon that the film then projects forward to.

In another manifestation diaspora explodes social space as well, its emphasis on difference making the bringing together of various cultural identities a highly contingent and transient affair.[14] Again, this risks abandoning the field to the kind of Black vs white simplicities which *Welcome II The Terrordome* is tapping into. The difficulty though is in formulating any basis for solidarity from within such a perspective. Here is Reece Auguiste from Black Audio Collective, responding to a question from Jim Pines who has asked whether the concept of diaspora can bring people from various cultural backgrounds together:

Not necessarily bring them together but to touch some of their sensibilities. The Hispanic experience is very different from the experiences of those who occupy the English-speaking Caribbean, because those experiences are structured by different engagements with Europe and different engagements within the geographical space that we call the diaspora. So there exists the possibility to tap into that diversity of sensibilities which might have, on a metaphysical level, a unitary dimension, but in its materiality that unitary field has no existence because of its diversity.[15]

Auguiste's theoretically informed reply is worlds away from the complacent empiricism which dominates mainstream (mostly white) cultural producers. But it is riven with problems for a politics of cross-cultural solidarity. Note the rapid retreat from any prospect of bringing people together; the emphasis on different experiences and a 'diversity of sensibilities' which refuses to entertain the possibility of any 'unitary dimension' to these admittedly 'different engagements'. Yet there is nothing 'metaphysical' about colonialism and despite its complex and diverse histories, there is a certain 'unity' in the capitalist logic through which it operated.

The South Asian diaspora was the direct result of the history of colonialism and imperialism. Labour shortages in the UK and labour surplus' in the ex-colonies led to the British government and employers appealing to Asians as well as Africans and Afro-Caribbeans to 'come home'.[16] Some Asians were already the product of a recent diaspora, having been relocated to East Africa as indentured labour.[17] But wherever they came from, migrants from the ex-colonies suffered similar conditions of discrimination in terms of poor housing and employment.[18] Thus the term 'Black' functioned as a political category to unify people of colour in the face of white racism.

For the white British, the crossing of Black people into the national space raised questions concerning national identity, it opened up what Brah calls a diasporic space that was inhabited not only by migrants and their descendants, 'but equally by those who are constructed and represented as indigenous.'[19] The indigenous are forced to 'reply' to their own existence in terms of 'movement and metamorphis'[20] so that some of the certainties about the timeless continuity of national identity are challenged and thrown open. The more queries one raises about 'origins', the more one finds that almost everyone is the product of some kind of distant or not so distant travel or displacement.

It is not only the movement of people, but the media itself which is involved in constructing numerous diasporic spaces. Globalisation has simultaneously increased both the flow of migrants and the 'images, narratives and information which cut across and challenge established national and cultural boundaries and identities.'[21] As we shall see, in both *Wild West* and *Bhaji On The Beach*, the deterritorialization of culture, as it is constructed in symbolic goods (videos, films, music) and exported across national boundaries, is inscribed into the narratives as important sites of identity negotiation. However, what is lacking in the British Asian films of the 1990s, is a conjoining of the principles of hybridity, transnational and intercultural mixing, with a more materialist, politicised sensibility. It is not impossible for cultural practices to articulate together hybridity and materialism. A flawed version of this articulation is found in *La Haine*, for example, while within Asian cultural practices, John Hutnyk notes how the band

Asian Dub Foundation have managed to articulate just such a militant hybridity.[22] However, hybridity theory, as Hutnyk notes, seems:

> to do very well at avoiding any discussion of Marxism, or indeed can be considered an elaborate displacement, a way of keeping Marx out of the academy at a time when a materialist method has never been more relevant.[23]

Take, for example, Arjun Appadurai's celebrated and in many ways, suggestive account of globalisation and its cultural implications.[24] He attempts to map the vast flows and 'disjunctures' between different forces which criss-cross the globe and impact upon cultural identities. Appadurai identifies five such flows: ethnoscapes (the vast movement of people, including tourists, immigrants, exiles and refugees); mediascapes ('image-centred, narrative-based accounts of strips of reality');[25] technoscapes (ever fluid global configurations of technology); finanscapes (the rapid shifts and flows of global capital); and ideoscapes (ideas and beliefs directly connected to political rights, struggles and power).

Appadurai's definition of the suffix 'scapes' is instructive. It is used partly to indicate the constantly shifting, expanding, contracting, amorphous nature of these flows. But it also signifies that theory can have little objective purchase on them. The terrain looks different depending on where you are positioned, that is whether your social being constitutes you as a multinational, the political elite, a sub-national grouping, etc., all the way down to the individual who is 'the last locus of this perspectival set of landscapes'.[26] This profoundly subjectivising approach interlocks with Appadurai's stress on the unpredictable directions which these flows have and the equally unpredictable consequences of their numerous intersections and divergences. Appadurai argues that the central issue he is attempting to theorise 'is the tension between cultural homogenisation and cultural heterogenization.'[27] But his model is far more attuned to heterogenization, that is to the differences generated by unpredictable disjunctive flows, than homogenisation. Appadurai's model allows us to conjure up a vision of the world in perpetual flux and turbulence, but any sense of the world having systemic qualities has been exploded. Where are the patterns, the cycles, the predictable processes, the continuities, the consolidations of position and power? Appadurai has taken what might be called the mode of production (the people, the technology, the capital) and the superstructure (the ideoscapes and mediascapes) and resolved the problems which the Marxist model raises about determinations of one social force on another by replacing it with an extreme multi-causal model in which any clear pattern to determination recedes in favour of a vortex of excess and unpredictability. In Appadurai's model, social being (the material determinants on life) is collapsed into culture; the solid and obdurate qualities of material reality are aestheticised, transformed into something as unpredictable as a surrealist game of association.

Black Film and Criticism

This difficulty in thinking through the relationship between social being and cultural identity, and the passage from a concern with the former to an emphasis on the latter, can also be traced in the emergence of Black British filmmaking and its critical reception. It is a tension which emerges in debates around aesthetics and the pros and cons of some kind of *realist* approach on the one hand (i.e. one which foregrounds the social determinations on peoples lives) or approaches which foreground subjectivity and culture (variously characterised as the unleashing of 'fantasy' or the deployment of avant-garde strategies). It should be noted how these debates concerning Black aesthetics have a distinctly British genealogy, mobilising the triadic terms of the 1930s and 1940s, where Griersonian/documentary realism, European Modernism and popular fantasy (e.g. Gainsborough melodramas) set the key terms for so much British filmmaking.

For Black British filmmaking, the more 'transparent' realist cinematic languages of the late 1970s and early 1980s focused on the material social determinations of their subjects' lives: *Pressure* (Horace Ove, 1975) *Blacks Britannica* (1978) *Burning An Illusion* (Menelik Shabazz, 1981). According to Kobena Mercer, these films were less adept at addressing 'the contradictory *subjective* experience of Black British identity ' or interrogating some of the ideological assumptions (of gender as well as 'race') encoded into the narrative realist forms they used.[28] As a result, Mercer and other critics welcomed and theorised the emergence during the 1980s of the avant-garde strategies deployed in such films as *Passion of Remembrance* (Maureen Blackwood/Isaac Julien, 1986) and *Handsworth Songs* (Black-Audio Film Collective, 1986). These strategies sought to self-reflexively interrogate the whole racialised culture of cinematic sound and image and the difficulty of speaking within that culture in a society for whom 'Black' and 'British' have traditionally been seen as mutually exclusive terms.

In line with European Modernism, the medium becomes less 'transparent' and an awareness of its mediation of representation is foregrounded; this in turn interlocks with a more general interest in questions of culture which cinema is a component of. However, something else is also stressed, not intrinsic to avant-garde strategies but specific to the new historical and theoretical context: a new stress on the plurality of identities (especially around gender and sexuality and ethnicity) at play across the term 'Black'.

These strategies achieved a more popular recognition and profile in the 'fantasy' aesthetics of *My Beautiful Laundrette* (Stephen Frears/Hanif Kureishi 1985) which Julien Henriques described as articulating 'the feelings, contradictions and imagination of the characters rather than any attempt to reflect reality.'[29] However, the film is not quite the break with 'realism' Henriques suggests, since it locates its representation of cultural identity and consciousness quite precisely in time and place (the era of Thatcherism, set in inner city London). The realist/fantasy couplet is a deeply embedded component of British film culture. However, in the British Asian films of the 1990s, the fantasy components are *not* yoked to a private consciousness as they usually are within British cinema. As we shall see later, even where fantasy is articulated in relation to a specific individual character, the fantasy retains a *collective* dimension. There are two reasons for this. Diasporic travels are, as we have seen, collective uprootings and therefore it is more difficult to privatise the meaning of travel and displacement even in a culture already profoundly commodified. Secondly, as Laura U. Marks notes, collective memory has a close relationship with diasporan cinema since the latter 'make[s] it clear, by virtue of their strained relation to dominant languages, that *no* utterance is individual.'[30]

Tensions between the 'poles' of interest (that is a focus on social being or identity) could provoke sharp disagreement in the critical reception of Black British cinema. For example, Mahmood Jamal criticised *My Beautiful Laundrette* for its avoidance of 'historically based contradictions', for its 'soggy liberalism' and its inability to represent 'harsh reality'.[31] In turn, *Majdhar* (Ahmed A. Jamal, 1984) produced by Mahmood Jamal was criticised by Henriques as illustrating 'the crippling weaknesses of realism for coming to terms with contemporary issues' (presumably of identity).[32] Certainly British Asian Films of the 1990s are indebted to these earlier theoretical debates and cinematic representations, while at the same time they are clearly locatable in a post-Thatcher era, where the urgency to address the *national* political context evident in the Kureshi/Frears films, has diminished.

What is interesting is that Black and Asian cultural producers were, through-out this period, interested in the relationship between cultural theory and practice. While fear and dismissal of theory characterises most white cultural producers, the marginality of ethnic minorities encourages a recourse to a language which is conceptual and analytical enough to understand the nature and implications of that marginality. As Gurinder Chadha notes when making *I'm British But [...]* , (1989) which tested out in the documentary genre many of the themes that would be fictionalised in *Bhaji On The Beach*:

> I was reading *There Ain't No Black in the Union Jack* every time I reached a stumbling point with *I'm British But [...]* Now what am I doing? How can I do this? And I would read it and everything would become clear. Brilliant. For the first time in my life I had a book which so closely related to what was going on in my head and that I could use.[33]

Unlike American postmodernism, which is obsessed with the image in a media saturated society, *Bhaji On The Beach* and *Wild West* are influenced by British cultural studies, which, despite the cultural turn, has since the early work of Williams and Hoggart, been interested in the lived experience of everyday life which has also been the realist aesthetic's special providence.

Unity and Difference

We have seen that within Black British film criticism, the 1980s saw a fissure between those who valued a focus on the contradictory subjective/cultural dynamics of Black experience and those who valorised an emphasis on social being. The idea that both might be possible did not seem to be an option. There is no doubt that it was the emphasis on the subjective/cultural which became the keynote of Black politics and film culture towards the end of the 1980s. I want to now concentrate for the sake of clarity on the work of Stuart Hall and offer a critique of the model of cultural politics and identity, which he has developed with some influential effect, during the late 1980s and 1990s. I want to identify a contradiction in Hall's work between his theoretical means and his political ends. My argument is that if one's desired political goals are, in Hall's words, to 'build those forms of solidarity and identification which make common struggle and resistance possible'[34] then this cannot be pursued on the basis of a politics of difference.

Hall's work is characterised by a particular kind of narrative of recent history and the story which this narrative tells is that the basis of political activity has made a passage from social being to cultural identity. Sometimes Hall explicitly rejects this kind of linear history, but the gravitational pull of his methodology reasserts precisely this linearity. His influential article, 'New Ethnicities' begins by discussing two 'moments' in the formation of Black politics. The first is organised around the unifying term 'Black', which sought to bind people across ethnic differences into a single 'racial' category as a defence against white racism. The second moment, the 'new ethnicities' represents an explosion out of the unifying category of 'Black' as various groups become very much more aware of questions around cultural identity. Hall appears to be adamant that these two 'moments' are 'two phases of the same movement which constantly overlap and interweave',[35] but the linear model is symptomatically present in the words used ('shift', 'change from' 'move towards'). Before long, Hall's caution evaporates and he is writing of 'the end' of the 'essential black subject.'[36] Important here is the way Hall equates Black identity with essentialism.

> What is at issue here is the recognition of the extraordinary diversity of subjective positions, social experiences and cultural identities which compose the category 'black'; that is, the recognition that 'black' is essentially a politically and culturally *constructed* category which cannot be grounded in a set of fixed trans-cultural or transcendental racial categories and which therefore has no guarantees in Nature.[37]

The implication is that the recognition of diversity equates with an understanding of a category's constructed quality, while a unifying term such as 'Black' intrinsically naturalises itself in order to hold all these differences subsumed under it in place. Hall goes onto to argue that:

> If the black subject and black experience are not stabilised by Nature or by some other essential guarantee, then it must be the case that they are constructed historically, culturally, politically – and the concept which refers to this is 'ethnicity'.[38]

This is a non sequitur. It begins by taking the signifier 'Black' and attaching it to the signified 'historically constructed identity' but it ends with 'ethnicity' replacing 'Black' as the signifier for that signified, leaving 'Black' tumbling towards an irredeemable association with Nature. The idea that the meaning of 'Black' might be a site of struggle does not appear to be an option, although it once was: ' […] we previously had to recuperate the term 'Black', from its place in a system of negative equivalences.'[39] But this no longer seems possible or desirable. It is time to move on and decouple ethnicity from its equivalence in dominant discourses, with nationalism, imperialism, racism and the state. So, it appears that there is quite a lot of work to do, especially for the theorist of discourse. But why it is not worth trying to decouple 'Black' from the homophobia and sexism which Hall rightly identifies as currents within Black politics, is not quite clear, unless, of course, 'Black' has passed into the category of Nature (a mistake Hall has just told us we should not make). Of course, 'Black' as a political identity is fissured by differences – just as the nation is. Indeed, with the rise of the Black middle class, it is fissured by this material difference as much as by ethnicity. My point though is that Hall rather too quickly dumps a category which indicates some (if problematic) shared interests in his rush to get to a politics *based* on cultural difference.

In a later essay, Hall returns to the question of cultural unity vs. cultural difference and tries once again to hold them in some kind of dynamic or tension, but again, his methodology ends up overwhelmingly privileging cultural difference while also exhibiting complete indifference towards the question of shared and divergent interests. A materialist analysis has no problem with Hall's emphasis on identity as something that is 'never complete, always in process, and always constituted within, not outside, representation.'[40] Understandably, Hall wants to shift the post-colonial identity away from a dominant view, which he associates with the colonial West, of identity as a fixed timeless essence. But in the essay 'Cultural Identity and Diaspora', Hall also wants to give some due (as 'resources of resistance') to the politics of cultural practices that assert the profound unities of experience forged by colonialism and slavery.[41] In suggesting that identity is constituted along two vectors, that of similarity and continuity and that of difference and rupture, it appears that Hall is giving each vector roughly equal weight. In fact, Hall arranges these vectors temporally, so that continuity and similarity are associated overwhelmingly with the past, while the present is characterised by the unfolding of the play of difference. This radically privileges the vector of difference and rupture, not least because any representation of the past, whether conscious of this or not, is shot through with the poignancy that the past is irrecoverable for both the object remembered (Africa say) and the subject (the post-colonial subject) are no longer what they once were. Again, a materialist analysis has no problem with this projection of difference back into the past and between the past and the present. But by arranging these two vectors only along a temporal axis, Hall not only prioritises difference, he avoids asking what, if anything, unifies the post-colonial subject *now*, in the present. How can solidarities be built in the present if they are always receding into the past, into an imaginary nostalgia, while the present turns on 'the experience of a profound discontinuity.'?[42] There is no projection of the vector of unity into social space.

The reason for this emphasis on difference is that Hall's understanding of why identity is never fixed but in process, is located not so much in history as in Derridean post-structuralist theories of language, meaning and representation.

Thus for Hall, '[m]eaning continues to unfold, so to speak, beyond the arbitrary closure which makes it, at any moment possible.'[43] Here process and change is rooted in the essence of signification, conceived as a constant leapfrogging or deferral in an endless chain of signs. What is evacuated is any sense of 'difference' being a clash between signs and any sense of difference and continuity having a structure or pattern.

Once we conceptualise the production of meaning in these more dialectical terms, it is a short (materialist) step to link meanings/representation/identities, to the real world of human activities and social relations.

It is at this point (the point where we link signifying constructs with social constructs) that we also have to make certain distinctions between culture and material interests. For all the talk about difference, this simple but crucial difference, is rarely invoked. We need to recognise that cultural similarities and continuities may be fissured by material differences (such as between the Black middle and working class), while the culturally different (the Moslem from a Turkish family and the white Catholic from Irish descent) may well share the same material interests as they work on the supermarket checkout tills. It is absolutely essential to insist, against the grain of Hall's new ethnicities, that culture and interests do not necessarily coincide.

What is interesting is the role of Channel Four, which funded many of the Black and Asian films that influenced Hall's thinking on ethnicity. As early as 1983, Paul Gilroy criticised Channel Four for fragmenting Black programming into ethnic compartments, breaking down the commonalities, 'which the communities have struggled to create' and consigning ' 'West Indians' to one ideological Bantustan and 'Asians' to another.'[44] Such apartheid was practised in the name of 'a pluralist or multicultural understanding of racial segmentation', which 'inflates the cultural aspects of racial differentiation to the exclusion of all other factors and makes them the determining agent in 'race relations'.[45]

Hall has precisely excluded 'all other factors' by collapsing interests into culture and then exploding the latter category into multiple identities. Looking at the fragments, Hall reaches for his trusty Gramscianism to hold out the tentative possibility of some contingent alliances. Hegemony, he suggests, occurs when 'a certain configuration of local particularities try to dominate the whole scene.'[46] Such a configuration of progressive politics though would be like the patterns temporarily arranged by the kaleidoscope. With each twist a new pattern would order itself while the machine which determines the patterns remains intact.

Bhaji On The Beach

Bhaji On The Beach practices what it preaches. Composed of Indian mythic fantasy sequences, British naturalism, and Carry On farce, the film valorises identities which work with hybridity, cultural mixing and fusion (e.g. the film's Punjabi version of Cliff Richard's 'We're All Going On A Summer Holiday' crossed with Bhangra). This is to say that it dramatises the diaspora in its *forward movement* as a series of cultural dispersals and reconfigurations. The film sets up a debate between this dynamic and that other definition associated with the diaspora which involves a symbolic movement back in time and space to reconnect with an imagined origin conceived as a unitary cultural sphere. It is this tension between identities based on fixed and timelessly conceived traditions and customs and identities which are provisional, permeable, open to change and recombination, which the film sets into motion.

Unlike other films about female travel and subsequent transformation, (e.g. *A Room With A View* (J. Ivory, 1985) and *Shirley Valentine* (L. Gilbert, 1989), the characters in

Bhaji On The Beach do not have to cross the legal/cultural boundary of the nation for travel to ask transformative questions of them. In a move that fuses the Asian characters with that most quintessential of English working-class activities (the seaside holiday trip) the characters only have to travel to the boundary of the nation (Blackpool, in this case). This reflects how much more ambivalent the question of 'home' already is for people negotiating the terms of their Britishness and Asianness in contemporary Britain.

This effects the narrative structure of the film. The plot transformations which leaving 'home' for a day brings, are actually continuations of plot lines that begin at 'home'. The film starts by introducing us to various relationships *already* in transition. We are introduced to Ranjit whose parents insist that 'English divorce' is not an option for his wife, Ginder, who has left him. Concerned with the continuation of the family line, his parents send him out to return Ginder and their son Amrit to the house. Ranjit then must travel to restore the status quo and traditional social relations based on custom. Ginder must travel into modernity and an uncertain future outside the traditional extended or even nuclear family unit. Then there is Hashida – who has been having a relationship, unknown to her parents, with Oliver, who is Black. She discovers she is pregnant, and initially at least, Oliver rejects Hashida. In this he is encouraged by his separatist friend. However, when they meet up in Blackpool the couple reaffirm their commitment to each other.

Thus for *Bhaji On The Beach* the transformations which the characters undergo as a result of their travels, are only the working through of plot lines which begin back in Birmingham – and this is because, the film suggests, transformation is part of their condition of life back at 'home'. This is in contrast to the dramatic structure of white films like a *A Room With A View,* or *Shirley Valentine.* In these films the geo-cultural spaces characters enter are both outside their normal cultural orbit and provoke profoundly new directions precisely because 'home' was conceived as such a fixed and stable point. These films operate around a firm demarcation between self and Other, familiar and foreign. *Bhaji On The Beach* deconstructs such binaries. It is significant I think that it does this by mobilising the collective rather than, what we might call, the individualising romantic gaze. John Urry associates the romantic gaze with undisturbed natural beauty, emphasising 'solitude, privacy and a personal, semi-spiritual relationship with the object of the gaze.'[47] The romantic gaze (evident in *Room With A View* and *Shirley Valentine*) works by distinguishing a cultured elite who are the *real* travellers, from the uncultured masses who are merely conceived as ignorant, dependent tourists.

By contrast the collective gaze depends on and acknowledges its roots in mass tourism and is unembarrassed by the presence of other people who are also tourists. The seaside resort and coach holiday are the quintessential sites/sights of and for the collective gaze.[48] The collective day out to Blackpool in *Bhaji On The Beach* fits this description perfectly. This more plebeian gaze has no need of an elitist distinction between tourist and traveller and therefore it has no need for the binary opposition between us and the Other. In one sense the film is arguing that everyone is a traveller. The film's narration is clearly on the side of contingency through interaction with difference: the very essence of the traveller. The key question which this raises though, is what happens to solidarity and alliances if everyone is *always* on the move? In another sense the film is also saying that we are all tourists by suggesting that we have as much chance of accessing an authentic culture or past as the tourist.

The position which the film constructs around diasporan contingency is contrasted with two other positions within the film. The first is separatism, represented by Oliver's friend, Ajay. When Oliver asks him what happened to Black solidarity, Ajay declares that:

> Black don't mean not white anymore [...] Forget the melting pot and respect the differences. But that's what's missing between us and them: respect [...] you try fusion and you get confusion.

Significantly, this exchange between Oliver and his friend is taking place in the university dorm kitchen where two Chinese students are also present. Ajay has an exchange with one of them who has accused him of stealing his eggs. This is significant because it nods – albeit obliquely – towards the question of material resources and how the struggle over them turns a separatism based on 'respect' to one of incomprehension and conflict.

The second alternative to diasporan hybridity is much more substantially engaged with during the course of the film: this is the position associated with nostalgia for a timeless, unchanged, unified home. According to Iain Chambers mobility and contingency makes the search for 'authentic' cultures and identities paradoxically, inauthentic.[49] Certainly *Bhaji On The Beach* could be enlisted to support this view, but it also cuts people off from other potentially more progressive resources of hope that may be emitted from the past. For example, I think there is something very powerful and liberating in the way that Shirley Valentine recaptures a lost aspect of her *personal* past in order to go forward. Nevertheless, *Bhaji On The Beach* offers a coherent critique of certain versions of remembering the past.

This point is made most clearly through the character of Asha. Significantly she runs an Indian video shop. These examples of travelling symbolic goods provide the cultural reference points beyond the British national imaginary. In her Southall-based ethnographic study, Gillespie notes how Hindi films on video are used as a form of cultural negotiation. She detects a generational difference though, suggesting that 'while young people use Indian films to deconstruct 'traditional culture', many parents use them to foster cultural and religious traditions.'[50] Asha's fantasies begin by investing cultural and religious traditions with unquestioned authority, but eventually crack under the pressures of modernity. In so doing, Asha travels across the generations to make some sort of alliance with the younger women.

To start with, Asha has a series of fantasies where she worries about the purity of Indian identity and customs being diluted by westernisation. In one fantasy, she projects these onto Hashida after she learns of Hashida's pregnancy. Her fantasy scenario appears to be located in a large white tent populated by various characters in traditional Indian dress. Hashida, however, visibly pregnant with her child from

Oliver, wears a short red dress, revealing top with glittering sequins, red boots, blonde wig and is smoking a cigarette. She is obviously enjoying the consternation of her parents and relatives. The fantasy ends with Hashida coughing on the cigarette. We cut back to the bus, on its way to Blackpool – and in fact it is Ginder who is coughing on the cigarette smoke of Rekha. This is an ironic piece of editing. For Rekha, is visiting from Bombay – but far from embodying a 'pure' Indianness, Rekha, with her sunglasses, short skirt, clutching her *Hello* magazine and smoking through a cigarette filter, is the most westernised of all the older women on the bus. Asha then, the film suggests, is looking backwards for her utopia, to a nostalgically constructed past. But what we must also note is the way her fantasy is contextualised within the ongoing debate and issues generated by the other characters and their trip to the seaside. It is a fantasy that is commenting on and is being influenced by what is happening around her. Asha's fantasy then retains a strong collective dimension, even when, as we shall see, she is fantasising directly about her own life.

Let us just consider a little more the significance of Blackpool. It is interesting that Birmingham and the route to Blackpool is figured as the territories where ethnicities are separating and confronting each other across a terrain of hostility and confusion. There is white on Asian racism, Asian on Asian racism (Ranjit's parents, for example, referring to Ginder, declare that 'you can't trust the dark ones'), Asian on Black racism, Black on Asian racism, etc.

Blackpool then becomes the site of another kind of response to the Other – this is the response not of fear, but of desire. The cultural historian John Mackenzie has argued, in relation to Orientalism in painting, that the Other, was not always, and perhaps not even typically, conceived as inferior. Rather, desires for things perceived to have been lost in the English identity could be imagined in the Other and so the latter could function as a vehicle for critiquing Englishness as presently constituted. Mackenzie notes the chivalric and medieval references in Orientalist paintings of the Arab world, the 'endless parade of equestrianism, of Arab knights bearing their long muskets like lances,' of hunting, and hawking.[51] He speculates that for the buyers of these cultural commodities, such paintings represented a lament concerning various aspects of capitalist modernity and its discontents. The fascination with the East lay less in a concern to provide a cultural legitimisation for its domination, as Edward Said has argued, than as a way of satisfying 'an atavistic reaction to modern industrialism.'[52]

Mackenzie argues that this desire to find what has been lost in the self via the Arab, suggests a pressing need for a theorisation of cross cultural influences rather more than theories of Otherness. However, desire and appreciation can still be motivated by the binary logic of Otherness, so that, for example, the latter is frozen in time, removed from history, serving primarily as a vehicle for the observer's fantasies. In this, Mackenzie's bourgeois patrons of Orientalist painting seem to me to be operating a highly touristic and Otherizing gaze, even though it is motivated by desire rather than fear.

Quite self-consciously, *Bhaji On The Beach* signifies Blackpool as the place where a nostalgic and mythical Englishness comes into contact with an assortment of exoticised Others. Fish and chips with curry powder, Union Jacks and cowboys, camels and mermaids, pythons and snake charmers. Here Asha meets the quintessential English gentleman, Ambrose Waddington. The film makes brilliant strategic use of this character. He takes her to see the white English clapping away to the Wurlitzer organ and then onto his beloved theatre – once the jewel in the crown of a now declining middlebrow culture. As they stand on the stage of the empty theatre, Ambrose conjures up the ghosts of audiences past while lamenting the decline of 'our popular culture'. The gaze with which he perceives Asha is similarly nostalgic and corresponds closely with Mackenzie's bourgeois patrons of Orientalist paintings. Ambrose mis-recognises in Asha his desire for a culture that (he imagines) holds steadfastly to its traditions and its past, checking the advance of history. Through Asha he expresses a similarly atavistic reaction to modernity. Ironically, his feeling that the white English have abandoned their proud cultural traditions parallels Asha's own anxieties concerning British Asians.

It is the very traditions and customs that Waddington admires which bring on another anxiety-fantasy for Asha – who is concerned that she has transgressed traditional customs by being alone with Waddington. But this time, Asha talks back to the Indian gods who berate her – declaring that 'duty' and 'sacrifice' have crushed her own educational and career ambitions. Crucially, this lays the ground for her defence of Ginder when she is attacked by Ranjit at the end of the film (again, fantasy feeds back into the collective). Asha comes to see the appeal to tradition and custom as legitimising resources for patriarchy. Despite the film's postmodern elements, some sense of authentic social being has been affirmed, for on what other basis can the film suggest that Ginder is better off without Ranjit?

At the start of the day trip, the organiser, Simi articulates, from the 'margins' of the storylines, the political voice of the text, rather like the Ricky Tomlinson character in *Riff Raff* (Ken Loach, 1991) or Bob's brother-in-law in *Raining Stones* (Ken Loach,1993). Simi urges the women to take this as an opportunity to escape from the 'double yoke' of racism and sexism, and although there are looks of bemusement from the older generation, by the end of the film, something like a collective anti-sexist and cross-generational identity *has* been forged. We have then, what Hall called 'a certain configuration of local particularities'[53] coming together. But this feminist hegemony can only be imagined, as Simi's speech makes clear, outside the established structures of racism and sexism: it can only be imagined in the escapism of the day out; it can only take root in the terrain of leisure and cultural pleasure; it is temporary, transient, the women are brought together on the bus for a day but the question of what happens to the women's solidarities once they have returned and dispersed to their established structures, remains a pressing and unanswered one. In this regard, the film's ability to imagine or pose only a temporary, transient alliance or configuration of particularities, demonstrates perfectly the weaknesses of the politics of difference argued for by Hall and the loss of focus on persistent, structural inequalities when, as with Appadurai, the real becomes aestheticised.

Wild West

The problem which any theory of cross-cultural exchange needs to address, is the material conditions of unequal relations of power which frame such an exchange. In one sense, *Wild West* is all about how far one can push 'the aesthetics of the diaspora, the aesthetics of creolization' as Hall puts it,[54] vis-a-vis the material conditions in which culture is produced and consumed. For Sivanandan, the refugees, migrants, and asylum-seekers constitute the 'flotsam and jetsam of latter-day imperialism', performing the dirty, low paid, insecure jobs, often 'rightless, rootless, peripatetic and temporary – illegal even.'[55] Now, this describes a particular fraction of people, none of whom appear in either of the films I am discussing. These films explore the intersection of being Asian and British, rooted *and* displaced. But it reminds us about questions of power which get concealed by some of the wilder flights of hybridity theory. Iain Chambers, for example, argues that 'the modern metropolitan figure is the migrant.' This theoretical framework and the fluid realities it explores downplays, as I have suggested, the continuities in the distribution of power which connect the past and the present and which therefore beg the question: what conceptual categories and histories do we need to hold onto? For Chambers, the migrant rewrites the 'urban script' as 'an earlier social order and cultural authority is now turned *inside out and dispersed*' (my emphasis).[56] To which one is tempted to reply: really? Obviously there have been cultural changes, but where is the sense of the repetition and reiteration of power?

Certainly *Wild West* explores the extent to which deterritorialization means that there is no necessary connection between culture and territory or, more radically, between culture and ethnicity. The film also testifies to the utopian dynamics underpinning the consumption of cultures which have travelled from elsewhere as well as the utopian impulse implicit in the travels of persons. Shot on location in London, Southall, the story concerns three Muslim brothers and a Sikh friend who have formed a country-and-western band. As Gillespie notes, Asian music has constructed identificatory connections between the American Indian and Asian Indian,[57] but here we have Asians appropriating the culture and ethnicity of white oppressors vis-a-vis both the American Indian and the Black American. The bedroom of the lead character, Zaf, is painted with pictures of the Lone Ranger. But if the racist assumptions governing that character were not enough, Zaf also has the American Confederate flag in his room, symbol of a racist South reluctant to abolish slavery.

In effect the band are refusing to let Black as a political category limit their cultural reference points or allow culture to have a fixed meaning. As culture travels via the media, so its indigenisation elsewhere transforms its meanings and/or provides a repertoire of meanings and cultural practices not available within the 'immediate' territory (whether locally or nationally). Although Zaf's mother tells him that 'there are no Pakistani cowboys', Zaf, dressed in jeans, ten-gallon hat, and country-and-western shirt, knows differently. Rather like the 'Arizona Jim' western stories in Jean Renoir's *The Crime Of Monsieur Lange* (1935), the music and the image of the American West represent a site of potential emancipation, the open road or landscape signifying social mobility and escape from oppression. Thus the film opens with Zaf cycling down an empty stretch of road and past a billboard displaying an American cowboy. This imagery is a utopian resource which the band use to fuel fantasies of escaping from the racism and diminished horizons which dominate Britain. 'This whole fucking shithole country's too small' as Zaf bluntly puts it.

The film has a brilliant fantasy sequence which articulates these utopian aspirations and connects this appropriation of country and western with the 'anti-capitalist aspects of black expressive culture' which Gilroy finds in various strands of Black music.[58] Here the collective dimensions of fantasy are retained by linking the fantasy with the band as a whole. The sequence begins at night as the band return from an unsuccessful evening at the 'Rising Asian' talent contest. They cross an industrial wasteland, passing the abandoned Southall Meat Factory where the brothers' father 'came off the land and into this shithole'. Their father was ground down by the time and motion rhythm of modern industrialisation. Zaf describes how 'they made a big man small.' As Gilroy notes, a critique of productivism, the labour process and the division of labour under capitalism, is a key core theme of Black music.

Having established the oppressive past and present from which a utopian escape is desired, the fantasy sequence really takes off when the band steal a police car. They transform it into an open top with a chainsaw, steal some guitars and head into the centre of town with the blue light flashing on top of the Sikh's turban. The appropriation and transformation of a vehicle owned by an oppressive and racist state connects with another core theme in Black music which revolves 'around a plea for the disassociation of law from domination.'[59] The geographical trajectory which the fantasy sequence maps is reminiscent of Hall's argument about the utopian appeal of the metropolitan centre for the diasporic masses.

> If you come from the sticks, the colonial sticks, where you really want to live is right on Eros Statue in Piccadilly Circus. You don't want to go and live in someone else's metropolitan sticks. You want to go right to the centre of the hub of the world.[60]

Here the movement is from the suburban sticks into Leicester Square where the band perform to and attract a large appreciative crowd. The song, called 'I ain't ever Satisfied' plays across the fantasy sequence, testifying to both the material realities which frustrate satisfaction and the utopian possibilities of both music and the musical as a cinematic genre.[61]

As with *Bhaji On The Beach* the different definitions and dynamics associated with the diaspora are mapped onto generational differences. Avtah Brah argues that the concept of the diaspora inscribes *'a homing desire while simultaneously critiquing discourses of fixed origins '* (original emphasis).[62] For the band and their manager, Jagdeep, who drives a convertible American saloon with buffalo horns strapped to the front grill, America represents precisely this homing desire. Jagdeep's ambition is to die in Beverly Hills. Zaf's mother also claims that she does not want to die in Britain, but she wishes to return 'home' to Pakistan, which she conceives precisely in terms of fixed origins. These are two very different journeys, very different dissatisfactions with Britain and very different proposed solutions. The tension is caught as Zaf, in country-and-western clothing, stands in the lounge framed in a low angle shot with a large portrait of President Zia, the former Pakistani dictator, dominating the background. Eventually his mother sells the home, claiming that she wants to return to her 'own kind' and lamenting the cultural 'confusion' which has afflicted her sons. They in turn reject her pleas to return with her to Pakistan.

In the meantime, the band's fortunes are finally changing. The film has mobilised a potential romance between Zaf and an Asian woman, Rifat, married to a white mini cab operator who is prone to physically abusing her. Rifat leaves her husband and joins the band as a singer. With her now fronting the band, their fortunes change and they are well received at an Irish pub which called them in at the last moment after their regular band is arrested by the anti-terrorist squad. From there, the band go into a recording studio and then with the demo tape, they get an appointment with the American-owned country-and-western music company, Wild West. Crucially, just as in *Bhaji On The Beach*, the heterosexual romance is not allowed to dominate the more collective story being told. Thus, although Rifat and Zaf do, as expected, end up in bed with each other, it is, rather unexpectedly, short lived. Rifat declares she wants Zaf as a friend, not a lover. This is crucial because it facilitates the key political point which the film ends on.

Invited to Wild West on the strength of their demo tape, the executive in a Stetson changes his tune when he actually sees the band. It is at this point that we and they learn that cultural hybridity takes place within certain material contexts. The executive, Hank Goldstein, and his partner, Yehudi (neither of them, obviously 'pure' Texans, whatever that may be), start to talk about marketing and salability and can see no future for an Asian country-and-western band in Texas. The commodification of music, the division between cultural producers and owners of the means of production suddenly and abruptly reminds us that while deterritorialization can in principle bring together any set of cultural combinations, the gate-keepers have to be satisfied of its exchange value. But then Hank and Yehudi close in on Rifat, saying that although she has the 'dusky looks' they can do something for her. Zaf persuades her to sign a contract with Wild West, while the band cash in the money gained from selling the house and buy their tickets to Nashville, where, we can assume, their utopian hopes of transcending the racist limitations of Britain, may not be entirely satisfied.

Conclusion

We have seen that the conceptualisation of diaspora within Black and Asian cultural theory and cinematic practice pulls in two very different directions. There is the ontological essentialist orientation, which spatially involves a return 'home' and temporally a freezing of time or projection back into the past. The other position, which has been much more attractive to cultural producers and theorists, conceives the diaspora spatially as an ongoing process of dispersion and settlement, in which identity is always already hybrid, plural, shifting, mixing and involved in crossing cultural borders and boundaries. But how does this square with identifying common interests and indeed, common enemies. As Avtah Brah (herself a hybridity advocate) notes:

> For several hundred years now a global economic system has been in the making. It evolved out of the transatlantic trade in human beings, it flourished during the Industrial Revolution, it has been nurtured by colonialism and imperialism, and now it has achieved a new vitality in this age of microchip technology and multinational

corporations. It is a system that has created lasting inequalities, both within nations and between nations. All our fates are linked within this system, but our precise position depends on a multiplicity of factors [...] [63]

It is this dilemma which theory has to grasp, this tension between the generalisation of interests which the expansion of commodity relations globally produces, so that indeed, all our fates are interlinked, and the other dynamic of commodity relations which produces a multiplicity of positions within this totality. It is once again the dialectic between history and histories.

I have attempted to discuss two British Asian films as a way of both illustrating these theoretical debates while according them their own cinematic specificity. The strength of these films are numerous: they display a sophisticated, self-reflexive, critical engagement with popular culture; they have an assured grasp of the fluidities of identity and subjectivity, breaking with the overpowering cloying nostalgia which grips so much British cinema. Like other Black British films they display what John Hill describes as an 'expanded sense of 'Britishness' [...] but also [...] sensitivity to social differences [...] within an identifiably and specifically British context.'[64] Both films play with the realist/fantasy aesthetics which have been so important to British film culture. In *Bhaji On The Beach,* fantasy is not equated with transgressive desire, but with the reality principle. The film explores the investments people have in the ideological fantasy of cultural purity and tradition. In *Wild West,* a rather different conception of fantasy is mobilised. Here it is yoked to cultural transgression and utopian hope. Yet both films ground these explorations of subjectivity and identification, within 'realist' frameworks which address racism, sexism, and class relations within a specifically British context.

The weakness of these films, like the theories I have discussed, lie along temporal and spatial axes. In terms of space, the films are only able to allude or briefly glimpse the solidarities necessary to address unequal concentrations of power. In terms of time, they live in the present, equating all memory, all tradition, with nostalgia, which is radically disabling. When in *Wild West* Zaf briefly remembers his father, his brother could almost be speaking for the film when he asks him not to talk about his father, as if it is too painful to bear. One may recall Walter Benjamin's advice on this matter of memory:

Social Democracy thought fit to assign to the working class the role of the redeemer of future generations, in this way cutting the sinews of its greatest strength. This training made the working class forget both its hatred and its spirit of sacrifice, for both are nourished by the image of enslaved ancestors rather than that of liberated grandchildren.[65]

References

1 N. Papastergiadis, 'Tracing hybridity in Theory', *Debating Cultural Hybridity, Multi-Cultural Identities and the Politics of Anti-Racism* (eds) P. Werbner & T. Modood, Zed Books, London, 1997, p. 260.

2 P. Werbner, 'The Dialectics of Cultural Hybridity', *Debating Cultural Hybridity*, p. 4.

3   A. D. Smith, 'Towards a Global Culture?' *Theory, Culture and Society*, Sage, London, vol, 7, 1990, p. 178.

4   A. Brah, *cartographies of diaspora, contesting identities,* Routledge, London, 1996, p. 181.

5   A. Brah, *cartographies of diaspora,* p. 193.

6   P. Gilroy, *The Black Atlantic, Modernity and Double Consciousness*, Verso, London, 1993, p. 32.

7   See for example the interview with Black Audio Collective in *Framework* no. 35, 1988, pp. 11–12.

8   P. Gilroy, *Sight and Sound*, vol.5, no.2, 1995, pp. 18–19.

9   P. Gilroy, *There Ain't No Black In The Union Jack*, Routledge, London, 1987, pp. 153–222.

10 A. Brah, *cartographies of diaspora,* p. 197.

11 I. Chambers, *migrancy, culture, identity,* Routledge/Comedia, London, 1994, p.16.

12 M. Gillespie, *Television, Ethnicity and Cultural Change*, Comedia/Routledge, London, 1995, p. 7.

13 F. Jameson, 'The Cultural Logic of Late Capitalism', *Postmodernism or, The Cultural Logic of Late Capitalism* Verso, 1991, London, p. 20.

14 B. Schwarz, 'Conquerors Of Truth: Reflections on Postcolonial Theory', *The Expansion of England, Race, ethnicity and cultural history*, (ed.) B. Schwarz, Routledge, 1996, p. 11.

15 'Interview with the Black Audio Collective', *Framework* 35, 1988, p. 11.

16 A. Brah, *cartographies of diaspora,* p. 21.

17 A. Brah, *cartographies of diaspora,* pp. 30–1.

18 A. Brah,*cartographies of diaspora,* p. 22.

19 A. Brah,*cartographies of diaspora,* p. 209.

20 I. Chambers, *migrancy, culture, identity,* p. 24.

21 M. Gillespie, *Television, Ethnicity and Cultural Change,* p. 3.

22 J. Hutnyk, 'Adorno At WOMAD: South Asian Crossovers and The Limits of Hybridity-Talk', *Debating Cultural Hybridity,* p. 119.

23 J. Hutnyk, 'Adorno at WOMAD', *Debating Cultural Hybridity,* p. 122.

24 A. Appadurai, 'Disjuncture and Difference in the Global Cultural Economy', *Global Culture, Nationalism, Globalization and Modernity* (ed.) M. Featherstone, Sage, London, 1995.

25 A. Appadurai, 'Disjuncture and Difference in the Global Cultural Economy', *Global Culture,* p. 299.

26 A. Appadurai, 'Disjuncture and Difference in the Global Cultural Economy', *Global Culture,* p. 296.

27 A. Appadurai, 'Disjuncture and Difference in the Global Cultural Economy', *Global Culture,* p. 295.

28 K. Mercer, 'Recoding Narratives of Race and Nation', *Black Film/British Cinema,* ICA Documents, No.7, 1988, (ed.) K. Mercer, pp. 10–11.

29 J. Henriques, 'Realism and the New Language', *Black Film/British Cinema,* p.19.

30 L. U. Marks, 'A Deleuzian politics of hybrid cinema', *Screen*, vol. 35, Autumn, 1994, p. 257.

31 M. Jamal, 'Dirty Linen', *Black Film/British Cinema,* pp. 21–2.

32 J. Henriques, *Black Film/British Cinema,* p. 19.

33 G. Chadha,*Third Text*, no. 27, Summer 1994, p. 57.

34 S. Hall, 'New Ethnicities', *Black Film/British Cinema,* p. 28.

35 S. Hall, 'New Ethnicities', *Black Film/British Cinema,* p. 27.

36 S. Hall, 'New Ethnicities', *Black Film/British Cinema,* p. 28.

37 S. Hall, 'New Ethnicities', *Black Film/British Cinema,* p. 28.

38 S. Hall, 'New Ethnicities', *Black Film/British Cinema,* p. 29.

39 S. Hall, 'New Ethnicities', *Black Film/British Cinema,* p. 29.

40 S. Hall, 'Cultural Identity and Diaspora', *Identity, Community, Culture, Difference* (ed.) J.Rutherford, Lawrence and Wishart, 1990, p. 222.

41 S. Hall, 'Cultural Identity and Diaspora', *Identity, Community, Culture, Difference*, p. 225.

42 S. Hall, 'Cultural Identity and Diaspora', *Identity, Community, Culture, Difference*, p. 227.

43 S. Hall, 'Cultural Identity and Diaspora', *Identity, Community, Culture, Difference*, p. 229.

44 P. Gilroy, 'C4 – Bridgehead Or Bantustan?', *Screen*, vol. 24, 4–5, 1983, p. 131.

45 P. Gilroy, 'C4 – Bridgehead Or Bantustan?', *Screen*, p. 131.

46 S. Hall, 'Old and New Identities, Old and New Ethnicities' *Culture, Globalization And The World System ,Contemporary Conditions For The Representation Of Identity*, (ed.) A. D. King, Macmillan, London, 1991, p. 67.

47 J. Urry, *The Tourist Gaze*, Sage, London, 1990, p. 45.

48 J. Urry, *The Tourist Gaze*, p. 46 and p. 95.

49 I. Chambers, *migrancy, culture, identity*, p. 72.

50 M. Gillespie, *Television, Ethnicity and Cultural Change*, p. 87.

51 J. M. Mackenzie, *Orientalism, history, theory and the arts*, Manchester University Press, Manchester, 1995, p. 55.

52 J. M. Mackenzie, *Orientalism, history, theory and the arts*, p. 59.

53 S. Hall, 'Old and New Identities, Old and New Ethnicities', *Culture, Globalization And The World System*, p. 67.

54 S. Hall, 'The Local and the Global: Globalization and Ethnicity' *Culture, Globalization and the World System*, p. 38.

55 A. Sivanandan, 'New Circuits of Imperialism', *Race and Class*, no.30. vol.4, 1989, pp. 15–16.

56 I. Chambers, *migrancy, culture, identity*, p. 23.

57 M. Gillespie, *Television, Ethnicity and Cultural Change*, p. 5.

58 P. Gilroy, *There Ain't No Black In The Union Jack*, pp. 199–209.

59 P. Gilroy, *There Ain't No Black In The Union Jack*, p. 199.

60 S. Hall, 'The Local and the Global', *Culture, Globalization And The World System*, p. 24.

61 R. Dyer, 'Entertainment and Utopia', *Movies and Methods Vol.2* (ed.) B. Nichols, University of California Press, 1985.

62 A. Brah, *cartographies of diaspora*, pp. 192–3.

63. A. Brah, *cartographies of diaspora*, p. 84.

64 J. Hill, 'The Issue Of National Cinema And British Film Production', *New Questions of British Cinema* (ed.) D. Petrie, BFI, 1992, p. 16.

65 W. Benjamin, 'Theses on the Philosophy of History', *Illuminations* Pimlico Press, 1999, p. 252.

Conclusion

This book has argued for a more materialist understanding of culture than is currently popular within film studies. Materialist questions keep on returning, like the repressed. In chapter five, I suggested that both contemporary cultural theory and film practices could not help but smuggle back into their discourse and representations, issues pertaining to material life, to social, cross-cultural solidarity and to universal principles (autonomy, freedom, opportunity) which were logically incompatible with their remorselessly hybridising, culturalising philosophy. Materialist analysis identifies the importance of social, economic and political power relations as key factors shaping cultural production and meanings. One of the major configurations of social, economic and political power that I have explored is that of the nation and the transfigured transnational context in which it increasingly operates. Louis Althusser once suggested that the ideological construction of the subject (the socio-historically formed individual) was characterised by the sense of being internally unified and free of oppressive external determinants.[1] This accords with the twin myths of national identity rather well. Culture plays a key role in this. For Gellner, nationalism 'is the political principle which maintains that similarity of culture is the basic social bond.'[2] Within nationalism, this bond, this feeling of being British, German or Serb, works to override the evident social fractures and diverging material interests within the nation. Freedom from coercive external forces has sometimes been partially articulated in terms of culture as well, particularly via the notion of 'Americanisation', a vulgar and incomplete critique of international power relations.

Despite the crisis of the nation, its mythic conceptualisations have sunk deep roots into our cultural and political apprehensions. Even a Marxist critic such as Fredric Jameson can, as we saw in chapter one, play down the internal class divisions of the nation-state in order to valorise it against the coercive homogenising effects of the global (American dominated) market. Or in the case of the Serbian films discussed in chapter four, despite agonised assessments of national identity, the films still clung to a disillusioned nationalism. A good example of the way the nation operates within and is determined by international forces, is evident at a cultural level in the case of British cinema. I explored in chapter two, how a dominant and conservative version of Britishness, albeit recently inflected with a pseudo-modernisation, circulates as an international commodity-image and how this shapes the production and profile of the images and meanings available (including the alternative and contesting images provided by a film like *Century*).

This example demonstrates one – and I would argue that it is the dominant one – dimension of globalisation: that is its homogenising effects on cultural diversity and in particular on the range of political perspectives and voices which cultural products such as film can articulate. Chapter one explored the economic determinants on the institutional arrangements of the film industry in more detail and argued that the consolidated power of Hollywood was homogenising insofar as it powerfully constrained the room for manoeuvre for European films. I argued that intervention into this most unfree market, at either national or European levels, if it was to be really effective, would have to address, at an economic level, the key question of *distribution/exhibition*; at a cultural level, such a policy would have to have ambitions somewhat different from merely protecting an assumed cultural uniqueness and pride. This is the culture of complacency and affirmation. The cultural production and consumption that needs to be fostered should be critical, interrogative, challenging assumed priorities and social, cultural orders. The assumption underlying my valorisation of anti-national, national films (best exemplified in this book by the French films discussed in chapter two) is that films do make some cumulative contribution over time to the perspective, values and understandings of self and society. As Henry A. Giroux has argued:

> As public pedagogies, texts…attempt to bridge the gap between private and the public discourses, while simultaneously putting into play particular ideologies and values that resonate with broader public conversations regarding how a society views itself and the world of power, events, and politics…They produce and reflect important considerations of how human beings should live, engage with others, define themselves, and address how a society should take up questions fundamental to its survival.[3]

In this respect, the emergence of a pan-European cinematic consciousness and a struggle around the nature of what that Europe of the future will be like, is of great significance. At this level of conceiving geo-cultural boundaries, we also found evidence of a 'critical regionalism' in such films such as *Land and Freedom, Three Colours Blue* and *White* and *Prometheus*. A new European cinema is now crystallising out of existing national cinemas, out of European film industry initiatives such as Eurimages, usually, although not exclusively involving co-productions, and out of the broader political and economic reconfiguration of Europe currently underway. This new European cinema is orientated to Europe as a determining context for the diegetic action, as a space for new utopian routes for individual change or dystopian 'state of Europe' surveys, and therefore the narratives often involve cross-border travels. Such a European cinema could act as the conscience of a continent being forged by instrumental economic and political forces.

The other dimension to globalisation, that of heterogenisation, is generated from all those 'scapes' and their potentially unpredictable configurations, which Appadurai maps out for us – the movement of finance, people, technology, media and ideas. Insofar as the movement of people, cultures and media may introduce signifying practices which challenges certain *nationally* dominant conceptions, perspectives and values, then this aspect of globalisation has critical potential. The British Asian films discussed in chapter five best represent these trends towards cultural difference and hybridity. Politically, these films are ambiguous, as are the theories that share their emphasis on cultural mutability. Disrupting the hermetic culture of the traditional nation-state, this transnational diasporan sensibility radically calls into question temporal continuity, cultural cohesion and fixed pure identities.

I suggested in chapter four that although the liberal multiculturalism associated with postmodernism and the 'cultural turn' are politically distant from the claims for ethnic purity, stable identities and cultural incompatibility which flourished in the Balkan wars of the 1990s, there was a secret thread connecting them: both positions repress the socio-economic realm in favour of culture, albeit radically different conceptions of cultural politics. Each side also errs on the question of temporality. If nationalism in effect smooths over historical changes to create a mythological continuity between past and present, a continuity which represses anything which does not fit in with legitimising the present order, then hybridity theory abolishes any conception of continuity or links or relationship with the past. This weakening of historicity was of course a key feature of postmodernism as diagnosed by Jameson.[4] The past as a critical resource thus becomes unusable just as it becomes difficult to gain a critical purchase on the present when it is viewed, through the lens of culture, as constantly shifting and protean.

It is remarkable how questions of cultural difference and identity have displaced other questions of equal significance. Cultural diversity may be an important goal, but what of social equality? A de-facto cultural diversity and even a celebration of it within official politics are not at all incompatible with a socially stratified society. Indeed if cultural similarity once legitimised the nation-state, then cultural diversity is fast becoming the new badge of inclusiveness, the new meritocracy. But it should be evident that a liberal European politics fixated on cultural diversity already has its terminus mapped out for it in America where the rising Black middle class, to be followed no doubt by a Hispanic middle class, share few material interests with the Black majority they have left behind and can be easily prised away from any effective solidarity with them by the political traditions which dominate America. Cultural identity meanwhile may be an important component of how individuals and collectives perceive themselves, but note how the question of identity has displaced the role of culture in forging cognitions of the world, in forging consciousness. An overwhelming emphasis on identity keeps us looking inwards and on a terrain largely uncoupled from the material world, where as the issue of consciousness orientates critical discourse outwards, into an engagement with the social world we find ourselves in.

In decoding European films in relation to that social world I have constructed a number of political and historical narratives (the intensification of globalisation, the emerging project of European integration, the collapse of the old Eastern communist bloc and the post-colonial legacy of migration) and contested a number of other narratives (the death of socialism, the rise of postmodernism and the rise of new ethnicities). These chronicles of recent times are framed by a larger totalising history, the structural tensions of an epoch dominated by capital and its discontents. The films which I have located in these narratives and the larger master-narrative, do not passively reflect these dramatic contours. Instead the films are active responses and interventions into history. But these interventions are not only diverse and conflicting between one example and another (a diversity threatened by Hollywood's economic power) they are to varying degrees, *internally* conflictual, not least at the level of the formal strategies deployed. To take a single 'unit ' of film language like the long shot, we have seen how in Ken Loach's *Land and Freedom* this facilitates the emergence into representation of a collective revolutionary social agent. But compare this with Angelopoulos's *Ulysses' Gaze*, where the long shot marks a crisis of agency, ethics and aesthetics as the film's camera records the horrors of social barbarism from a resolutely non-participative position. Or take a film like Kusturica's *Undergound* which reveals its particular relations to history in its contradictory amalgamation of a cosmopolitan postmodernism (national identity is a fiction), an indigenous nationalist surrealist Romanticism (the Serbs have a peasant vitality) and an allegorical and realist critique of class differences (the Communist Party was an exploiting elite).

This book on European cinema is coming to a close. But the histories and film practices which it provides a brief and obviously cursory snapshot of, continues to unfold. Hopefully the reader will feel that some of the themes and approaches of this book can be taken on into that still open-ended future.

Notes

1   L. Althusser, 'Ideology and Ideological State Apparatuses', *Lenin and Philosophy and other essays*, Monthly Review Press, New York, 1971, pp. 172–3.

2   E. Gellner, *Nationalism*, Phoenix, London, 1997, p. 6.

3   Henry A. Giroux, 'Private Satisfactions and Public Disorders, *Fight Club*, Patriarchy, and the Politics of Masculine Violence', *Third Text*, no. 53, Winter 2001, pp. 39–40.

4   F. Jameson, 'The Cultural Logic of Late Capitalism', *Postmodernism, Or The Cultural Logic of Late Capitalism*, Verso, 1991, p. 6.

Index

Index